THE ENVIRONMENT
AND
ECONOMICS

A Reader from

DOLLARS&SENSE

Edited by Bryan Snyder and the *Dollars & Sense* Collective

D0165751

THE ENVIRONMENT AND ECONOMICS

A Reader from Dollars & Sense. *Edited by Bryan Snyder and the* Dollars & Sense *collective.*

ISBN: 978-1-878585-90-5

Published by:

Economic Affairs Bureau, Inc. d/b/a *Dollars & Sense*

1 Milk Street, 5th floor, Boston, MA 02109

617-447-2177; dollars@dollarsandsense.org.

For order information, contact Economic Affairs Bureau or visit: www.dollarsandsense.org.

The *Dollars & Sense* Collective also publishes *Dollars & Sense* magazine and the classroom books *Real World Macro, Real World Micro, The Economic Crisis Reader, Current Economic Issues, Real World Globalization, Real World Latin America, Real World Labor, Real World Banking and Finance, The Wealth Inequality Reader, The Environment in Crisis, Introduction to Political Economy, Unlevel Playing Fields: Understanding Wage Inequality and Discrimination, Striking a Balance: Work, Family, Life,* and *Grassroots Journalism.*

The 2012 *Dollars & Sense* Collective: Ben Collins, Leibiana Feliz, Ben Greenberg, Vera Kelsey-Watts, Shirley Kressel, James McBride, Neal Meyer, John Miller, Linda Pinkow, Paul Piwko, Lauren Price, Smriti Rao, Dan Schneider, Bryan Snyder, Chris Sturr, and Jeanne Winner.

Editor of this volume: Bryan Snyder

Editorial Assistant: Jason Allen

Layout and production: Sandra Korn

Cover design and layout: Chris Sturr

Cover conception: Bryan Snyder

Cover images: "The Great Wave off Kanagawa," by Katsushika Hokusai (1760-1849); Lindsay Lohan's mug shot, Los Angeles County Sheriff's Department (September 24, 2010).

This reader is designed to accompany Eban Goodstein's *Economics and the Environment,* 6th edition (Wiley 2011 ISBN: 978-0-470561-09-6). Resources are available for instructors and students at bcs.wiley.com.

Printed in U.S.A.

CONTENTS

INTRODUCTION

"The purpose of studying economics is not to acquire a set of ready-made answers to economic questions, but to learn how to avoid being deceived by economists."

—*Joan Robinson*

In the Spring of 1991, I first taught the subject of environmental economics at Burlington College in Burlington, Vt. At the time, I wasn't quite sure what the content and parameters of the course would be, but I knew that it would have to fill an enormous void left from what at the time was known as "natural resource economics." Natural resource economics was a cul-de-sac of neoclassical economic theory in which the invisible hand of the market was thought to act as a mechanism that would efficiently allocate resources for the best of all possible social welfare outcomes. If "externalities" occasionally arose, the state could assist the market mechanism to properly "internalize" the externalities and the problem would be promptly solved.

Natural resource economics was a lovely theory—rational, internally consistent, and somewhat elegant; its only problem was that it didn't work. The real-world relationship between people and the environment we live in was notably absent from the economic theory. The failure of natural resources economics raises the following questions for any study of economics and the environment:

1. How do we use economics as a tool of analysis for the relationship between ourselves and our environment?
2. What are the strengths and weaknesses of neoclassical economic theory with respect to the environment?
3. Can we build a better an analytic framework or method of analysis?

These three questions are a tall order indeed! Where should we begin our study of the subject?

I have found that E.F. Schumacher's *Small is Beautiful: Economics as if People Mattered* was a fine starting point. This book, written in 1973, established a context to begin analyzing people in the environment beyond the "commodity fetishism" of neoclassical economics.

Some of the issues Schumacher first raised in 1973 we now treat as standard. He introduced the distinction between renewable and non-renewable resources, what we now casually refer to as "sustainability." Schumacher was also acutely aware of the "disconnect" between human economic systems and complex natural systems. It is here, at this disjuncture, that we find the really interesting stuff of our inquiry.

Nature has a way of confounding even the best-laid plans of human beings. "Unanticipated consequences" and "self-reinforcing effects" often arise when natural systems respond to human activity. A wonderful example of this is the heartwarming saga of "cats and rats." Beginning in the mid 1990s, rice farmers in northern Vietnam began selling their cats to merchants, who shipped the cats north to China. Rising wealth in southern China had lead to an increase in consumption of all sorts of consumer goods but especially luxury goods, including the delectable dish known as "The Little Tigers." The price of cats skyrocketed and the rural rice farmers were more than happy to part with their "working" cats. (Pythons and other rodent-eating snakes also became culinary prizes.) The problem became apparent by 1997. The rice field rat population exploded, and these rapacious rodents consumed the primary source of income for these rice farmers. This led to a regional crop failure and made the farmers worse off than if they had never sold off their cats in the first place.

Notice the structure of our little story here. A human action, in this case a change in tastes brought on by a rise in incomes, changes the demand for an animal that was vital in suppressing the rodent population. The price of cats rises, their numbers fall. The rat population responds accordingly, and regional catastrophe of comprehensive crop destruction results.

What is evident is that human economic systems are often at odds with natural and or biological systems. Modern economics inspires the arrogant and incorrect assumption that an artificial market mechanism can adequately respond to the awkward relationship between humans and nature.

Nature is complex. Our economic relationship to nature is imperfect and full of surprises. E.F. Schumacher was correct in noting that a serious study of this subject should bring with it a sense of humility and respect. We should proceed with humility and respect both for the knowledge we do have and for the limitations of our knowledge.

We are pleased to present this reader as a supplement to Eban Goodstein's *Economics and the Environment* (6th edition). We have used the chapter structure of Goodstein's text to help organize recent articles from *Dollars & Sense* and our earlier reader, *The Environment in Crisis* (3rd edition) in such a way as to provide real-world examples of the economic tools and theory presented in Goodstein's textbook.

We have split Goodstein's Part 1, **How Much Pollution Is Too Much?**, into two chapters. Chapter 1 presents articles on population, growth, and consumption. First, Abby Scher explores the idea of a "New Economy" as presented by the New Economics Institute in its 2012 conference, and explains various visions and models of a sustainable and people-centered economy. Next, in "The Growth Consensus Unravels," Jonathan Rowe notes the irony of speaking of economic "growth" while ignoring externalities like environmental destruction. Alan Durning's "Enough is

Enough" and Thad Williamson's "America Beyond Consumerism" both investigate the present and future of consumption, sufficiency, and sustainability. David Holtzman's "Ecological Footprints" warns that countries with "modern" economies, like the United States, have disproportionately large ecological footprints. In "Is the U.S. Making Progress?" Marc Breslow notes the flaws of the Gross Domestic Product as a measure of economic progress. William E. Rees's article "Let's Just Assume We're Sustainable" advocates for a model of "strong sustainability." Peter Barnes argues that by "Sharing the Wealth of the Commons," we can fix a flawed economy. Finally, Samuel Scott and Michelle Sheehan present case studies on the fisheries of the Northwest Atlantic and land trusts of U.S. farmland.

Chapter 2 of Part 1 accompanies Goodstein's opening case study of climate change. The articles in this section argue that "cost-benefit analysis" cannot be effectively applied to climate change. The chapter begins with three case studies. First, Ben Greenberg interviews Monique Harden, an environmental justice activist, to gain insights into the ways in which economic practices compound environmental injustice. Next, Alejandro Reuss's article "Car Trouble" explores the environmental and public health problems associated with a transportation system that depends on passenger automobiles. Finally, in "Extinction is Forever," Jan Clausen uses the case study of the Northwest salmon crisis to shed light on the delicate balance between profits and conservation.

The articles in the second part of the chapter shift to explore the broader consequences of cost-benefit analysis. Liz Heinzerlind and Frank Ackerman's article "Pricing the Priceless" critiques the practice of cost-benefit analysis. Then, Frank Ackerman's article "Climate Economics in Four Easy Pieces" addresses more specifically the way in which cost-benefit models fail when applied to climate change. In her article "The Costs of Extreme Weather," Heidi Garrett-Peltier notes some of the often-ignored costs of climate change. Amy Gluckman's article "A Greater Threat? Federal Spending on the Military vs. Climate Change" exemplifies one significant consequence of skewed cost-benefit analysis. Finally, Larry Peterson's interview with Joel Kovel on "Climate Change and Ecosocialism" presents a new way of conceptualizing climate change.

Part 2, **Is Government Up To The Job?**, contains a number of articles relating to the institution of the government. The articles in this section explore the government's ability to act and enforce environmental regulation upon corporations.

Bob Feldman's "War on the Earth" describes the detrimental effects that U.S. military bases have had on local environments across the globe. In "Industry Attacks on Dissent, from Rachel Carson to Oprah," Laura Orlando details how the mainstream media and corporations have attacked and downplayed critiques of environmentally unsound corporate practices. Jonathan Latham's article "Way Beyond Greenwashing" notes that big conservation nonprofits like the World Wide Fund for Nature have also bowed to corporate pressures. In their article "Bankruptcy as Corporate Makeover," Anne Fischel, Mara Kardas-Nelson, and Lin Nelson provide a case study of how corporations can use bankruptcy to escape accountability for environmental degradation—with the complicity of federal and state governments.

The second half of Part 2 focuses on the ways in which environmentalism relates to labor, and presents visions of how the governmental can create an economy that is both sustainable and good to workers. Alan Durning's article "Between the Devil and the Deep Blue Sea," explains how the environmentally destructive practices of corporations can also hurt workers, necessitating an alliance between environmentalism and labor. In "We Need a Green Jobs Program," Jeannette Wicks-Lim demands that the federal government invest in clean-energy industry. "Saving Energy Creates Jobs" by Heidi Garrett-Peltier calls for the Obama administration to include energy efficiency in plans for job creation. Lastly, "The Phantom Menace," also by Garrett-Peltier, defends environmental regulation against those who have accused it of being a "job-killer."

Part 3, **How Can We Do Better?**, offers a number of innovative ways to harness both the visible and invisible hand to address environmental issues ranging from climate change to water rights. The section opens with John Miller's article "Climate Reality Eludes the Business Press," which critiques the *Wall Street Journal*'s interpretation of cap-and-trade. Next, David L. Levy's article "Business and Climate Change" and Kevin Murray's article "Whose Right to Water?" explore the consequences of privatization on environmental regulation and water rights. Thad Williamson envisions "What an Environmentally Sustainable Economy Looks Like," calling for more intentional ecological governance. Next, an excerpt from a book by Jerome M. Segal, entitled "Achieving the Good Life," explores the idea of "simple living." Lastly, Skip Barry interviews John Bellamy Foster, who raises systemic critiques of "Capitalism and Environmental Destruction."

Part 4, **Can We Resolve Global Issues?**, addresses global aspects of the ecological crisis. Most of the world's environmental problems are now global in scope. Climate change, energy use, water issues, and resource depletion are but a few of the issues that show little regard for national borders. This part presents a number of examples of environmental challenges faced by people in developing countries around the world. First, Ross Gelbspan's article "Toward a Global Energy Transition" critiques international efficiency standards and emissions-reduction strategies. In "Sustainable Sanitation," Laura Orlando calls for a new approach to global sanitation that takes economic and environmental sustainability into account. Eugenio Gonzales and Liz Stanton's case study, "Filipino Dump Activists Turn Waste Into Wealth," presents a vision for simultaneous environmental protection and poverty reduction. Maurice Dufour's satirical article "Hooked on Hydrocarbons" riffs on the idea that the United States is "addicted to oil" as a way of criticizing the exploitation of Alberta's oil sands.

David Bacon's article "Blood on the Palms" describes community activism in Colombia against corporate land development, detailing the ways in which U.S. policies have contributed to hurting Afro-Colombian communities. Next, we have included two letters, a response to Bacon's article by the Embassy of the U.S. in Colombia and a response by Colombian activists. The next article, "Keep it in the Ground" by Elissa Dennis, provides another case study of community organizing against environmental destruction, this time to oppose oil extraction in Ecuador. William G. Moseley's article "Famine Myths" debunks common misunderstandings about the 2011 famine in the Horn of Africa, revealing that U.S. foreign policy and corporate land grabs contributed more to the famine than overpopulation or inadequate food production. Next, Frank Ackerman asks "Is the United States a

Pollution Haven?", arguing that the U.S. corn industry is destroying both the environment and traditional farming methods. Finally, we close this part with an article by Anuradha Mittal and Peter Rosset, "Genetic Engineering and the Privatization of Seeds," arguing that the biotechnology industry has presented a false vision of how to feed the world.

A s we note the complexity of economic development, growth, resource utilization, and globalization, we will test the new-found analytical tools provided to you by Goodstein's textbook. Is *Economics and the Environment* up to the task of adequately assessing and addressing environmental issues in developing countries? Or will will need to add a few more tools?

—Bryan Snyder, Concord, Mass, August 2012

PART 1

HOW MUCH POLLUTION
IS TOO MUCH?

CHAPTER 1:

POPULATION, GROWTH, AND CONSUMPTION

Article 1.1.1

GREETINGS FROM THE NEW ECONOMY

In a race against climate change, a new movement seeks to build a just, sustainable world.

BY ABBY SCHER
July/August 2012

"**A**re you ready for a new economy? Are you ready for a new politics?" The challenge at the podium came from Gus Speth, the courtly co-founder of the Natural Resources Defense Council, now a professor at Vermont Law School, who is on the board of the newly created New Economics Institute (NEI). The occasion was the founding conference of NEI, held at Bard College in early June, and Speth was making a call for "an economy whose very purpose is not to grow profit...but sustain people and the planet."

NEI is the remade E.F. Schumacher Society, the group based in Massachusetts' Berkshire mountains that promoted the wisdom of the author of *Small Is Beautiful: Economics as if People Mattered* for over 30 years. In honor of this early champion of a sustainable, just economy and the idea that big is not necessarily better, the Society nurtured economic innovations that support community building—community supported agriculture, local currencies, local land trusts.

With the help of the London-based New Economics Foundation, the Schumacher Society rethought what kind of "think and do" tank is needed to transform our fossil fuel-powered, finance-bloated, inegalitarian economy into one that is resilient, just, and sustainable in the environmental and economic transition given true urgency by climate change. And with the help of some deep pockets, it relaunched as NEI and pulled together, all in one place on Bard's rural campus on the Hudson, some of the thinkers and organizers who might have a piece of the puzzle.

People reimagining ownership and work on the job or in the academy, ex-Wall Streeters revealing the secrets of how to curb the power of big finance, community people reclaiming the commons—taking air, water, and land out of the market—and rebuilding local economies from the bottom up, advocates struggling with government to make it responsive, and social scientists who are remaking our economic indicators—they may never have talked with one another before the Strategies for

1

a New Economy conference. But as Bob Massie, the new executive director of NEI said, together they created "raw energy."

Beyond Growth and Finance

The "New Economy" moniker is bubbling around lately, with a meaning recast far from President Bill Clinton's neoliberal usage 20 years ago. The venerable Washington DC-based Institute for Policy Studies has its New Economy Working Group, a partnership with Yes! magazine and the 22,000-member Business Alliance for Local Living Economies (BALLE). At the core of the call for a New Economy is an effort to come up with practical alternatives that democratize the control of the economy—including workplaces, finance, and the structure of the firm—in ways that are ecologically sustainable.

The focus on finance—on shrinking a dangerously unstable, extractive banking sector and nurturing an alternative one—is powered by such people as John Fullerton, the former JPMorgan managing director who launched Capital Institute to promote the idea of finance "not as master but as servant" and sees a role for "social impact" investing in the New Economy.

It is in the New Economy movement that you'll hear people talk about how to build a "no-growth" economy that shares more and taxes the earth less, a view promoted in the United States most notably by Boston College professor Juliet Schor. On the board of the new NEI are thinkers like Peter Victor of York University in Toronto, author of 2008's *Managing Without Growth: Smaller by Design Not Disaster,* and Stewart Wallis, head of London's New Economics Foundation, which has been popularizing the no-growth idea for years.

"Even if everybody was to rediscover Keynes, that's not the answer," Wallis told the NEI crowd, referring to the British economist who popularized government investment in the economy during downturns, even if it means running deficits, in order to boost demand and employment. "We can have an economy with high well-being, high social justice" that destroys the planet. "We need a new model, an economy that runs on very different metrics, maximizing returns to scarce ecological resources, maximizing returns [to] human well-being, good jobs."

"We have to move from talking about ourselves as consumers to [regarding ourselves as] stewards." But the New Economy movement is a big tent, and for some growth isn't the question. For Marjorie Kelly, author of *Owning Our Future: The Emerging Ownership Revolution*, and a fellow of the Tellus Institute, the Boston-based think tank focused on sustainability, growth isn't the focus. In a chat at the conference "bookstore," she said,

The problem is not growth but too much finance. You have the overlap of debt, unemployment, lack of jobs for youth.... We can't have capital markets run the economy. It has a destructive focus. It's starting to fall apart. That's terrifying. You hold on desperately to what you have as it collapses. But no, you have an alternative. You have the Right, cutting taxes, deregulating. No serious thinker believes that those are the solutions. ...There's an inevitable sorting process. There's some loony ideas and we haven't sorted that out yet. But they said that about democracy.

NOT THE SAME OLD "NEW ECONOMY"

Today's movement isn't the first time the term "New Economy" has been used. Many of us remember the Clinton-era "New Economy" of the 1990s, when computers and the Internet were hyped as having ushered in a new age of permanent prosperity. Then the dot.com bubble burst, ushering in recession of the early 2000s instead.

But there's an even more cringe-worthy precedent: back in the late 1920s, the longest continuous expansion in the U.S. economy until that time was regarded as a "New Economy." Irving Fisher, the leading economist of the day, claimed the stock market had reached a "permanently high plateau." We all know how that vision ended in October of 1929.

Whereas these precedents were founded on denial of the boom-and-bust cycles of capitalism, today's New Economy and Solidarity Economy movements, coming in the wake of the most severe economic crisis since the Great Depression, are acutely aware of capitalism's shortcomings—speculation, the growth imperative, and the dominance of finance—and seek to move beyond them.

Sources: Doug Dowd, "The New Era of the 1920's and the New Economy of Today: Birds of a Feather?" Znet (zcommunications.org), 2001; James Cypher, "Beyond Keynesianism," *Dollars & Sense*, January/February 2011.

Following the NEF and Schumacher, the New Economy umbrella also covers those promoting more realistic economic indicators that measure people's well-being and ecological costs, including the Green GDP. It considers which business forms—not just worker-owned companies but also so-called B-Corporations that consider social impact—might be compatible with a just, sustainable economy. It covers those challenging the decontextualized, value-free world of neoclassical economics because, as Massie said, "our current theories have blinded us." In late June, this was the agenda of Juliet Schor's week-long Summer Institute in New Economics at Boston College, where graduate students sat at the feet of Gar Alperovitz of the University of Maryland, James Boyce of the University of Massachusetts-Amherst, Duncan Foley of the New School, and others.

It's a big tent, and feels a bit like the Progressive Movement of the early 20th century, when many elites and middle-class people began questioning and even challenging how capitalism was organized. Partly because of its high price tag, the Bard gathering was almost entirely white and highly educated, deploring poverty but not necessarily touched by it, yet highly motivated to build a more communal, cooperative economy. How these middle-class reformers will share leadership with low-income immigrants, progressive unions, and co-ops—key social bases for the movement—is a bit of a mystery. It's no mystery, however, that any massive change in the U.S. political economy needs all these sectors pulling toward change.

Andrew Simms, the Brit known for his creative leadership in The Other Economic Summits (which dogged G-7 meetings for years before turning into London's New Economy Foundation), put class and political power on the table when he told the meeting, "When I hear people talk about sustainable capitalism, they are making a strategic error," adding "If we could get where we need to be by writing reports, we would have gotten there." The knowledge that the activists need to raise their game ran through the conference. In his plenary, Massie acknowledged who largely was not represented in the room: unions, communities of color, youth, business. He asked his audience to ask in turn, "How can we work together? How can we make this bigger and make the New Economy a reality?"

Solidarity and Division

It was only April 2009, at University of Massachusetts-Amherst, that the U.S. Solidarity Economy Network held its own sizeable gathering. That brought together people in progressive unions, worker co-ops, credit unions, food co-ops, green jobs initiatives, and even the peace movement. Inspired by the U.S. Social Forum in Atlanta in 2007 and Solidarity Economy movements in Latin America and Quebec, the network was soon celebrating the United Steel Workers' announcement that it would try to take over smaller enterprises for worker ownership, based on the example of Spain's Mondragón cooperatives—an effort slowed by the impact of the economic crisis on the union. Canadian unions reported using their pension funds to support worker ownership.

There is some overlap between the Solidarity Economy and New Economy networks. The NEI conference sought out sustainable business networks and social venture funders while the solidarity framework inspired more lower-income people and people of color. Worker co-ops came to the New Economy gathering at Bard. The green Cleveland co-ops—the complex including industrial laundry and urban farm—received a rousing reception. And NEI board member and plenary speaker Gar Alperovitz is one of worker ownership's most vocal academic champions. But as Donnie Maclurcan, of Australia's Post-Growth Institute asked me at the opening session: "Where is the acknowledgment of the custodians? [Thanking the janitors] is standard in Australia." A participant set up a sign on a picnic table during lunch asking people to come over and talk about race and class. The divide is deep. Speth was another who took on the divisions in the movements directly but warned the group they had to overcome it:

Critical here is a common progressive platform. It should embrace a profound commitment to social justice, job creation, and environmental protection; a sustained challenge to consumerism and commercialism and the lifestyles they offer; a healthy skepticism of growth mania and a democratic redefinition of what society should be striving to grow; a challenge to corporate dominance and a redefinition of the corporation, its goals and its management and ownership; a commitment to an array of prodemocracy reforms in campaign finance, elections, the regulation of lobbying; and much more. A common agenda would also include an ambitious set of new national indicators beyond GDP to inform us of the true quality of life in America.

WORKER COOPERATIVES GROWING

More than 400 people attended the National Worker Cooperative Conference in late June in Boston, more than double the number that attended the U.S. Federation of Worker Cooperatives conference two years earlier. Is something brewing? The 300+ worker co-ops in the United States are enterprises wholly owned by the people who work there and considered a key way to democratize the workplace. The 11,000-strong Employee Stock Ownership Plans, while much more common, are far less likely to be democratically managed, giving workers risk without responsibility.

A large showing of co-ops led by immigrant workers made possible the first national caucus of immigrant cleaners to gather as they took advantage of one of the "open space" sessions of the conference. Indeed, immigrant-led co-ops are the fastest growing sector of the movement. People from Opportunity Threads in North Carolina made the conference t-shirts, and spoke on a panel along with the Beyond Care child-care co-op in Brooklyn, Team Works, the 13-member cleaning co-op in Silicon Valley, and Apple Eco-Friendly, the cleaning co-op in Williamsburg, Brooklyn.

The Madison, Wisc. interpreter co-op, with the help of equipment from the local Service Employees International union, ensured that monolingual cooperators understood their allies.

This past year, the U.S. Federation created an alliance with the Canadian and Mexican worker co-op federations that is now linked with the Latin American and international networks, including the International Organisation of Industrial, Artisanal and Service Producers' Cooperatives (CICOPA). At a keynote, José Hernán Orbaiceta, the Argentinian co-op leader who has been coaching the North American federation to position itself for growth, advised those gathered to see themselves as part of the larger economic justice movement and find allies there, particularly among unions.

Meanwhile, three participants—a Los Angeles Steel Workers organizer teaming with immigrant car wash workers to launch a co-op, a Food and Commercial Worker staffer supporting the launch of a cooperative farm in Cincinnati, and a Communications Workers of America activist creating a web workers co-op—led another "open session" during lunch and promoted the Union Co-ops Council of the U.S. Federation which is building bridges between the progressive union and worker co-op movement. Its goal is nothing less than creating a "worker-driven cooperative economy with workplace and economic democracy for all."

Thinkers like Alperovitz support democratizing our economy by building out our existing network of land trusts, consumer and worker cooperatives, employee stock ownership programs with workers participating in governance, and credit unions—building off institutions crisscrossing the country. He mourns the age of unions as past, noting that more workers are in worker co-ops or ESOPs than private-sector unions. He sees these cooperative endeavors as providing a key base for building the future. He gives a political blueprint calling for redirecting federal, state and local government support toward these enterprises from corporations. This echoes the "cooperative commonwealth" envisioned by some 19th-century populists, and has healthy if long-lost roots in American thought. Markets are left intact but so is government action for the common good.

With a much greater ecological consciousness than many of her peers, Juliet Schor (like Costas Panayotakis in his new book *Remaking Scarcity*) calls for a struggle over our subjectivity and how we define our needs in building a more egalitarian, sustainable economy. While Schor was unable to attend the conference, in some ways she captures the downshifting philosophy of much of the audience better than keynoter Alperovitz. She warns us that capitalism's ability to nimbly create new needs and intensify consumerism needs to be challenged on an ecological and moral basis. Can we remake the common-sense values that are lodged at the core of our current system?

Schor lays out the more explicit vision of what almost seems like a social crusade, yet relies on individual action. She argues we need to remove ourselves from the market, step by step where we can: by working part-time, making do with less disposable cash income, and doing more on our own... That means everything from cooking to making clothes to home construction. Drawing on the alternative economy movements promoted by the old Schumacher Society, Schor champions local time dollar schemes, freecycle sharing, and barter. These schemes seek to intensify community values by intensifying your web of support with your neighbors. Ultralocal, home-based solar energy production should spread. People should embrace the slow money movement by investing locally through credit unions other other local networks, not through big finance. Meanwhile, she supports expanding the welfare state so that we are not subject to markets when it comes to our health, to expand living-wage jobs and in protecting the commons.

Slow Money

While the thinkers and policy heads dominated the panels at Bard, in the hallways I met an organic farmer who is a soil activist and writer, a big-city organizer trying to launch a Cleveland-style worker-owned initiative in an impoverished area, an Occupier, a member of a worker coop, and a Rhode Island man hoping to launch a community currency so that impoverished residents can find value in their skills. I also met Frank Nuessle of the Public Banking Institute, which is championing state banks modeled on North Dakota's, and Sean McGuire, Maryland's director of sustainability who championed the Genuine Progress Indicator so the state now measures economic growth with an eye to its social and ecological costs. Attending in force were Transition Woodstock members. These last are part of the international Transition movement begun in the U.K. that tries to encourage communities to downshift and take up resilient, ecologically sound practices so that we respond to climate change in an egalitarian way. NEI's London partner, New Economy Foundation, actively supports the Transition movement.

One of my deepest conversations was with Bonnie Rukin, regional coordinator of Slow Money Maine, which holds events matching people who can give loans or grants to enterprises creating a local sustainable food system. That might mean an organic member-owned restaurant or seaweed harvesters. Inspired by Woody Tasch, the former venture capitalist who founded Slow Money, the Maine group is one of the more successful regional spinoffs. Other people at the conference reported struggling projects in Ohio and Colorado. "A funder meets a farmer. A farmer meets a legislator. We have a lot of networking time at our meetings," said Rukin, a 62-year-old former organic farmer with a nonprofit background. "We catalyzed the flow of $3 million … and untold amounts of awareness. In terms of hunger needs, we're second in the country. We're on par with Alabama. We want to develop the social fabric."

"We started with 30 people gathering and we're up to 450 people," said Rukin. "They're each given 10 to 15 minutes to tell what they did…then the bell would ring," said Jonathan Lee, a Belfast, Maine Slow Money activist. He describes the scene: "People in the audience are from foundations, government…" Some skilled businesspeople offer their time.

Jonah Fertig, a member of the Sprouts cooperative restaurant funded through Slow Money Maine, said simply, "It's helped us to connect to different resources and people," including fellow "farmers, cooks, food proccessors…"

American Sustainable Business Association

Less explicitly anti-capitalist than many of the alternative economy folks are some of the business-oriented elements of the New Economy movement that wrestle to reform traditional market-based tools so they create incentives toward sustainable, socially just practices. Or sometimes they just try to create a counterforce to the big-business lobby. "Policies that provide social benefit are called bad for business," David Levine, founding director of the American Sustainable Business Association reported to the Bard gathering. "It was time to ask, 'Bad for whose business?'"

The ASBA formed after the election of President Obama to provide lobbying muscle and build political power for policies that tackle global warming and invest in job growth. "That means showing up before the Energy and Commerce committee and say why regulations are very important for business." It now networks 150 existing local and specialized business associations representing 150,000 members. The New Mexico Green Chamber of Commerce and women's business associations are among their members.

"We can actually produce chemicals that are not toxic. We can produce materials that are recyclable," said Levine. "What are we up against? It's the $200 million budget of the U.S. Chamber of Commerce. While we might not have the money, we can show up and have a voice."

B-Corporations

Being obsessed with profit and growth comes with costs that don't show up in the numbers. Community stakeholders and goals are ignored in corporate ratings, and companies are captive to Wall Street's short-termism. And Wall Street's goals are written into corporate law. A former bond trader came up with a new corporate form, B-corporations, that allows companies to be evaluated by their social performance, not just their economic bottom line. Since 2010, laws allowing B-corps have been enacted in eight states, most recently in Louisiana. Nathan Gilbert's job at B-Lab, a New York-based nonprofit, is to make it spread.

Strategists who think investors will voluntarily make better decisions if they knew the true impact of companies are also creating alternatives like GIIRS, the Global Impact Investing Rating System, to reveal what businesses are doing for the environment, job creation, and job quality.

But only 500 companies are chartered as B-corporations, mostly small firms. "They have $3 billion total capitalization—that's cappuccino money at Apple," said Allen K. White, vice president of Tellus, another speaker. Still, he said, "Ownership does matter. It has a moral and operational quality."

Meanwhile, he pointed out, most of the world's economic activity is controlled by the 1,000 largest corporations, untouched by many of these ideas and local movements. Richard Branson of Virgin may have told Davos, the gathering of the high and mighty, that we are seeing "the end of capitalism," as White noted. And indeed the Solidarity Economy and New Economy movements are debating what should replace it.

The stakes are high. The environmental writer and campaigner Bill McKibben was on hand to give the conference a sense of urgency to curb corporations' destructive power before the imminent damage caused by climate change is irreversible. "It is a fundamentally altered planet," he told a packed auditorium. Given our interconnection, it's not enough to work in our home communities. "If we don't take care of this large global crisis, we won't realize the future toward which we are all working.

"This is not only a huge practical dilemma but a moral one too," he said, reporting on the dengue fever epidemic he just faced in Bangladesh which he survived when undernourished people died. "Today we learned this spring was the worst spring and the most extreme. Saudi Arabia had the hottest rainstorm recorded on this planet—109 degrees. We're building a science fiction story and I don't know if we can stop it."

"Here's the good news: Most of what we need to do to deal with global warming will also help [people]," he said. With those marching orders, his middle-class reform army filed out. ❑

Sources: Juliet Schor, *True Wealth: How and Why Millions of Americans Are Creating a Time-rich, Ecologically Light, Small-scale, High-satisfaction Economy*, Penguin, 2011; Bill Mckibben, *Earth: Making a Life on a Tough New Planet*, *New York Times*, 2010; Costas Panayotakis, *Remaking Scarcity: From Capitalist Inefficiency to Economic Democracy*, Pluto, 2011; James Gustave Speth, *The Bridge at the Edge of the World: Capitalism, the Environment, and Crossing from Crisis to Sustainability*, Yale University Press, 2008; Marjorie Kelly, *Owning Our Future: The Emerging Ownership Revolution*, Berrett-Koehler, 2012; Tim Jackson, *Prosperity without Growth: Economics for a Finite Planet*, Earthscan, 2009; Gar Alperovitz, *America beyond Capitalism: Reclaiming Our Wealth, Our Liberty, and Our Democracy*, Democracy Collaborative/Dollars & Sense, 2011; E. F. Schumacher, *Small Is Beautiful: Economics as If People Mattered*, Harper & Row, 1973; Peter

Victor, *Managing Without Growth: Smaller by Design Not Disaster*, Edward Elgar Publishing, Inc. 2008; David Brancaccio, "Fixing the Future," pbs.org; The Democracy Collaborative, community-wealth.org; New Economics Institute, neweconomicsinstitute.org; The New Economics Foundation, neweconomics.org; The U.S. Federation of Worker Cooperatives, usworker.coop.

Article 1.1.2

THE GROWTH CONSENSUS UNRAVELS

BY JONATHAN ROWE

July/August 1999

Economics has been called the dismal science, but beneath its gray exterior is a system of belief worthy of Pollyanna. Yes, economists manage to see a dark cloud in every silver lining. Downturn follows uptick, and inflation rears its ugly head. But there's a story within that story—a gauzy romance, a lyric ode to Stuff. It's built into the language. A thing produced is called a "good," for example, no questions asked. The word is more than just a term of art. It suggests the automatic benediction which economics bestows upon commodities of any kind.

By the same token, an activity for sale is called a "service." In conventional economics there are no "dis-services," no actions that might be better left undone. The bank that gouges you with ATM fees, the lawyer who runs up the bill—such things are "services" so long as someone pays. If a friend or neighbor fixes your plumbing for free, it's not a "service" and so it doesn't count.

The sum total of these products and activities is called the Gross Domestic Product, or GDP. If the GDP is greater this year than last, then the result is called "growth." There is no bad GDP and no bad growth; economics does not even have a word for such a thing. It does have a word for less growth. In such a case, economists say growth is "sluggish" and the economy is in "recession." No matter what is growing—more payments to doctors because of worsening health, more toxic cleanup—so long as there is more of it, then the economic mind declares it good.

This purports to be "objective science." In reality it is a rhetorical construct with the value judgments built in, and this rhetoric has been the basis of economic debate in the United States for the last half century at least. True, people have disagreed over how best to promote a rising GDP. Liberals generally wanted to use government more, conservatives less. But regarding the beneficence of a rising GDP, there has been little debate at all.

If anything, the Left traditionally has believed in growth with even greater fervor than the Right. It was John Maynard Keynes, after all, who devised the growth-boosting mechanisms of macroeconomic policy to combat the Depression of the 1930s; it was Keynesians who embraced these strategies after the War and turned the GDP into a totem. There's no point in seeking a bigger pie to redistribute to the poor, if you don't believe the expanding pie is desirable in the first place.

Today, however, the growth consensus is starting to unravel across the political spectrum and in ways that are both obvious and subtle. The issue is no longer just the impact of growth upon the environment—the toxic impacts of industry and the like. It now goes deeper, to what growth actually consists of and what it means in people's lives. The things economists call "goods" and "services" increasingly don't strike people as such. There is a growing disconnect between the way people experience growth and the way the policy establishment talks about it, and this gap is becoming an unspoken subtext to much of American political life.

The group most commonly associated with an antigrowth stance is environmentalists, of course. To be sure, one faction, the environmental economists, is trying to put green new wine into the old bottles of economic thought. If we would just make people pay the "true" cost of, say, the gasoline they burn, through the tax system for example, then the market would do the rest. We'd have benign, less-polluting growth, they say, perhaps even more than now. But the core of the environmental movement remains deeply suspicious of the growth ethos, and probably would be even if the environmental impacts somehow could be lessened.

In the middle are suburbanites who applaud growth in the abstract, but oppose the particular manifestations they see around them—the traffic, sprawl and crowded schools. On the Right, meanwhile, an anti-growth politics is arising practically unnoticed. When social conservatives denounce gambling, pornography, or sex and violence in the media, they are talking about specific instances of the growth that their political leaders rhapsodize on other days.

Environmentalists have been like social conservatives in one key respect. They have been moralistic regarding growth, often scolding people for enjoying themselves at the expense of future generations and the earth. Their concern is valid, up to a point—the consumer culture does promote the time horizon of a five year old. But politically it is not the most promising line of attack, and conceptually it concedes too much ground. To moralize about consumption as they do is to accept the conventional premise that it really is something chosen—an enjoyable form of self-indulgence that has unfortunate consequences for the earth.

That's "consumption" in the common parlance—the sport utility vehicle loading up at Wal-Mart, the stuff piling up in the basement and garage. But increasingly that's not what people actually experience, nor is it what the term really means. In economics, consumption means everything people spend money on, pleasurable or not. Wal-Mart is just one dimension of a much larger and increasingly unpleasant whole. The lawyers' fees for the house settlement or divorce; the repair work on the car after it was rear-ended; the cancer treatments for the uncle who was a three-pack-a-day smoker; the stress medications and weight loss regimens—all these and more are "consumption." They all go into the GDP.

Cancer treatments and lawyer's fees are not what come to mind when environmentalists lament the nation's excess consumption, or for that matter when economists applaud America's "consumers" for keeping the world economy afloat. Yet increasingly such things are what consumption actually consists of in the economy today. More and more, it consists not of pleasurable things that people choose, but rather of things that most people would gladly do without.

Much consumption today is addictive, for example. Millions of Americans are engaged in a grim daily struggle with themselves to do less of it. They want to eat less, drink less, smoke less, gamble less, talk less on the telephone—do less buying, period. Yet economic reasoning declares as growth and progress that which people themselves regard as a tyrannical affliction.

Economists resist this reality of a divided self, because it would complicate their models beyond repair. They cling instead to an 18th century model of human psychology—the "rational" and self-interested man—which assumes those complexities away. As David McClelland, the Harvard psychologist, once put it, economists "haven't even discovered Freud, let alone Abraham Maslow." (They also haven't discovered the Apostle Paul, who lamented that "the good that I would I do not, but the evil that I would not, that I do.")

Then too there's the mounting expenditure that sellers foist upon people through machination and deceit. People don't choose to pay for the corrupt campaign finance system or for bloated executive pay packages. The cost of these is hidden in the prices that we pay at the store. The *Washington Post* recently reported that Microsoft hired Ralph Reed, former head of the Christian Coalition, and Grover Norquist, a right-wing polemicist, as lobbyists in Washington. When I bought this computer with Windows 95, Bill Gates never asked me whether I wanted to help support a bunch of Beltway operators like these.

This is compulsory consumption, not choice, and the economy is rife with it today. People don't choose to pay some $40 billion a year in telemarketing fraud. They don't choose to pay 32% more for prescription drugs than do people in Canada. ("Free trade" means that corporations are free to buy their labor and materials in other countries, but ordinary Americans aren't equally free to do their shopping there.) For that matter, people don't choose to spend $25 and up for inkjet printer cartridges. The manufacturers design the printers to make money on the cartridges because, as the *Wall Street Journal* put it, that's "where the big profit margins are."

Yet another category of consumption that most people would gladly do without arises from the need to deal with the offshoots and implications of growth. Bottled water has become a multibillion dollar business in the United States because people don't trust what comes from the tap. There's a growing market for sound insulation and double-pane windows because the economy produces so much noise. A wide array of physical and social stresses arise from the activities that get lumped into the euphemistic term "growth."

The economy in such cases doesn't solve problems so much as create new problems that require more expenditure to solve. Food is supposed to sustain people, for example. But today the dis-economies of eating sustain the GDP instead. The food industry spends some $21 billion a year on advertising to entice people to eat food they don't need. Not coincidentally there's now a $32 billion diet and weight loss industry to help people take off the pounds that inevitably result. When that doesn't work, which is often, there is always the vacuum pump or knife. There were some 110,000 liposuctions in the United States last year; at five pounds each that's some 275 tons of flab up the tube.

It is a grueling cycle of indulgence and repentance, binge and purge. Yet each stage of this miserable experience, viewed through the pollyanic lens of economics, becomes growth and therefore good. The problem here goes far beyond the old critique of how the consumer culture cultivates feelings of inadequacy, lack and need so people will buy and buy again. Now this culture actually makes life worse, in order to sell solutions that purport to make it better.

Traffic shows this syndrome in a finely developed form. First we build sprawling suburbs so people need a car to go almost anywhere. The resulting long commutes are daily torture but help build up the GDP. Americans spend some $5 billion a year in gasoline alone while they sit in traffic and go nowhere. As the price of gas increases this growth sector will expand.

Commerce deplores a vacuum, and the exasperating hours in the car have spawned a booming subeconomy of relaxation tapes, cell phones, even special bibs. Billboards have 1-800 numbers so commuters can shop while they stew. Talk radio thrives on traffic-bound commuters, which accounts for some of the contentious, get-out-of-my-face tone. The traffic also helps sustain a $130 billion a year car wreck industry; and if Gates succeeds in getting computers into cars, that sector should get a major boost.

The health implications also are good for growth. Los Angeles, which has the worst traffic in the nation, also leads—if that's the word—in hospital admissions due to respiratory ailments. The resulting medical bills go into the GDP. And while Americans sit in traffic they aren't walking or getting exercise. More likely they are entertaining themselves orally with a glazed donut or a Big Mac, which helps explain why the portion of middle-aged Americans who are clinically obese has doubled since the 1960s.

C. Everett Koop, the former Surgeon General, estimates that some 70% of the nation's medical expenses are lifestyle induced. Yet the same lifestyle that promotes disease also produces a rising GDP. (Keynes observed that traditional virtues like thrift are bad for growth; now it appears that health is bad for growth too.) We literally are growing ourselves sick, and this puts a grim new twist on the economic doctrine of "complementary goods," which describes the way new products tend to spawn a host of others. The automobile gave rise to car wash franchises, drive-in restaurants, fuzz busters, tire dumps, and so forth. Television produced an antenna industry, VCRs, soap magazines, ad infinitum. The texts present this phenomenon as the wondrous perpetual motion machine of the market— goods beget more goods. But now the machine is producing complementary ills and collateral damages instead.

Suggestive of this new dynamic is a pesticide plant in Richmond, California, which is owned by a transnational corporation that also makes the breast cancer drug tamoxifen. Many researchers believe that pesticides, and the toxins created in the production of them, play a role in breast cancer. "It's a pretty good deal," a local physician told the East Bay Express, a Bay Area weekly. "First you cause the cancer, then you profit from curing it." Both the alleged cause and cure make the GDP go up, and this syndrome has become a central dynamic of growth in the U.S. today.

Mainstream economists would argue that this is all beside the point. If people didn't have to spend money on such things as commuting or medical costs, they'd simply spend it on something else, they say. Growth would be the same or even greater, so the actual content of growth should be of little concern to those who promote it. That view holds sway in the nation's policy councils; as a result we try continually to grow our way out of problems, when increasingly we are growing our way in.

To the extent conventional economics has raised an eyebrow at growth, it has done so mainly through the concept of "externalities." These are negative side effects suffered by those not party to a transaction between a buyer and a seller. Man buys car, car pollutes air, others suffer that "externality." As the language implies, anything outside the original transaction is deemed secondary, a subordinate reality, and therefore easily overlooked. More, the effects upon buyer and seller—the "internalities" one might say—are assumed to be good.

Today however that mental schema is collapsing. Externalities are starting to overwhelm internalities. A single jet ski can cause more misery for the people who reside by a lake, than it gives pleasure to the person riding it.

More importantly, and as just discussed, internalities themselves are coming into question, and with them the assumption of choice, which is the moral linchpin of market thought.

If people choose what they buy, as market theory posits, then—externalities aside—the sum total of all their buying must be the greatest good of all. That's the ideology behind the GDP. But if people don't always choose, then the model starts to fall apart, which is what is happening today. The practical implications are obvious. If growth consists increasingly of problems rather than solutions, then scolding people for consuming too much is barking up the wrong tree. It is possible to talk instead about ridding our lives of what we don't want as well as forsaking what we do want—or think we want.

Politically this is a more promising path. But to where? The economy may be turning into a kind of round robin of difficulty and affliction, but we are all tied to the game. The sickness industry employs a lot of people, as do ad agencies and trash haulers. The fastest-growing occupations in the country include debt collectors and prison guards. What would we do without our problems and dysfunctions?

The problem is especially acute for those at the bottom of the income scale who have not shared much in the apparent prosperity. For them, a bigger piece of a bad pie might be better than none.

This is the economic conundrum of our age. No one has more than pieces of an answer, but it helps to see that much growth today is really an optical illusion created by accounting tricks. The official tally ignores totally the cost side of the growth ledger—the toll of traffic upon our time and health for example. In fact, it actually counts such costs as growth and gain. By the same token, the official tally ignores the economic contributions of the natural environment and the social structure; so that the more the economy destroys these, and puts commoditized substitutes in their places, the more the experts say the economy has "grown." Pollute the lakes and oceans so that people have to join private swim clubs and the economy grows. Erode the social infrastructure of community so people have to buy services from the market instead of getting help from their neighbors, and it grows some more. The real economy—the one that sustains us—has diminished. All that has grown is the need to buy commoditized substitutes for things we used to have for free.

So one might rephrase the question thus: how do we achieve real growth, as opposed to the statistical illusion that passes for growth today? Four decades ago, John Kenneth Galbraith argued in *The Affluent Society* that conventional economic reasoning is rapidly becoming obsolete. An economics based upon scarcity simply doesn't work in an economy of hyper-abundance, he said. If it takes a $200 billion (today) advertising industry to maintain what economists quaintly call "demand," then perhaps that demand isn't as urgent as conventional theory posits. Perhaps it's not even demand in any sane meaning of the word.

Galbraith argued that genuine economy called for shifting some resources from consumption that needs to be prodded, to needs which are indisputably great: schools, parks, older people, the inner cities and the like. For this he was skewered as a proto-socialist. Yet today the case is even stronger, as advertisers worm into virtually every waking moment in a desperate effort to keep the growth machine on track.

Galbraith was arguing for a larger public sector. But that brings dysfunctions of its own, such as bureaucracy; and it depends upon an enlarging private sector as a fiscal base to begin with. Today we need to go further, and establish new ground rules for the economy, so that it produces more genuine growth on its own. We also need to find ways to revive the nonmarket economy of informal community exchange, so that people do not need money to meet every single life need.

In the first category, environmental fiscal policy can help. While the corporate world has flogged workers to be more productive, resources such as petroleum have been in effect loafing on the job. If we used these more efficiently the result could be jobs and growth, even in conventional terms, with less environmental pollution. If we used land more efficiently—that is, reduced urban sprawl—the social and environmental gains would be great.

Another ground rule is the corporate charter laws. We need to restore these to their original purpose: to keep large business organizations within the compass of the common good. But such shifts can do only so much. More efficient cars might simply encourage more traffic, for example. Cheap renewable power for electronic devices could encourage more noise. In other words, the answer won't just be a more efficient version of what we do now. Sooner or later we'll need different ways of thinking about work and growth and how we allocate the means of life.

This is where the social economy comes in, the informal exchange between neighbors and friends. There are some promising trends. One is the return to the traditional village model in housing. Structure does affect content. When houses are close together, and people can walk to stores and work, it encourages the spontaneous social interaction that nurtures real community. New local currencies, such as Time Dollars, provide a kind of lattice work upon which informal nonmarket exchange can take root and grow.

Changes like these are off the grid of economics as conventionally defined. It took centuries for the market to emerge from the stagnation of feudalism. The next organizing principle, whatever it is, most likely will emerge slowly as well. This much we can say with certainty. As the market hurtles towards multiple implosions, social and environmental as well as financial, it is just possible that the economics profession is going to have to do what it constantly lectures the rest of us to do: adjust to new realities and show a willingness to change. ❏

Article 1.1.3

ENOUGH IS ENOUGH

Why more is not necessarily better than less.

BY ALAN DURNING
June 1991, updated May 2009

> "Our enormously productive economy...demands that we make consumption our way of life, that we convert the buying and use of goods into rituals, that we seek our spiritual satisfaction, our ego satisfaction, in consumption... We need things consumed, burned up, worn out, replaced, and discarded at an ever increasing rate."
>
> *—Victor Lebow, U.S. retailing analyst, 1955*

Across the country, Americans have responded to Victor Lebow's call, and around the globe, those who could afford it have followed. And many can: Worldwide, on average, a person today is four-and-a-half times richer than were his or her great-grandparents at the turn of the last century.

Needless to say, that new global wealth is not evenly spread among the earth's people. One billion live in unprecedented luxury; one billion live in destitution. Overconsumption by the world's fortunate is an environmental problem unmatched in severity by anything except perhaps population growth. Surging exploitation of resources threatens to exhaust or unalterably disfigure forests, soils, water, air, and climate. High consumption may be a mixed blessing in human terms, too. Many in the industrial lands have a sense that, hoodwinked by a consumerist culture, they have been fruitlessly attempting to satisfy social, psychological, and spiritual needs with material things.

Of course, the opposite of overconsumption—poverty—is no solution to either environmental or human problems. It is infinitely worse for people and bad for the natural world. Dispossessed peasants slash and burn their way into Latin American rain forests, and hungry nomads turn their herds out onto fragile African range land, reducing it to desert. If environmental destruction results when people have either too little or too much, we are left to wonder how much is enough. What level of consumption can the earth support? When does having more cease to add appreciably to human satisfaction?

The Consuming Society

Consumption is the hallmark of our era. The headlong advance of technology, rising earnings, and cheaper material goods have lifted consumption to levels never dreamed of a century ago. In the United States, the world's premier consuming society, people today on average own twice as many cars, drive two-and-a-half times as far, and travel 25 times further by air than did their parents in 1950. Air conditioning spread from 15% of households in 1960 to 64% in 1987, and color televisions from 1% to 93%. Microwave ovens and video cassette recorders reached almost two-thirds of American homes during the 1980s alone.

Japan and Western Europe have displayed parallel trends. Per person, the Japanese today consume more than four times as much aluminum, almost five times as much energy, and 25 times as much steel as they did in 1950. They also own four times as many cars and eat nearly twice as much meat. Like the Japanese, Western Europeans' consumption levels are only one notch below Americans'.

The late 1980s saw some poor societies begin the transition to consuming ways. In China, the sudden surge in spending on consumer durables shows up clearly in data from the State Statistical Bureau: Between 1982 and 1987, color televisions spread from 1% to 35% of urban Chinese homes, washing machines quadrupled from 16% to 67%, and refrigerators expanded their reach from 1% to 20%. By 2002 there were 126 color televisions, 93 washing machines, and 87 refridgerators for every 100 urban Chinese households.

Few would begrudge anyone the simple advantages of cold food storage or mechanized clothes washing. The point, rather, is that even the oldest non-Western nations are emulating the high-consumption lifestyle. Long before all the world's people could achieve the American dream, however, we would lay waste the planet.

The industrial world's one billion meat eaters, car drivers, and throwaway consumers are responsible for the lion's share of the damage humans have caused common global resources. Over the past century, the economies of the wealthiest fifth of humanity have pumped out two-thirds of the greenhouse gases threatening the earth's climate, and each year their energy use releases three-fourths of the sulfur and nitrogen oxides causing acid rain. Their industries generate most of the world's hazardous chemical wastes, and their air conditioners, aerosol sprays, and factories release almost 90% of the chlorofluorocarbons destroying the earth's protective ozone layer. Clearly, even one billion profligate consumers is too much for the earth.

Beyond the environmental costs of acquisitiveness, some perplexing findings of social scientists throw doubt on the wisdom of high consumption as a personal and national goal: Rich societies have had little success in turning consumption into fulfillment. Regular surveys by the National Opinion Research Center of the University of Chicago reveal, for example, that no more Americans report they are "very happy" now than in 1957.

Likewise, a landmark study by sociologist Richard Easterlin in 1974 revealed that Nigerians, Filipinos, Panamanians, Yugoslavians, Japanese, Israelis, and West Germans all ranked themselves near the middle of a happiness scale. Confounding any attempt to correlate affluence and happiness, poor Cubans and rich Americans were both found to be considerably happier than the norm.

If the effectiveness of consumption in providing personal fulfillment is questionable, perhaps environmental concerns can help us redefine our goals.

In Search of Sufficiency

By examining current consumption patterns, we receive some guidance on what the earth can sustain. For three of the most ecologically important types of consumption—transportation, diet, and use of raw materials—the world's people are distributed unevenly over a vast range. Those at the bottom clearly fall below the "too little" line, while those at the top, in the cars-meat-and-disposables class, clearly consume too much.

Approximately one billion people do their traveling, aside from the occasional donkey or bus ride, on foot. Unable to get to jobs easily, attend school, or bring their complaints before government offices, they are severely hindered by the lack of transportation options.

Another three billion people travel by bus and bicycle. Kilometer for kilometer, bikes are cheaper than any other vehicle, costing less than $100 new in most of the Third World and requiring no fuel.

The world's automobile class is relatively small: Only 8% of humans, about 400 million people, own cars. The automobile makes itself indispensable: Cities sprawl, public transit atrophies, shopping centers multiply, workplaces scatter.

The global food consumption ladder has three rungs. According to the latest World Bank estimates, the world's 630 million poorest people are unable to provide themselves with a healthy diet. On the next rung, the 3.4 billion grain eaters of the world's middle class get enough calories and plenty of plant-based protein, giving them the world's healthiest basic diet.

The top of the ladder is populated by the meat eaters, those who obtain close to 40% of their calories from fat. These 1.25 billion people eat three times as much fat per person as the remaining four billion, mostly because they eat so much red meat. The meat class pays the price of its diet in high death rates from the so-called diseases of affluence—heart disease, stroke, and certain types of cancer.

The earth also pays for the high-fat diet. Indirectly, the meat-eating quarter of humanity consumes nearly 40% of the world's grain—grain that fattens the livestock they eat. Meat production is behind a substantial share of the environmental strains induced by agriculture, from soil erosion to overpumping of underground water.

In consumption of raw materials, such as steel, cotton, or wood, the same pattern emerges. A large group lacks many of the benefits provided by modest use of nonrenewable resources—particularly durables like radios, refrigerators, water pipes, tools, and carts with lightweight wheels and ball bearings. More than two billion people live in countries where per capita consumption of steel, the most basic modern material, falls below 50 kilograms a year.

Roughly 1.5 billion live in the middle class of materials use. Providing each of them with durable goods every year uses between 50 and 150 kilograms of steel. At the top of the heap is the industrial world or the throwaway class. A typical resident of the industrialized fourth of the world uses 15 times as much paper, 10 times as much steel, and 12 times as much fuel as a Third World resident.

In the throwaway economy, packaging becomes an end in itself, disposables proliferate, and durability suffers. Americans toss away 180 million razors annually, enough paper and plastic plates and cups to feed the world a picnic six times a year, and enough aluminum cans to make 6,000 DC-10 airplanes. Similarly, the Japanese use 30 million "disposable" single-roll cameras each year, and the British dump 2.5 billion diapers.

The Cultivation of Needs

What prompts us to consume so much? "The avarice of mankind is insatiable," wrote Aristotle 23 centuries ago. As each of our desires is satisfied, a new one appears in its place. All of economic theory is based on that observation.

What distinguishes modern consuming habits, some would say, is simply that we are much richer than our ancestors, and consequently have more ruinous effects on nature. While a great deal of truth lies in that view, five distinctly modern factors play a role in cultivating particularly voracious appetites: the influence of social pressures in mass societies, advertising, the shopping culture, various government policies, and the expansion of the mass market into households and local communities.

In advanced industrial nations, daily interactions with the economy lack the face-to-face character prevailing in surviving local communities. Traditional virtues such as integrity, honesty, and skill are too hard to measure to serve as yardsticks of social worth. By default, they are gradually supplanted by a simple, single indicator—money. As one Wall Street banker put it bluntly to the *New York Times*, "Net worth equals self-worth."

Beyond social pressures, the affluent live completely enveloped in pro-consumption advertising messages. The sales pitch is everywhere. One analyst estimates that the typical American is exposed to 50 to 100 advertisements each morning before nine o'clock. Along with their weekly 22-hour diet of television, American teenagers are typically exposed to three to four hours of TV advertisements a week, adding up to at least 100,000 ads between birth and high school graduation.

Advertising has been one of the fastest-growing industries during the past half-century. In the United States, ad expenditures rose from $198 per capita in 1950 to $498 in 1989 to $930 for every man, woman, and child in the country in 2007. Worldwide, over the same period, per person advertising expenditures grew from $15 in 1950 to $46 in 1989 and $71 in 2002. In developing countries, the increases have been astonishing. Advertising billings in India jumped fivefold in the 1980s; newly industrialized South Korea's advertising industry grew 3540% annually in the late 1980s.

Government policies also play a role in promoting consumption and in worsening its ecological impact. The British tax code, for example, encourages businesses to buy thousands of large company cars for employee use. Most governments in North and South America subsidize beef production on a massive scale.

Finally, the sweeping advance of the commercial mass market into realms once dominated by family members and local enterprise has made consumption far more wasteful than in the past. More and more, flush with cash but pressed for time, households opt for the questionable "conveniences" of prepared, packaged foods, miracle cleaning products, and disposable everything—from napkins to shower curtains. All these things cost the earth dearly.

Like the household, the community economy has atrophied—or been dismembered—under the blind force of the money economy. Shopping malls, superhighways, and strips have replaced corner stores, local restaurants, and neighborhood theaters—the very places that help create a sense of common identity and community. Traditional Japanese vegetable stands and fish shops are giving way to supermarkets and convenience stores, and styrofoam and plastic film have replaced yesterday's newspaper as fish wrap.

All these things nurture the acquisitive desires that everyone has. Can we, as individuals and as citizens, act to confront these forces?

The Culture of Permanence

The basic value of a sustainable society, the ecological equivalent of the Golden Rule, is simple: Each generation should meet its own needs without jeopardizing the prospects of future generations to meet theirs.

For individuals, the decision to live a life of sufficiency—to find their own answer to the question "how much is enough?"—is to begin a highly personal process. Social researcher Duane Elgin estimated in 1981—perhaps optimistically—that 10 million adult Americans were experimenting "wholeheartedly" with voluntary simplicity. India, the Netherlands, Norway, Western Germany, and the United Kingdom all have small segments of their populations who adhere to a nonconsuming philosophy. Motivated by the desire to live justly in an unjust world, to walk gently on the earth, and to avoid distraction, clutter, and pretense, their goal is not ascetic self-denial but personal fulfillment. They do not think consuming more is likely to provide it.

Realistically, voluntary simplicity is unlikely to gain ground rapidly against the onslaught of consumerist values. And, ultimately, personal restraint will do little if not wedded to bold political and social steps against the forces promoting consumption. Commercial television, for example, will need fundamental reorientation in a culture of permanence. As religious historian Robert Bellah put it, "That happiness is to be attained through limitless material acquisition is denied by every religion and philosophy known to humankind, but is preached incessantly by every American television set."

Direct incentives for overconsumption are also essential targets for reform. If goods' prices reflected something closer to the environmental cost of their production, through revised subsidies and tax systems, the market itself would guide consumers toward less damaging forms of consumption. Disposables and packaging would rise in price relative to durable, less-packaged goods; local unprocessed food would fall in price relative to prepared products trucked from far away.

The net effect might be lower overall consumption as people's effective purchasing power declined. As currently constituted, unfortunately, economies penalize the poor when aggregate consumption contracts: Unemployment skyrockets and inequalities grow. Thus arises one of the greatest challenges for sustainable economics in rich societies—finding ways to ensure basic employment opportunities for all without constantly stoking the fires of economic growth. ❏

Article 1.1.4

AMERICA BEYOND CONSUMERISM
Has capitalist economic growth outlived its purpose?

BY THAD WILLIAMSON
May/June 2008

O ne of the great benefits of studying the history of economic ideas is coming to the recognition that the founding figures of capitalist economics, and in particular Adam Smith, author of the pivotal *Wealth of Nations*, were often deeply ambivalent about the acquisitive way of life. Consider the famous parable of the poor man's son, presented by Smith in his *Theory of Moral Sentiments*:

The poor man's son, whom heaven in its anger has visited with ambition, when he begins to look around him, admires the condition of the rich. He finds the cottage of his father too small for his accommodation, and fancies he should be lodged more at his ease in a palace. He is displeased with being obliged to walk a-foot, or to endure the fatigue of riding on horseback. He sees his superiors carried about in machines, and imagines that in one of these he could travel with less inconveniency. … He thinks if he had attained all these, he would sit still contentedly, and be quiet, enjoying himself in the thought of the happiness and tranquility of his situation. He is enchanted with the distant idea of this felicity. It appears in his fancy like the life of some superior rank of beings, and, in order to arrive at it, he devotes himself forever to the pursuit of wealth and greatness. To obtain the conveniencies which these afford, he submits in the first year, nay in the first month of his application, to more fatigue of body and more uneasiness of mind than he could have suffered through the whole of his life from want of them. He studies to distinguish himself in some laborious profession. With the most unrelenting industry he labours night and day to acquire talents superior to all his competitors. He endeavours next to bring those talents into public view, and with equal assiduity solicits every opportunity of employment. For this purpose he makes his court to all mankind; he serves those whom he hates, and is obsequious to those whom he despises. Through the whole of his life he pursues the idea of a certain artificial and elegant repose which he may never arrive at, for which he sacrifices a real tranquility that is at all times in his power, and which if in the extremity of old age, he should at last attain to it, he will find to be in no respect preferable to that humble security and contentment which he had abandoned for it. It is then … that he begins at last to find that wealth and greatness are mere trinkets of frivolous utility, no more adapted for procuring ease of body or tranquility of mind than the tweezer-cases of the lover of toys; and like them too, more troublesome to the person who carries them about with him than all the advantages they can afford him…

In his heart he curses ambition, and vainly regrets the ease and the indolence of youth, pleasures which are fled for ever, and which he has foolishly sacrificed for what, when he has got it, can afford him no real satisfaction.

Adam Smith, traditionally regarded as the patron saint of capitalist economics, here avers that the fundamental engines of the market economy—ambition and acquisitiveness—rest on what he terms a "deception," the illusion that all the objects we spend our days striving for will make us happy.

Fast forward over 200 years. Here is how a contemporary economist, Juliet Schor of Boston College, describes "Greg," a sixth grader in a Boston suburb, in her 2004 book *Born to Buy: The Commercialized Child and the New Consumer Culture*:

> Greg is an avid consumer. He loves professional wrestling, Gameboy, Nintendo, television, movies, junk food, and CDs (especially those with parental advisories). Since he came to live with his [father and step-mother], they've had a succession of incidents, most of which resulted in Greg's losing privileges to one or another of these things. He isn't allowed to do wrestling moves on his younger sister, but he does, and he loses the right to watch wrestling. He's supposed to do his homework, but he has lied and said he doesn't have any so he can spend his time playing a new Gameboy. He's supposed to tell the truth, but he stole [his stepmom's] Snickers bar and denied it. He knows he's not allowed to have CDs with parental advisories, but he went behind [his parents]' back and asked his [biological] mother to buy them for him…
>
> Another couple described their son Doug as "the ultimate consumer." He wanted to buy every product he saw advertised on television. Doug was now in sixth grade, and they were fighting constant battles. He would stay on the computer all day if they let him. He has a weakness for fast food. He has a lot of trouble holding on to money. His mother even described trying to sneak out to the store without him to avoid conflicts about buying stuff.

Schor was stunned to find that persistent parent-child conflicts over money and goods were widespread, not confined to a few severe cases like Greg and Doug. In a survey of some 300 Boston-area fifth and sixth graders, Schor found strong evidence of a causal relationship between heavier involvement in consumer culture and strained relationships with parents, greater feelings of boredom and physical pain, higher levels of depression and anxiety, and lower self-esteem.

This finding is troubling precisely because corporate advertisers, as Schor and others have amply documented, have become increasingly brazen in the past 10 to 15 years about marketing directly to children, with the explicit purpose of establishing brand identifications and consumer loyalty as early as possible. By age ten, the average American kid is aware of over 300 specific brand names. A particular goal of this marketing is to persuade children to nag their parents to buy them things. A recent study reveals that the average American child aged three to eight now nags his or her parents nearly five times a day for material goods. Furthermore, research shows that over 80% of parents respond positively to such nagging at least some of the time, and marketers have estimated that up to one-half of sales of popular products for kids are a direct result of children nagging their parents. Probably not coincidentally, since the 1970s, as the impact of commercial culture on childhood has increased, the observed mental and physical health outcomes of American children, including levels of depression, obesity, and attention deficit disorder, have worsened.

So maybe it's not good to be obsessed with consumer goods, or to be, consciously or subconsciously, the slave of some advertising executive who knows how to play on your insecurities, self-image, and aspirations. But isn't money, at some level, necessary to make us happy?

Here the answer is slightly more complicated, but a large body of research—much of it usefully summarized by political scientist Robert Lane in his 2000 book *The Loss of Happiness in Market Democracies*—suggests it is not at all inconsistent with the view Aristotle expressed over 2,000 years ago: we need some material goods to be happy, but not an excess of them. Consider evidence from the Social Capital Community Benchmark Survey, a survey of some 33,050 Americans conducted by the Saguaro Center for Civic Engagement at Harvard in 2000. Among many other topics, this survey asked people how happy they are, allowing researchers to assess the most important predictors of greater happiness. How does income stack up in importance compared to having friends, confidantes, and close family relationships, and to being an active member of the community?

The survey data suggest that holding other demographic factors equal, an individual who earns $30,000 to $50,000 a year, visits with relatives three times a month, has at least ten "close friends" and at least three people he or she can confide in, and belongs to a religious congregation as well as three other organizations has a 47.5% likelihood of self-reporting as "very happy." In contrast, consider someone demographically alike in all other respects who earns over $100,000 a year, but visits with relatives just one time a month, has only one to two "close friends," has only one person to confide in, is not part of a religious congregation, and belongs to only one organization. That person—richer in income but poorer in social connections—is estimated to have just a 28.6% chance of feeling "very happy."

Now, it's true that higher income, while not connected at all to family visits, is somewhat correlated with having more friends and confidantes and even more strongly associated with increased group memberships. Nor can anyone deny that economic circumstances influence well-being: controlling for other factors, moving from $30,000-$50,000 to over $100,000 a year in income is associated with a substantial rise in the likelihood of being "very happy"—from 34.4% to 45.3%. But the projected increase in the likelihood of being "very happy" associated with moving from having just three to five friends and two confidantes to over ten friends and at least three confidantes is even more substantial (from 32.2% to 44.2%). For most people, making five new friends and developing one or two especially close friendships are more realistic goals than doubling their income. The evidence suggests that expanding social ties is also a better strategy for finding happiness—especially if the alternative, chasing after more income, comes at the cost of fewer friends and weaker social connections. Income matters in shaping subjective well-being, but social connections matter more.

It would be misleading to leave the story at that, however. So far we have only been discussing raw income figures. But a closer look reveals that what people value more than their raw income is a sense of being *satisfied* with their economic circumstances. When we include both measures in statistical models predicting individual happiness, economic satisfaction predominates; it's a far more powerful predictor of well-being than absolute income. *Controlling for income level,* individuals who are "very satisfied," "somewhat satisfied," or "not at all satisfied" with their economic circumstances have sharply divergent chances of being very happy: 48.7%, 33.3%, and 20.8% respectively. In contrast, if we control for people's level of economic satisfaction, more income does relatively little to promote happiness: a leap from the $30,000–$50,000 income bracket to the over-$100,000 bracket implies an increase of just four percentage points in the predicted likelihood of being "very happy," from 34.8% to 38.9%. Put another way, a person earning $30,000 to $50,000 who reports being "very satisfied" with her financial condition has, controlling for other factors, a 48.8% likelihood of being "very happy," whereas a person earning over $100,000 who is only "somewhat satisfied" with her financial condition has just a 37.5% likelihood of being "very happy." How much money one earns is, in itself, not an overwhelmingly decisive factor driving individual well-being, but being satisfied with what one has certainly is.

What is it that allows people to be happy with what they have? It could be that people who are psychologically disposed to be happier also tend to look more positively on whatever economic circumstances they find themselves in. But it's equally if not more plausible to think that two other factors drive economic satisfaction: a sense of economic security—in other words, knowing that you will be able to sustain your current lifestyle in the future—and freedom from the compulsion to compare your own versus others' income and consumption. But as scholars like Jacob Hacker and Robert Frank have pointed out, recent political-economic trends in the United States have had precisely the effect of weakening economic security and encouraging social comparisons. In his recent book *Falling Behind*, Frank insightfully discusses how the explosion in consumption by the super-rich in the last 20 years has shaped the behavior of middle- and upper-middle-class households, who feel that they too should have a bigger house or, to take Frank's favorite illustration, a more expensive barbecue grill.

If Consuming More Doesn't Make Us Happier, What's the Point of Capitalism?

This brings us back to Adam Smith, who anticipated much of this body of evidence when he described the poor man's son who forsakes enjoyment of life for a life of industry and self-advancement as suffering from a fundamental delusion. Yet this insight did not lead Smith to reject capitalism. On the contrary, he thought this deception had a socially productive purpose: namely, helping to fuel economic progress, the advancement of industry, and the gradual rise of living standards—not just the living standards of the rich, but the living standards of average working people as well.

Indeed, in the subsequent 200 years, capitalism—or more accurately, capitalism modified by a range of state interventions, public spending, social welfare programs, and labor laws—has been remarkably successful in lifting overall living standards in places like the United Kingdom and the United States (albeit with often enormous social costs borne by millions of nameless workers who labored for capitalist employers under horrific conditions, enforced by the threat of hunger, and in some cases literally at gunpoint). In the 20th century alone, per capita income in the United States increased eightfold and life expectancy rose from 49 to 77 years.

That's the good news. The bad news is, median wage growth has stalled in the United States in the last 30 years, and has gone backwards for the least educated Americans. Total hours worked per household have risen as women work longer hours without a corresponding reduction in men's work hours. The hope of a secure, stable job has all but disappeared—hence today's widespread feelings of economic insecurity and dissatisfaction across income brackets. More to the point, there is good reason to doubt that simply continuing to "grow the economy" is going to address any of these concerns—or make most people any happier.

Consider just how rich a society this is. The U.S. Gross Domestic Product now stands at $13.8 trillion. If it were divided equally, that would come to over $180,000 for a family of four, or about $125,000 in take-home pay assuming an effective tax rate of 30%. In other words, the U.S. economy is large enough to provide a very comfortable life for each and every American.

But it doesn't. Why not?

A skyrocketing degree of economic inequality is one reason. The median income for married couple households in 2006 was $70,000, with of course many families making far, far less. While the income and wealth of the top 1% spike to unimaginable levels, many Americans simply do not have enough money to get by. With inequality comes not just poverty, but also widening disparities in status which themselves help fuel ever-greater levels of consumption as people spend more and more to try to keep up with the (ever-richer) Joneses.

The second reason is the widespread fact of economic insecurity. People whose jobs, health coverage, wage levels, and pensions are fragile naturally feel pressure to accumulate and advance as far as they can, lest they fall behind and lose what they now have. And, every week, we read about workers and communities who do in fact lose what they have as layoffs and plant shutdowns are announced. As we have seen, survey data (as well Adam Smith's intuitions) suggest that what matters most for well-being is the sense that one has enough and can feel comfortable about the future—that is, the very thing that the American economy fails to provide to the vast majority of families.

This insecurity is most potent in blue-collar America, but the middle class does not escape it either. Consider the life pattern of the average white-collar American. To go to college and get ahead, you have to borrow money and incur debt; to pay off the debt, you're under pressure to land a high-paying job; when you start a family, financial responsibilities multiply: you take on a mortgage, begin paying for child care or else accept a drop in household income, and within a few years face the stark realization that unless you make enough to either pay for private education or live in a neighborhood with good public schools, your children's education will suffer; and by the time you are finally done paying your children's college costs, it's already past time to begin building a nest egg for retirement and a cushion against illness. At no point does it seem to most people prudent—or even possible—simply to get off the treadmill.

Little wonder, then, that the Harvard social capital survey found just 26% of Americans to be "very satisfied" with their economic status (including just 54% of those making over $100,000 a year). It is impossible to address the issue of runaway consumerism without also addressing the issue of economic security. Indeed, as Knox College psychologist Tim Kasser, author of *The High Price of Materialism*, notes, a host of studies by psychologists and others demonstrate a strong relationship between numerous kinds of insecurity, especially economic insecurity, and the development of a materialist outlook on life.

This brings us to the third major reason the U.S. economy fails to foster a comfortable life for most Americans: long hours and overwork. Stress, fatigue, and sleep deprivation have become hallmarks of the American way of life. Over three-quarters of Americans report feeling stressed at least "sometimes," with a full one-third saying they experience stress "frequently." (The figures are higher still for persons holding jobs and for parents.) Likewise, roughly one-half of all Americans—including three-fifths of employed workers, parents, and persons aged 18 to 49—say they do not have enough time to do what they would like to in daily life, such as spend time with friends. Harvard political scientist Robert Putnam reports that the percentage of Americans regularly eating dinner together declined by one-third between 1977 and 1999. Research by the Families and Work Institute indicates that almost two-thirds (63%) would like to work fewer hours. On average those questioned said they would reduce their work week by more than ten hours if they could. But what people want and what the political economy provides are two different things: in the past generation, the centuries-long trend towards reducing the length of the work week has come to a screeching halt.

So the U.S. economy, as presently constituted, produces tremendous inequality, insecurity, and overwork. Nor is there reason to think that growing from a $14 trillion to, say, a $20 or $25 trillion economy will change these destructive trends.

It doesn't have to be this way. There is no inherent reason why we could not cease to regard more income as a good in itself, but instead alter our political economy so that it provides what Americans really need and want: greater employment security, stronger protection against the pitfalls of poverty, and more free time. We could choose to have the public guarantee employment opportunities for every willing worker, to put a floor on income, to decommodify health care and education, to reduce the gross inequalities of income and status which themselves help fuel consumerism, and to take future productivity growth in the form of more time, not more stuff.

To be sure, doing so would not be easy, and would require substantial institutional changes, possibly even a shift to a system that, as economist Gar Alperovitz puts it, lies "beyond capitalism." Many careful analysts, including Alperovitz and Schor, have thought long and hard about just how that could happen; indeed, there has been a rich debate in the past 15 years about the long-term possibilities of alternative political-economic frameworks that would reshape the logic of our current system.

It would be very easy to dismiss these ideas as "crazy" or "utopian." But, I submit, the moral task Adam Smith set for capitalism—that of making it economically possible for each and every person to live a materially comfortable life—has been achieved, at least in the advanced industrialized countries. The acquisitive life that goes with capitalism Smith never endorsed as good in itself. Neither should we, especially given the unhealthy consequences of an excessive consumerism that is now warping children's lives from their earliest years, and given the potentially planet-melting consequences of a way of life based on continual increases in consumption and economic activity.

That wasn't what Adam Smith wanted. Nor was it what the most influential and pragmatic of 20th-century economists, John Maynard Keynes, the man many credit with saving capitalism from itself, wanted. In a famous but too often neglected essay called "Economic Possibilities for Our Grandchildren," Keynes looked to a time when at last it would be possible for humanity (at least in the affluent nations) to turn its attention away from acquisition and toward broader moral concerns— such as "how to use his freedom from pressing economic cares, how to occupy the leisure, which science and compound interest will have won for him, to live wisely and agreeably and well."

That time has not yet come. But the remaining barriers to it are political, not economic; and the great task of this century is to assure that our prodigious economic capacities are directed towards supplying the real goods of human life: material security, meaningful work, and plentiful time for the friends and family who are the most lasting source of human happiness. ❑

Sources: Adam Smith, *The Theory of Moral Sentiments* (1759) (Liberty Fund, 1984); Juliet Schor, *Born to Buy: The Commercialized Child and the New Consumer Culture* (Scribner, 2004); Tim Kasser, *The High Price of Materialism* (MIT Press, 2002); "Half of Americans are Pressed for Time; A Third Are Stressed Out," *Gallup News Svc*, May 3, 2004; "No time for R&R," *Gallup News Svc*, May 11, 2004; "Who Dreams, Perchance to Sleep?" *Gallup News Svc*, Jan. 25, 2005; Robert Putnam, *Bowling Alone: The Collapse and Revival of American Community* (Simon & Schuster, 2000); J. Bond, E. Galinsky, and J. Swanberg, *The 1997 National Study of the Changing Workforce*, Families and Work Institute, 1998; Gar Alperovitz, *America Beyond Capitalism: Reclaiming Our Wealth, Our Liberty, and Our Democracy* (Wiley, 2004); Jerome Segal, *Graceful Simplicity: Towards a Philosophy and Politics of Simple Living* (Henry Holt, 1999); Juliet Schor, *A Sustainable Economy for the 21st Century* (Open Media, 1995); John Maynard Keynes, *Essays in Persuasion* (W.W. Norton, 1963); Jacob S. Hacker, *The Great Risk Shift* (Oxford Univ. Press, 2006); Robert H. Frank, *Falling Behind: How Rising Inequality Harms the Middle Class* (Univ. of Calif. Press, 2007); Robert E. Lane, *The Loss of Happiness in Market Democracies* (Yale Univ. Press, 2000); Robert M. Biswas-Diener, "Material Wealth and Subjective Well-Being," in M. Eid and R. J. Larsen, eds., *The Science of Subjective Well-Being* (Guilford Press, 2008).

Article 1.1.5

ECOLOGICAL FOOTPRINTS

BY DAVID HOLTZMAN
July/August 1999

What is to blame for global warming, depleting fossil fuels, and other environmental problems? Overpopulated Third World countries with lax environmental standards, as the Heritage Foundation and other conservative think tanks assert, or overconsuming First World economies, as most environmentalists maintain?

Mathis Wackernagel and William Rees, two community planners at the University of British Columbia in Canada, developed an innovative way to answer this question in the 1996 book *The Ecological Footprint*. Their statistical measure—what they call an ecological footprint—reveals the impact each country has on the world's resources. Not surprisingly, "modern" economies, such as the United States, have the largest ecological footprints. These economies require far more land, energy, and water, and emit much more of the carbon dioxide that is so harmful to people's health and the atmosphere, than do poorer nations, even though poor nations are home to most of the world's population.

The ecological footprint measures the resources consumed by a community or a nation, whether they come from the community's backyard or around the globe. Earlier studies had determined a community or nation's "carrying capacity"—the number of people a society can support before it loses its ability to support itself. Wackernagel and Rees' innovation adds in richer countries' use of trade and technology to import resources they don't possess.

Wackernagel and Rees ask how many hectares or acres are needed per person to support a nation's consumption of food, housing, transportation, consumer goods, and services. They calculate how much fossil energy use, land degradation, and garden, crop, pasture, and forest space it takes to produce all the consumers buy.

For example, Wackernagel and Rees determined that Vancouver, British Columbia, their home, runs a large "ecological deficit" with the rest of the world. As they calculate it, Vancouver needs an area 19 times larger than its 4,000 square kilometers to support the food production, forest products, and energy consumption of the region.

Compared globally, the Wackernagel and Rees results are stunning. Based on 1991 figures, the U.S. ecological footprint was 5.1 hectares per person, or over 12.5 acres. In contrast, each resident of India, which has a population three times the size o the United States, requires 0.4 hectares or just over two acres to maintain his or hr livelihood per year. he implications of these ecological footprints for world development are profoundly disturbing.

For instance, for everyone on Earth to enjoy the ecological standards of average residents in Canada and the United States, an additional planet or two might be necessary. And while the material wealth of people in the rich countries increased during the 20th century, the First World exploited so much space and resources in the process that little is left for poor countries hoping to obtain a similar standard of living in the same manner.

To sustain these inequitable ecological footprints, most rich countries run large ecological deficits with the rest of the world. The United States, one of the most land-rich modern economies, is one of the few exceptions. If the ecological marks left by all the world's people are to be distributed more equitably, then Americans, Canadians, and other residents of wealthy countries are going to have to change their habits radically. A modest first step in that direction would be to require that the industries and governments that drive the world economy include an analysis of their impacts on the environment, or ecological footprint, in their economic forecasts. ❏

Resources: Mathis Wackernagel and William Rees, *Our Ecological Footprint: Reducing Human Impact on the Earth* (New Society Publishers, 1996); www.wri.org/data/matflows. To determine your own ecological footprint, visit www.myfootprint.org.

Article 1.1.6

IS THE U.S. MAKING PROGRESS?

Unlike the GDP, a new measure says "no."

BY MARC BRESLOW
March/April 1996

Suppose a factory in your community has been producing valuable chemicals for several decades. It employs hundreds of workers, purchases materials and services from nearby towns, and yields high profits. Then inspectors for the Environmental Protection Agency discover that the factory owners have been dumping hazardous wastes onto the company's land, polluting the local water supply. Under the federal "Superfund" law, EPA orders a cleanup and tries to make the company pay for the damages. In turn, the company resists the EPA in court.

What do these events mean for society? Contrary to common sense, all are counted as positive by the nation's primary measure of economic output, Gross Domestic Product, or GDP. This indicator includes not only the dollar value of constructing the factory, paying wages to employees, and generating profits for the owners—but also the millions of dollars spent to clean up toxic wastes and to restore the purity of the water supply. GDP even includes the health care expenses of anyone who contracts cancer or other illnesses from drinking contaminated water. And, the money spent by EPA to regulate the polluter, and by the company on lawyers and experts to defend itself against regulation, both add to the official measure of national output.

Not only does the GDP count as "progress" many things that do not deserve the label, but it fails to count items that genuinely improve national welfare. Try another example. You and your domestic partner Jean are both working full-time, while your three-year-old daughter Kim is in day care 40 hours a week, at a cost of $10,000 a year. Both Jean and you are exhausted by the hectic schedule of going to work, picking Kim up from her center, and then caring for her as soon as you get home. You feel guilty about how much time Kim is in an institutional setting, and wish you could be with her more. On the plus side, both your salaries and the day care expenses add to the nation's GDP.

But then an amazing thing happens. The company that you work for, and the government agency where Jean works, both decide to allow part-time work. You cut back to three days a week, Jean cuts back to four days, and you keep Kim in day care for three days. Kim is happier, you enjoy being with her more, both you and Jean have more free time, and your relationship improves. Money is tighter, but you can still pay the bills.

A happy ending? Yes, except that the economic statisticians will hate you. By cutting your wages, and by reducing your payments to the day care center, you have harmed the GDP. And, the extra two days a week that you and Jean spend caring forKim yourselves count for nothing, since no one is paying you to do it. These are not extreme examples. GDP, the primary method by which economic progress is measured in the United States and throughout the world, is a highly misleading index. While the adjective "economic" could be viewed as a tipoff that "progress" includes many other things, in practice GDP is often treated as the sole measure of how human welfare is changing.

Even if its meaning is limited to the value of economic output, GDP is fatally flawed. First, as the child care example shows, GDP rises when unpaid household labor is replaced by paid wage labor, even if real "output" has not changed. Second, GDP fails to note that as production rises annually, we are depleting the earth's stocks of fossil fuels, minerals, forests, wetlands, and fish. Unlike business firms, which subtract "depreciation" of their equipment and buildings from annual income, the GDP makes no adjustment for depletion of natural resources.

When GDP's purpose is extended to measuring human welfare, it has even less relevance, since it fails to distinguish between desirable output ("goods") and undesirable output ("bads"). As the pollution example demonstrates, the costs of controlling environmental damages from production, and of repairing our health once the byproducts of production have harmed it, add to the GDP no differently than do the food, clothing, and entertainment that we actually get pleasure from consuming. GDP also fails to account for how production and consumption create environmental problems that threaten future generations, such as global warming and destruction of the ozone layer. And it ignores the worsening of social problems in modern-day America, such as inequality, crime, and loss of leisure time.

TAXES FOR PROGRESS

Having a better statistical measure of progress is a good idea, but by itself will not change the course of industrial civilization. To help accomplish this goal, Redefining Progress proposes that the United States inhibit pollution and resource depletion by placing severe taxes on the use of resources such as energy fuels.

As the World Resources institute did in its book *Green Fees*, Redefining Progress arguesthat such taxes would have a dual benefit. First, they would discourage the use of fuels, thereby limiting global warming and acid rain, and conserving resources for our descendants.

Second, the resulting revenues would allow the government to reduce or eliminate its taxation of labor and capital investment. The latter are activities that we wish to encourage, but instead discourage at present by taxing them heavily. Redefining Progress estimates that a tax on resources and pollution in California would bring in sufficient revenues to enable abolishing all other state and local taxes. Such a change could, by reducing the cost of hiring employees and investing in plant and equipment, prove to be a great boon to workers and to real economic growth.

Redefining Progress

These deficiencies in the "national income" accounts of the United States and other nations have been critiqued by environmentalists, feminists, and those who see social development faltering even as the GDP grows. The United Nations Development Program (UNDP), for example, has for years modified GDP scores by examining the health and educational status of each nation's population, deriving a "Human Development Index."

Recently the group "Redefining Progress," based in San Francisco, created its own alternative to GDP, called the "Genuine Progress Indicator," or GPI. According to Clifford Cobb, Ted Halstead, and Jonathan Rowe, the authors of the group's study: Much of what we now call growth or GDP is really just one of three things in disguise: fixing blunders from the past, borrowing resources from the future, or shifting functions from the traditional realm of household and community to the realm of the monetized economy.

While the GPI rose somewhat between 1950 and the early 1970s, it has been falling steadily since then. By 1994 the GPI was 26% lower than it had been in 1973. Since the U.S. population has been growing, what really matters is "progress" per person, which the GPI measures as having fallen by an astounding 42% since 1970! These figures are consistent with wage and productivity trends that show economic welfare, measured by workers' paychecks, falling since the same year. But the 42% drop is far more severe than the decline in wages. If the GPI accurately reflects reality, then the U.S. economy must be in a dramatic decline.

Upon closer examination, most of Redefining Progress' adjustments to the GDP are based on depletion of natural resources and long-term damage to the environment. So while the welfare of the current generation of Americans has stagnated, but perhaps not dropped greatly, the GPI indicates that we are severely compromising the ability of future generations to enjoy the fruits of the earth. Many experts will question details of how the GPI was constructed, and will not accept the specifics of their numbers. But there is widespread agreement that Redefining Progress' effort to construct an alternative to the GDP is well-founded. Hundreds of economists, including such mainstream figures as Nobel Laureate Herbert Simon and former president of the American Economics Association Robert Eisner, have called for new measures of economic progress.

Inequality, Underemployment, and Overwork

The conventional GDP is a combination of three main elements: consumption, meaning the food, clothing, housing and other expenses of all individuals in the United States; investment by business in items such as machinery and buildings; and spending by government bodies on items such as roads, schools, and the military. The new GPI breaks each of these elements down more specifically, looking at whether particular expenses are "goods" or "bads." But it still begins with consumption, which increased by an impressive 55%, or $6,200, per person between 1970 and 1994 (all figures in 1994 inflation-adjusted dollars). If we stopped here, we would, as do true believers in the free market, think that life is pretty rosy in

America. But it is now well known that gains in wealth, income, and therefore consumption have been concentrated in the upper classes in recent decades, while wages have fallen for most people and government has cut the real value of assistance for the poor. For its index of inequality, Redefining Progress uses the share of income received by the lowest-income 20% of the population, which was a meager 3.9% in 1990. Counting inequality as a "bad," the per capita GPI falls by $3,700 due to the drop in this share from 1970 to 1994—canceling out more than half of the gain from higher consumption.

While there is no "objective" means of weighting the harm from inequality, the GPI's adjustment appears to be well justified. Government data shows that between 1970 and 1992 the average incomes of the bottom three-fifths of U.S. households were virtually unchanged. Thus, less than half the population has gained from the large rise in consumption.

The GPI also has downward adjustments for two other results of America's destructive labor market—underemployment and loss of leisure time. In recent decades average unemployment has risen slightly in the United States, but "under-employment" —meaning people who want full-time jobs but can only get part-time work during part or all of the year—has skyrocketed. Redefining Progress uses the average real wage as the basis for valuing this involuntary idleness.

The U.S. economy is causing seemingly contradictory difficulties, since at the same time that underemployment is rising for some people, overwork is rising for most others. Due to the simultaneous demands of paid labor and unpaid child care, leisure time has been falling consistently. Based on research by Laura Leete-Guy and Juliet Schor (author of The Overworked American), Redefining Progress estimates that hours of leisure per fully employed member of the workforce fell by an average of more than 100 per year, or two hours per week, from 1969 to 1989.

Clifford Cobb and his co-authors have also made adjustments for other social problems, including the costs of households protecting themselves from crime, of increasing rates of family breakdown, of longer commuting times to work, and of auto accidents. But while these are conceptually important, the authors' methodology makes them small numerically relative to labor market and environmental factors. In several cases the GPI appears to underestimate social damages. For example, it limits the costs of crime to the value of stolen goods and to spending on locks, burglar alarms and other "defensive" measures. But surely these are only minor parts of the real damage from rising crime and exploding rates of incarceration. There are now more than a million Americans in prison, a figure that has doubled in the past decade. Is not the loss in freedom to these prisoners far more important than the expenses of buying alarm systems? And what about increasing social division, as most people who can afford to do so move out of urban neighborhoods, partially to escape from crime?

Destroying the Earth

While the GPI may underestimate the social costs of life in modern-day America, it probably overestimates the environmental costs. Redefining Progress asserts that destruction of old-growth forests, elimination of farmland and wetlands, depletion of non-renewable resources (principally oil), destruction of the ozone layer, and global warming are in combination the most important reasons to discard Gross Domestic Product as a measure of progress. The GPI counts these failures to conserve the bounties Mother Earth as subtracting $4,900 per person from the 1994 GDP—much more than the adjustments for rising inequality, loss of leisure time, and higher underemployment combined.

Although resource destruction is accelerating in the United States and worldwide, the GPI indicates that more "traditional" environmental problems—water and air pollution—have not gotten worse in the United States since 1970. In fact, while the costs of water pollution have remained constant, those from air pollution have been cut in half. Redefining Progress estimates that while air quality deteriorated in the United States during the 1950s and 1960s, it began improving by 3% per year in the 1970s, due to the Clean Air Act of 1970.

Perhaps these results are not surprising, given that government policies have been focused on restricting pollution but not on controlling the use of resources. But how should we view our overuse of the earth? Should all of us alive today, who enjoy using our four-wheel drive autos, building houses in the far reaches of suburbia on former farmlands or wetlands, and using our ozone-destroying air conditions, feel guilty that our grandchildren will have less because we have more?

Most economists—including many who consider themselves environmentalists —would disagree with this perspective. They would argue that with each succeeding generation the economy's capacity to produce becomes greater, and levels of technology improve, so that human "welfare" can rise even as resources become more scarce.

Take, for example, the depletion of petroleum stocks, which is the largest negative adjustment that Redefining Progress makes to the GDP. There have been scares about declining oil supplies for more than a century, with the most recent being the oil "crises" of 1973 and 1979, when the Organization of Petroleum Exporting Countries (OPEC) sharply raised its prices.

But as new supplies of oil have been discovered throughout the world, OPEC's power has declined, and with it the price of crude oil. Gasoline prices in the United States (adjusted for inflation) are only slightly higher today than they were in 1973. Many economists, politicians, and perhaps the general public have concluded that there is no reason to worry about the availability of oil supplies for the next generation. But Redefining Progress argues that the failure of prices to rise today is weak evidence for believing that our children and grandchildren will not be faced with true resource scarcities. And Cobb et al. may be right. Since oil supplies are currently abundant, prices will only rise if their owners restrict supply by keeping oil in the ground today, while hoping to sell at higher prices in future decades. But if owners are interested only in short-term profits, then they will fail to conserve oil until a true shortage develops. To account for potential scarcity, and for the current costs of keeping prices low, the GPI treats oil consumption as a loss to society. The index values this loss at the high price of producing a renewable motor fuel—specifically "gasohol" derived from sugar cane or other organic materials. This is estimated at $75 a barrel (as of 1988)—about five times the current cost of buying crude oil on the world market! With oil consumption constituting a significant fraction of all U.S. spending, the $75 estimate causes a huge downward adjustment to the GDP. While most environmental analysts would probably agree with making some adjustment for resource scarcity, they would question the magnitude of Redefining Progress' estimate. It is likely that succeeding generations will face rising real oil prices over the next century, but Redefining Progress has not provided evidence to support a dramatic fivefold price rise.

Redefining Progress also makes large subtractions from the GDP to account for global warming, ozone depletion, and the gradual destruction of forests, farmland, and wetlands. While the principle behind this is undeniable, the reliability of their specific calculations is again uncertain. Concerning global warming, the Intergovernmental Panel on Climate Change has forecasted that average worldwide temperatures are likely to rise 2.5 degrees centigrade by the year 2025, and economist William Cline has estimated that this would cause $120 billion annually in losses to society. Warming is primarily due to releases of carbon dioxide to the atmosphere, and such releases are mainly a function of burning fossil fuels. To account for this, Cobb et al. take the cumulative consumption of oil, coal, and natural gas since 1900 and count $1 per barrel of oil (or its equivalent for coal and gas) as a long-term environmental cost. They make the same adjustment for electricity production from nuclear power plants, in view of the long-term threat from disposal of radioactive wastes. This yields a reduction of $645 billion, or more than one-tenth, to the 1994 Gross Domestic Product(!)—far higher than Cline's research justifies. Although their numbers are debatable, Redefining Progress has focused our attention on a critical problem, and has begun the necessary process of developing a more meaningful indicator of human welfare—one that would take into account the needs of future generations. As the GPI's authors say, if economists don't like their numbers, then the progression should begin the difficult task of developing better ones. In the meantime, the Genuine Progress Indicator is a serious effort to place values on resource depletion, environmental destruction, the household sector, inequality, and social costs. Even if it is a flawed effort, policymakers would do far better to pay attention to the GPI than to the absurdities of the Gross Domestic Product. ❏

Resources: The Genuine Progress Indicator: Summary of Data and Methodology, Clifford Cobb, Ted Halstead, and Jonathan Rowe, *Redefining Progress*, September 1995; "The Green Revenue Path: For Healthy Growth, ashington Should Tax Resources, Not Labor," Halstead and Rowe, *Washington Post*, September 10, 1995; "If The GDP Is Up, Why Is America Down?" Cobb, Halstead, and Rose, *Atlantic Monthly*, October 1995; Accounts Overdue: National Resource Depreciation in Costa Rica, World Resources Institute, December 1991.

Article 1.1.7

LET'S JUST ASSUME WE'RE SUSTAINABLE

BY WILLIAM E. REES
May/June 1997

"If it is very easy to substitute other factors for natural resources, then ... the world can, in effect, get along without natural resources, so exhaustion is just an event not a catastrophe." So wrote Nobel-winning economist Robert Solow in 1974. If we don't think about it much, this statement seems innocuous enough. The internal logic is impeccable and very comforting to those nervous about the state of the world. Probe a little deeper, however, and we find that Solow's message lies at the heart of a major controversy among economists concerning whether the economy—and society—are sustainable despite increasingly depleted and polluted resources in the long run.

Those on Solow's side believe that technology can substitute for nature. If we run out of some resource, human ingenuity and inventiveness will rally to find a replacement. Most economists in wealthy countries generally accept this argument.

But their ecologically minded colleagues question Solow's assumption that it is "very easy" to find substitutes for natural resources and processes. The ozone layer, for instance, may not be easily replaceable. If not, then our present economy is not organized in an "environmentally sustainable" way.

The controversy is tied to recent advances in capital theory. In the past decade, economists have begun to recognize that resources are a unique type of capital capable of producing income indefinitely into the future. For example, every year properly managed fish stocks can produce a catch that can be sustained into the future; if left intact, stratospheric ozone delivers continuous protection against harmful ultraviolet radiation. So-called "natural capital" has thus gained the same weight and theoretical status as the more familiar human-made capital—factories, machinery, and equipment.

This expanded concept of capital is now being used by both sides in the debate to develop measures of sustainability. From the perspective of capital theory, no economy is sustainable if it depletes productive assets, whether natural or human-made. An economy is only sustainable if it passes on the same per capita stock of capital from one generation to the next. But while this basic principle has gained wide acceptance in recent years, controversy remains over the degree to which manufactured capital can substitute for natural capital.

Neoclassical economists and other analysts generally assume that the two forms of capital are interchangeable. By this interpretation, depleting natural resources—natural capital—does not matter so long as part of the money generated by resource use is invested in manufactured capital of equivalent value. Because the neoclassical view makes no distinction between natural and human-made assets, this variation on the theme is referred to as "weak sustainability."

To many non-economists, it is a long stretch to assume that natural and humanmade capital can just substitute for one another. However, the argument is not entirely groundless. Economists assume (yes, another assumption) that you can measure the scarcity of a good by its market price. Repeated studies since the 1960s have shown that the real prices of most resources bought and sold on the market have remained stable or have actually fallen over the past century. Economists take this as evidence that any hint of scarcity for a natural commodity stimulates human ingenuity to find a substitute, thus conserving the original resource. Sometimes the substitution is the functional equivalent, as when metal studs replace wooden ones in construction. As often, however, we invent an entirely new technology with different or educed material requirements. Think of how much copper wire has been saved by the developmentof microwave communication, the adoption of printed circuit boards, and the invention of optical fibers. (These fibers are as thin as a human hair and can carry more information more accurately than a thick bundle of copper wires.)

Examples like this are sometimes used to press the substitution argument to extremes. For instance, because optical fiber is itself not found in nature but is made fromsilicon (the second-most abundant element in the Earth's crust), technological optimists proclaim that resources are actually more the product of the human mind than of nature. Thus, in 1990, Walter Block, then senior economist at the Fraser Institute (a Canadian neoconservative think tank), argued the benefits of continuous population growth on the grounds that "additional people can create more resources than they useup, thanks to technological improvements..." More recently, the University of Maryland's famed growth advocate, Julian Simon, wrote: "Technology exists now to produce in virtually inexhaustible quantities just about all the products made by nature..."

Extremes aside, most economists and planners today do favor the "weak sustainability" model. Indeed, it undergirds their model of international development driven by continuous material growth, globalization, liberalized trade—and the depletion of natural capital.

Ecological economists, on the other hand, are less sanguine about human prospects than their mainstream colleagues. They observe that natural and manufactured capital often complement each other in the production process and cannot always substitute for one another. For example, more fishing boats are no substitute for a depleted stock of fish. In fact, since human-made capital is made from natural capital and requires natural resources to function, then natural capital is a prerequisite for manufactured capital.

In any event, it is becoming clear that certain crucial goods and services of nature are essential to human life and the economy. They cannot be substituted, and if lost, they are lost forever. Exhausting the stock of certain types of natural capital could therefore be catastrophic (as may be the case with stratospheric ozone, currently being depleted by CFCs and other industrial chemicals made from chlorine and bromine). It seems, therefore, that Solow's assumption is false, and if so, both the notion of weak sustainability and the prevailing model of global development collapse.

Ecologically minded analysts therefore support a "strong sustainability" argument instead. This is a more cautious model in which renewable natural capital and manufactured capital must each be maintained intact for the next generation.

Strong sustainability implies that humankind must learn to live on the annual income of goods and "life support services" of air, water and the like, generated by the natural capital stocks we have left. If the population grows, so should our natural capital stocks.

There are other reasons to be suspicious of the weak sustainability model. Economists measure the natural capital stock using customary accounting methods, including market prices. But markets only work well with familiar, easily quantified material and energy commodities. The assimilation of wastes, "life support," aesthetic and spiritual values—all important services provided by the environment—are difficult to price or are simply invisible to conventional analysis. These may be lost forever as the stocks that produce them are liquidated or converted to human-made capital. For example, as forests are clear-cut for lumber and wood fiber, we lose their carbon sink functions—a key to the stability of the globe's climate—their water regulation and flood control services, and their biodiversity and spiritual values. How can we have confidence in a view of sustainability that does not account for such enormous wealth simply because it cannot be priced in the marketplace?

If the prevailing system of costs, prices and incentives fails absolutely as an indicator of impending scarcity, it is no surprise that conventional economic analyses raise few concerns about potential unsustainability. Instead, those who sound the ecological alarm are usually biologists and others who work with physical data on the state of the world.

One final problem. It turns out that many countries cannot meet standards for even weak sustainability. Worse, many that do, such as Germany, the Netherlands, Japan, and the United States, survive only by appropriating the ecological output of a land and sea area vastly larger than their own domestic territories. While they may seem economically sustainable, these high-income economies are running massive "ecological deficits" with the rest of the world. They draw on the Third World for resources, locate high-polluting industries and landfills there, and generally abuse the global commons. Thus, their high-flying lifestyles cannot be extended sustainably to all of humanity using prevailing technology.

No wonder the international community is having such difficulty defining a criterion for sustainability that is ecologically rigorous. Accepting strong sustainability would require significant government intervention in the economy and a radical transformation of consumer values and behavior. Weak sustainability is certainly easier to swallow—it virtually assumes we are already sustainable. ❏

Resources: Steady State Economics, Herman Daly (Island Press, 1991); "Capital Theory and the Measurement of Sustainable Development: An Indicator of Weak Sustainability," David W. Pearce and Giles D. Atkinson, *Ecological Economics* 8, 1993; "Ecological Footprints and Appropriated Carrying Capacity: Measuring the Natural Capital Requirements of the Human Economy," William Rees and M. Wackernagel, in A.M. Jansson et al., *Investing in Natural Capital: The Ecological Economics Approach to Sustainability* (Island Press, 1994); "How Strong Is Weak Sustainability?" P. Victor et al., *Economie Applique* XLVIII, 1995; "The Economics of Resources or the Resources of Economics," Robert Solow, *American Economics Review* 2, 1974; "The State of Humanity: Steadily Improving," Julian Simon, The Cato Institute, 1995.

Article 1.1.8

SHARING THE WEALTH OF THE COMMONS

BY PETER BARNES
November/December 2004

We're all familiar with private wealth, even if we don't have much. Economists and the media celebrate it every day. But there's another trove of wealth we barely notice: our common wealth.

Each of us is the beneficiary of a vast inheritance. This common wealth includes our air and water, habitats and ecosystems, languages and cultures, science and technologies, political and monetary systems, and quite a bit more. To say we share this inheritance doesn't mean we can call a broker and sell our shares tomorrow. It does mean we're responsible for the commons and entitled to any income it generates. Both the responsibility and the entitlement are ours by birth. They're part of the obligation each generation owes to the next, and each living human owes to other beings.

At present, however, our economic system scarcely recognizes the commons. This omission causes two major tragedies: ceaseless destruction of nature and widening inequality among humans. Nature gets destroyed because no one's unequivocally responsible for protecting it. Inequality widens because private wealth concentrates while common wealth shrinks.

The great challenges for the 21st century are, first of all, to make the commons visible; second, to give it proper reverence; and third, to translate that reverence into property rights and legal institutions that are on a par with those supporting private property. If we do this, we can avert the twin tragedies currently built into our market-driven system.

Defining the Commons

What exactly is the commons? Here is a workable definition: The commons includes all the assets we inherit together and are morally obligated to pass on, undiminished, to future generations.

This definition is a practical one. It designates a set of assets that have three specific characteristics: they're (1) inherited, (2) shared, and (3) worthy of long-term preservation. Usually it's obvious whether an asset has these characteristics or not.

At the same time, the definition is broad. It encompasses assets that are natural as well as social, intangible as well as tangible, small as well as large. It also introduces a moral factor that is absent from other economic definitions: it requires us to consider whether an asset is worthy of long-term preservation. At present, capitalism has no interest in this question. If an asset is likely to yield a competitive return to capital, it's kept alive; if not, it's destroyed or allowed to run down. Assets in the commons, by contrast, are meant to be preserved regardless of their return.

This definition sorts all economic assets into two baskets, the market and the commons. In the market basket are those assets we want to own privately and manage for profit. In the commons basket are the assets we want to hold in common and manage for long-term preservation. These baskets then are, or ought to be, the yin and yang of economic activity; each should enhance and contain the other. The role of the state should be to maintain a healthy balance between them.

The Value of the Commons

For most of human existence, the commons supplied everyone's food, water, fuel, and medicines. People hunted, fished, gathered fruits and herbs, collected firewood and building materials, and grazed their animals in common lands and waters. In other words, the commons was the source of basic sustenance. This is still true today in many parts of the world, and even in San Francisco, where I live, cash-poor people fish in the bay not for sport, but for food.

Though sustenance in the industrialized world now flows mostly through markets, the commons remains hugely valuable. It's the source of all natural resources and nature's many replenishing services. Water, air, DNA, seeds, topsoil, minerals, the protective ozone layer, the atmosphere's climate regulation, and much more, are gifts of nature to us all.

Just as crucially, the commons is our ultimate waste sink. It recycles water, oxygen, carbon, and everything else we excrete, exhale, or throw away. It's the place we store, or try to store, the residues of our industrial system.

The commons also holds humanity's vast accumulation of knowledge, art, and thought. As Isaac Newton said, "If I have seen further it is by standing on the shoulders of giants." So, too, the legal, political, and economic institutions we inherit—even the market itself—were built by the efforts of millions. Without these gifts we'd be hugely poorer than we are today.

To be sure, thinking of these natural and social inheritances primarily as economic assets is a limited way of viewing them. I deeply believe they are much more than that. But if treating portions of the commons as economic assets can help us conserve them, it's surely worth doing so.

How much might the commons be worth in monetary terms? It's relatively easy to put a dollar value on private assets. Accountants and appraisers do it every day, aided by the fact that private assets are regularly traded for money.

This isn't the case with most shared assets. How much is clean air, an intact wetlands,

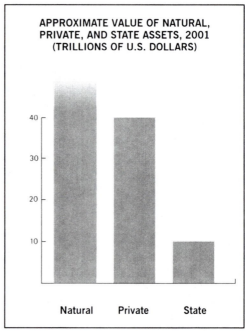

APPROXIMATE VALUE OF NATURAL, PRIVATE, AND STATE ASSETS, 2001 (TRILLIONS OF U.S. DOLLARS)

Natural   Private   State

or Darwin's theory of evolution worth in dollar terms? Clearly, many shared inheritances are simply priceless. Others are potentially quantifiable, but there's no current market for them. Fortunately, economists have developed methods to quantify the value of things that aren't traded, so it's possible to estimate the value of the "priceable" part of the commons within an order of magnitude. The surprising conclusion that emerges from numerous studies is that the wealth we share is worth more than the wealth we own privately.

This fact bears repeating. Even though much of the commons can't be valued in monetary terms, the parts that can be valued are worth more than all private assets combined.

It's worth noting that these estimates understate the gap between common and private assets because a significant portion of the value attributed to private wealth is in fact an appropriation of common wealth. If this mislabeled portion was subtracted from private wealth and added to common wealth, the gap between the two would widen further.

Two examples will make this point clear. Suppose you buy a house for $200,000 and, without improving it, sell it a few years later for $300,000. You pay off the mortgage and walk away with a pile of cash. But what caused the house to rise in value? It wasn't anything you did. Rather, it was the fact that your neighborhood became more popular, likely a result of the efforts of community members, improvements in public services, and similar factors.

Or consider another fount of private wealth, the social invention and public expansion of the stock market. Suppose you start a business that goes "public" through an offering of stock. Within a few years, you're able to sell your stock for a spectacular capital gain.

Much of this gain is a social creation, the result of centuries of monetary-system evolution, laws and regulations, and whole industries devoted to accounting, sharing information, and trading stocks. What's more, there's a direct correlation between the scale and quality of the stock market as an institution and the size of the private gain. You'll fetch a higher price if you sell into a market of millions than into a market of two. Similarly, you'll gain more if transaction costs are low and trust in public information is high. Thus, stock that's traded on a regulated exchange sells for a higher multiple of earnings than unlisted stock. This socially created premium can account for 30% of the stock's value. If you're the lucky seller, you'll reap that extra cash—in no way thanks to anything you did as an individual.

Real estate gains and the stock market's social premium are just two instances of common assets contributing to private gain. Still, most rich people would like us to think it's their extraordinary talent, hard work, and risk-taking that create their well-deserved wealth. That's like saying a flower's beauty is due solely to its own efforts, owing nothing to nutrients in the soil, energy from the sun, water from the aquifer, or the activity of bees.

The Great Commons Giveaway

That we inherit a trove of common wealth is the good news. The bad news, alas, is that our inheritance is being grossly mismanaged. As a recent report by the advocacy group Friends of the Commons concludes, "Maintenance of the commons is terrible, theft is rampant, and rents often aren't collected. To put it bluntly, our common wealth—and our children's—is being squandered. We are all poorer as a result."

Examples of commons mismanagement include the handout of broadcast spectrum to media conglomerates, the giveaway of pollution rights to polluters, the extension of copyrights to entertainment companies, the patenting of seeds and genes, the privatization of water, and the relentless destruction of habitat, wildlife, and ecosystems.

This mismanagement, though currently extreme, is not new. For over 200 years, the market has been devouring the commons in two ways. With one hand, the market takes valuable stuff from the commons and privatizes it. This is called "enclosure." With the other hand, the market dumps bad stuff into the commons and says, "It's your problem." This is called "externalizing." Much that is called economic growth today is actually a form of cannibalization in which the market diminishes the commons that ultimately sustains it.

Enclosure—the taking of good stuff from the commons—at first meant privatization of land by the gentry. Today it means privatization of many common assets by corporations. Either way, it means that what once belonged to everyone now belongs to a few.

Enclosure is usually justified in the name of efficiency. And sometimes, though not always, it does result in efficiency gains. But what also results from enclosure is the impoverishment of those who lose access to the commons, and the enrichment of those who take title to it. In other words, enclosure widens the gap between those with income-producing property and those without.

Externalizing—the dumping of bad stuff into the commons—is an automatic behavior pattern of profit-maximizing corporations: if they can avoid any out-of-pocket costs, they will. If workers, taxpayers, anyone downwind, future generations, or nature have to absorb added costs, so be it.

For decades, economists have agreed we'd be better served if businesses "internalized" their externalities—that is, paid in real time the costs they now shift to the commons. The reason this doesn't happen is that there's no one to set prices and collect them. Unlike private wealth, the commons lacks property rights and institutions to represent it in the marketplace.

The seeds of such institutions, however, are starting to emerge. Consider one of the environmental protection tools the U.S. currently uses, pollution trading. So-called cap-and-trade programs put a cap on total pollution, then grant portions of the total, via permits, to each polluting firm. Companies may buy other firms' permits if they want to pollute more than their allotment allows, or sell unused permits if they manage to pollute less. Such programs are generally supported by business because they allow polluters to find the cheapest ways to reduce pollution.

Public discussion of cap-and-trade programs has focused exclusively on their trading features. What's been overlooked is how they give away common wealth to polluters.

To date, all cap-and-trade programs have begun by giving pollution rights to existing polluters for free. This treats polluters as if they own our sky and rivers. It means that future polluters will have to pay old polluters for the scarce—hence valuable—right to dump wastes into nature. Imagine that: because a corporation polluted in the past, it gets free income forever! And, because ultimately we'll all pay for limited pollution via higher prices, this amounts to an enormous transfer of wealth—trillions of dollars—to shareholders of historically polluting corporations.

In theory, though, there is no reason that the initial pollution rights should not reside with the public. Clean air and the atmosphere's capacity to absorb pollutants are "wealth" that belongs to everyone. Hence, when polluters use up these parts of the commons, they should pay the public—not the other way around.

Taking the Commons Back

How can we correct the system omission that permits, and indeed promotes, destruction of nature and ever-widening inequality among humans? The answer lies in building a new sector of the economy whose clear legal mission is to preserve shared inheritances for everyone. Just as the market is populated by profit-maximizing corporations, so this new sector would be populated by asset-preserving trusts.

Here a brief description of trusts may be helpful. The trust is a private institution that's even older than the corporation. The essence of a trust is a fiduciary relationship. A trust holds and manages property for another person or for many other people. A simple example is a trust set up by a grandparent to pay for a grandchild's education. Other trusts include pension funds, charitable foundations, and university endowments. There are also hundreds of trusts in America, like the Nature Conservancy and the Trust for Public Land, that own land or conservation easements in perpetuity.

If we were to design an institution to protect pieces of the commons, we couldn't do much better than a trust. The goal of commons management, after all, is to preserve assets and deliver benefits to broad classes of beneficiaries. That's what trusts do, and it's not rocket science.

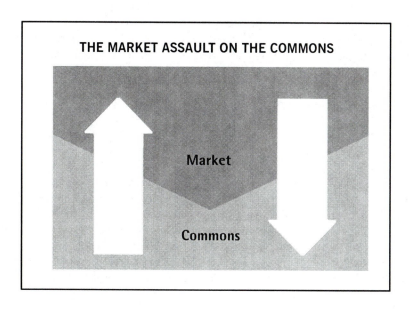

THE MARKET ASSAULT ON THE COMMONS

Market

Commons

Over centuries, several principles of trust management have evolved. These include:

- Trustees have a fiduciary responsibility to beneficiaries. If a trustee fails in this obligation, he or she can be removed and penalized.
- Trustees must preserve the original asset. It's okay to spend income, but don't invade the principal.
- Trustees must assure transparency. Information about money flows should be readily available to beneficiaries.

Trusts in the new commons sector would be endowed with rights comparable to those of corporations. Their trustees would take binding oaths of office and, like judges, serve long terms. Though protecting common assets would be their primary job, they would also distribute income from those assets to beneficiaries. These beneficiaries would include all citizens within a jurisdiction, large classes of citizens (children, the elderly), and/or agencies serving common purposes such as public transit or ecological restoration. When distributing income to individuals, the allocation formula would be one person, one share. The right to receive commons income would be a nontransferable birthright, not a property right that could be traded.

Fortuitously, a working model of such a trust already exists: the Alaska Permanent Fund. When oil drilling on the North Slope began in the 1970s, Gov. Jay Hammond, a Republican, proposed that 25% of the state's royalties be placed in a mutual fund to be invested on behalf of Alaska's citizens. Voters approved in a referendum. Since then, the Alaska Permanent Fund has grown to over $28 billion, and Alaskans have received roughly $22,000 apiece in dividends. In 2003 the per capita dividend was $1,107; a family of four received $4,428.

What Alaska did with its oil can be replicated for other gifts of nature. For example, we could create a nationwide Sky Trust to stabilize the climate for future generations. The trust would restrict emissions of heat-trapping gases and sell a declining number of emission permits to polluters. The income would be returned to U.S. residents in equal yearly dividends, thus reversing the wealth transfer built into current cap-and-trade programs. Instead of everyone paying historic polluters, polluters would pay all of us.

Just as a Sky Trust could represent our equity in the natural commons, a Public Stock Trust could embody our equity in the social commons. Such a trust would capture some of the socially created stock-market premium that currently flows only to shareholders and their investment bankers. As noted earlier, this premium is sizeable—roughly 30% of the value of publicly traded stock. A simple way to share it would be to create a giant mutual fund—call it the American Permanent Fund—that would hold, say, 10% of the shares of publicly traded companies. This mutual fund, in turn, would be owned by all Americans on a one share per person basis (perhaps linked to their Social Security accounts).

To build up the fund without precipitating a fall in share prices, companies would contribute shares at the rate of, say, 1% per year. The contributions would be the price companies pay for the benefits they derive from a commons asset, the large, trusted market for stock—a small price, indeed, for the hefty benefits. Over time, the mutual fund would assure that when the economy grows, everyone benefits. The top 5% would still own more than the bottom 90%, but at least every American would have some property income, and a slightly larger slice of our economic pie.

Sharing the Wealth

The perpetuation of inequality is built into the current design of capitalism. Because of the skewed distribution of private wealth, a small self-perpetuating minority receives a disproportionate share of America's nonlabor income.

Tom Paine had something to say about this. In his essay "Agrarian Justice," written in 1790, he argued that, because enclosure of the commons had separated so many people from their primary source of sustenance, it was necessary to create a functional equivalent of the commons in the form of a National Fund. Here is how he put it:

> There are two kinds of property. Firstly, natural property, or that which comes to us from the Creator of the universe—such as the earth, air, water. Secondly, artificial or acquired property—the invention of men. In the latter, equality is impossible; for to distribute it equally, it would be necessary that all should have contributed in the same proportion, which can never be the case .... Equality of natural property is different. Every individual in the world is born with legitimate claims on this property, or its equivalent.

Enclosure of the commons, he went on, was necessary to improve the efficiency of cultivation. But:

> The landed monopoly that began with [enclosure] has produced the greatest evil. It has dispossessed more than half the inhabitants of every nation of their natural inheritance, without providing for them, as ought to have been done, an indemnification for that loss, and has thereby created a species of poverty and wretchedness that did not exist before.

The appropriate compensation for loss of the commons, Paine said, was a national fund financed by rents paid by land owners. Out of this fund, every person reaching age 21 would get 15 pounds a year, and every person over 50 would receive an additional 10 pounds. (Think of Social Security, financed by commons rents instead of payroll taxes.)

A Progressive Offensive

Paine's vision, allowing for inflation and new forms of enclosure, could not be more timely today. Surely from our vast common inheritance—not just the land, but the atmosphere, the broadcast spectrum, our mineral resources, our threatened habitats and water supplies—enough rent can be collected to pay every American over age 21 a modest annual dividend, and every person reaching 21 a small start-up inheritance.

Such a proposal may seem utopian. In today's political climate, perhaps it is. But consider this. About 20 years ago, right-wing think tanks laid out a bold agenda. They called for lowering taxes on private wealth, privatizing much of government, and deregulating industry. Amazingly, this radical agenda has largely been achieved.

It's time for progressives to mount an equally bold offensive. The old shibboleths—let's gin up the economy, create jobs, and expand government programs—no longer excite. We need to talk about fixing the economy, not just growing it; about income for everyone, not just jobs; about nurturing ecosystems, cultures, and communities, not just our individual selves. More broadly, we need to celebrate the commons as an essential counterpoise to the market.

Unfortunately, many progressives have viewed the state as the only possible counterpoise to the market. The trouble is, the state has been captured by corporations. This capture isn't accidental or temporary; it's structural and long-term.

This doesn't mean progressives can't occasionally recapture the state. We've done so before and will do so again. It does mean that progressive control of the state is the exception, not the norm; in due course, corporate capture will resume. It follows that if we want lasting fixes to capitalism's tragic flaws, we must use our brief moments of political ascendancy to build institutions that endure.

Programs that rely on taxes, appropriations, or regulations are inherently transitory; they get weakened or repealed when political power shifts. By contrast, institutions that are self-perpetuating and have broad constituencies are likely to last. (It also helps if they mail out checks periodically.) This was the genius of Social Security, which has survived—indeed grown—through numerous Republican administrations.

If progressives are smart, we'll use our next New Deal to create common property trusts that include all Americans as beneficiaries. These trusts will then be to the 21st century what social insurance was to the 20th: sturdy pillars of shared responsibility and entitlement. Through them, the commons will be a source of sustenance for all, as it was before enclosure. Life-long income will be linked to generations-long ecological health. Isn't that a future most Americans would welcome? ❏

Article 1.1.9

HUNTERS OR SHEPHERDS OF THE SEA?
Understanding the fisheries crisis of the Northwest Atlantic

BY SAMUEL SCOTT
January/Febrary 2001

On October 29, 2000, the Portland, Maine, fishing community gathered on the city's Fish Pier to hold a memorial service for Carlyle "Butch" Minot. Minot's body had been recovered four days earlier, 35 miles off the coast. Caught between declining catches and restrictions on the amount of time that can be spent at sea, fishers are accepting greater risks in an already dangerous industry. Minot, the fifth member of the Portland fishing community lost at sea in the year 2000, had been fishing by himself when he was lost. Another fisher said of Minot's decision to go out alone, "It's stupid. It shouldn't be done. I've done it myself and it's stupid." In coastal communities throughout the northeast United States and Atlantic Canada, however, fishers face a crushing dilemma of working harder and at greater risk than ever before,or getting out of the life altogether.

Throughout the 500-year history of commercial fishing in the northwest Atlantic, there has been one constant: the fishers harvesting the sea have worked at the limits of their ships, their gear, and their bodies. At a high cost in both lives and vessels, they have worked hard to catch as many fish as they could, as fast as they could, and for as long as they could. In the process, they have created an industrial culture that emphasizes working at high risk to maximize the catch. The introduction over the last half century of new technologies in fishing, food processing, and food distribution has created an unbearable burden on the ecosystems of the northwest Atlantic. The crisis will require a fundamental shift not only in how fisheries are managed, but also in how the peoples and communities living along the shores of this region understand their relationship to the sea.

To the Limit

While the fishers of the 19th century, like their present-day counterparts, pushed themselves and their equipment as far as they could, their maximum catch remained well within the sustainable limits of the northwest Atlantic ecosystem. The fishing grounds were so productive, in fact, that contemporary experts predicted that they could never be exhausted. As long as the fishers worked from sailing vessels with hook and line, these predictions might have held true. However, two crucial developments, occurring on either side of the turn of the 20th century, destroyed the balance: the introduction of the steel-hulled fishing trawler and the perfection of refrigeration and frozen foods.

The change in vessel in the late 19th century allowed for a entirely new method of catching fish. The net replaced the hook and line as the primary method of capture. The new boats could drag an enormous sack-shaped net across the ocean bottom where the most highly prized species of fish lived. This method was called trawling, and the word trawler soon became synonymous with fishing boat throughout the North Atlantic. Trawlers immediately began landing catches six times greater than the fishing schooners. The fishers, used to driving both themselves and their vessels to the breaking point, now had a vessel whose endurance and durability were far greater than before. Fishers from the United States and Canada were joined in their traditional waters by Europeans—English, French, and Spanish—who used the speed and endurance of the new trawlers to extend their scope far west from Europe.

The unprecedented catches were fed into a market radically enlarged by the introduction of frozen-food technology in the early decades of the 20th century. The emergence of distribution centers like the large fish markets in Boston and New York were a boon to seafood processors. Focused distribution allowed them to control most of the catch without needing to invest directly in fishing vessels and crews. Freezing and fast transportation allowed them to extend the market for fresh fish to consumers living far from the smell of salt air. As a result, fishers had every economic incentive to use their new vessels to their fullest extent.

Below the waters, however, the marvelous fishing grounds that had supported centuries of intensive harvesting were beginning to change. As the vast amounts of fish being harvested began to strain the fish population, the method of capture was damaging the ecosystem's ability to recover. The bottom-dragging trawls that could sweep tons of fish from the ocean floor also caused significant damage to the fishes' habitat. It did not take long for the double stress of overfishing and habitat destruction to cause noticeable declines in the catch. The fishers responded with the customary aggressiveness. More powerful vessels and more efficient gear were employed by fishers working ever harder to sustain the catch levels they had come to expect. The fishers were whipped into an even greater sense of urgency by the intense competition among the multinational fleets present on the fishing grounds. The predictable result was an accelerated degradation of the ecosystem.

By the 1960s the inability of the northwest Atlantic ecosystem to sustain the level of harvest was undeniable. The response by the fishing nations was one of nationalprotectionism. The extension of national sovereignty over vast expanses of ocean took some time to emerge, but by the mid-1970s most nations had laid claim to exclusive fishing rights up to 200 miles from their shores. The lucrative fishing grounds of the northwest Atlantic largely fell to the United States and Canada, and their respective fishing fleets immediately reaped the benefits. So great was the prize of the grounds that the two nations could not agree where the demarcation line between the two zones fell. An international court arbitrated nearly a decade later. The resulting Hague Line, established in 1984, pleased no one, and has been a source of contention ever since, particularly because the line bisects George's Bank, one of the region's richest grounds.

The 200-mile limits, and the resulting departure of the international fleets from their waters, brought good days for the U.S. and Canadian fishing industries. This windfall only served to reinforce an industrial culture that pushed body and boat to the limit. It took very little time for the domestic fishing fleets to make up for the capacity of the departed foreign fleets. In fact, they soon both outstripped the industry's prior harvest capacity and brought the total catch to unprecedented levels. By the end of the 1980s the assault on the fish populations finally reached catastrophic proportions and the fish stocks began to collapse.

The fishing communities bore the economic brunt of the ecological crisis. Unemployment in Gloucester and New Bedford, two of the largest fishing ports in Massachusetts, for example, consistently exceeds the statewide rate—sometimes by nearly double. Traditional structures of credit, whereby fishers could fuel, provision, and maintain their vessels based on the return of future voyages, are deteriorating and disappearing throughout the Massachusetts fishing ports. In 1994, Gloucester's fishing population numbered around 400, down from 2,000 at mid-century. In the same year, the National Marine Fisheries Service estimated that the Gloucester fishing fleet was twice as large as the current fish stocks could sustain. In the year 2000, a report to the New England Fishery Management Council concluded that fish populations were well below the targets necessary for rebuilding stocks and recommended further reductions in both the overall fishing effort and the fleet capacity.

Too Little, Too Late

Faced with the protests of the fishing communities and criticism from environmentalists, the Canadian and U.S. governments tried various belated strategies to shore up the plummeting fish populations. In the aftermath of the 200-mile limits, the Canadian government promoted the integration of the fishing industry as part of an economic- development package for the depressed Atlantic provinces. It fostered local fish-processing facilities that owned their own fleets of trawlers. Ultimately, these large concerns came to own almost half of the Canadian fleet capacity. Canadian regulations tried to capitalize on this concentration of vessel ownership—emphasizing limited entry into the industry and catch quota systems. The United States, which always had a much more decentralized industrial structure, focused on limiting the type of gear used and closing certain areas to fishing altogether. These partial regulatory schemes failed partially because they were instituted too late. Worldwatch Institute researcher Anne Platt McGinn has shown that the governments only acted in the face of immediate environmental collapse. To succeed, McGinn argues, regulators would have had to take a precautionary approach—monitoring environmental indicators more closely, and implementing regulations when the indicators pointed to a coming crisis, rather than after the crisis itself had occurred.

In the aftermath of failed attempts at regulation, both the United States and Canada resorted to widespread closures of fishing grounds. The 200-mile limits themselves posed a tremendous obstacle to effective management. The fishing grounds are part of a single ecosystem. To work, any system of regulation would have to address the ecosystem in its entirety. Instead, the 200- mile limits divided the grounds between Canadian and U.S. sovereignty, often in an atmosphere of national fervor and acrimony. This thwarted the development of an overarching authority that could work across boundaries in governing the whole ecosystem.

Perhaps the most uncontrollable of the challenges to effective fisheries management, however, is the voracious world market for fish. Many of the largest seafood producers shop regularly on the international market. Gorton's Foods, for example, is actually located in Gloucester, Massachusetts, but has not used locally landed fish in its products for nearly 30 years. The company relies instead on a world supply of quick-frozen fish that is more readily available and cheaper than the local supply. The world fish market protects the big seafood concerns from fluctuations in the local catch—isolating the impact to the local level. Reductions in a regional catch, whether for ecological or regulatory reasons, do not necessarily mean increased prices for regional fishers, as there are ready substitutes from fisheries around the world. As the traditional Atlantic cod and halibut have disappeared from the fish counters they have been seamlessly replaced with Chilean sea bass, mahi mahi, and other white fish with similar texture and appearance.

Regulations limiting the catch have clashed with the tightly knit culture of professional fishers, sparking resentment among the fishing communities and provoking an unwillingness to comply with the measures imposed. Fishers have continued under their customary mode of operation—pushing their own limits and those of the ecosystem. Today's fishing technology, however, is simply too efficient for the traditional aggressive mode of harvest to be practiced in a sustainable way. If the fisheries are to be restored, the very culture of fishing is going to have to change.

New Approaches

Various proposed regulatory structures have tried to grapple with the fisheries crisis. Maritime anthropologist Evelyn Pinkerton has advocated the novel approach of involving the fishing communities themselves in fisheries management. Numerous case studies show that organizations of fishers can become active participants in the development and enforcement of fisheries policy, with the sustainability of the harvest as a key objective. Salmon fishers in southeastern Alaska, for example, formed an organization that included all types of harvest technologies and worked effectively with state environmental bodies to guarantee the benefits of the industry for all participants—including commercial and sport fishers. Such examples of cooperative fisheries management, while usually working on a small scale, are particularly encouraging because they show fishing communities changing their relationship to their fisheries—from simple harvester to active custodian. The goal of management of the northwest Atlantic fisheries cannot be to restore fish stocks to a level where intensive fishing can be resumed. This would only perpetuate the fishing culture that has proved so destructive and lead to future environmental disasters and industrial collapse. Introducing restraint into the fishing culture of the northwest Atlantic will probably be the greatest challenge for future regulatory policy. If there is any silver lining to the current crisis, however, it is that the fishers' shared sense of economic desperation could help engender the collective identity necessary for them to assume a central role in the management of the fisheries.

Fisheries management is a global problem with intense local consequences. The depletion of the northwest Atlantic fishing grounds has meant not only economic disaster for local fishing communities, but also increased pressure on other grounds around the world to make up the difference. Managing the fisheries of the northwest

Atlantic will require the establishment of an international oversight institution. To sustain the fishing communities that line the shores, the fishers will need to be active and central players in the development and implementation of fisheries policy. If a successful system can be developed, every effort should be made to apply it to other threatened fishing grounds throughout the world's oceans. Ultimately, the role of the fisher will have to be reshaped—from hunter to shepherd of the seas. ❑

Resources: Mark Kurlansky, Cod: *A Biography of the Fish that Changed the World*, 1997; Peter B. Doeringer and David G. Terkla, *Troubled Waters: Economic Structure, Regulatory reform, and Fisheries Trade*, 1995; Anne Platt McGinn, *Rocking the Boat: Conserving Fisheries and Protecting Jobs*, Worldwatch Paper 142, Worldwatch Institute, 1998; Evelyn Pinkerton, ed., *Co-operative Management of Local Fisheries*, 1989; Linda Greenlaw, *The Hungry Ocean: A Swordboat Captain's Journey*, 1999; Sebastian Junger, The Perfect Storm, 1997; "Five dead: 'What's happening here?'" *Portland Press Herald*, October 27, 2000.

Article 1.1.10

THE LAND TRUST SOLUTION
Land trusts ease control of U.S. farmland away from developers.

BY MICHELLE SHEEHAN

It was back in the early 1970s that Steven and Gloria Decater of Covelo, Calif., first started farming an unused plot of land belonging to a neighbor. Over many years, they turned the fallow plot into fertile farmland that yielded a bounty of organic vegetables. They named it "Live Power Community Farm" and launched California's first successful community supported agriculture (CSA) program there in 1988. But the Decaters' hold on the land was vulnerable. Without ownership rights, they risked losing the farm to encroaching development. The couple wanted to buy the property but could not afford the land into which they had poured their lives.

The Decaters found a solution to their land-tenure challenge that gave them ownership rights *and* ensured the land would remain an active organic farm. Their solution creates an important precedent—and a possible path for other small tenant farmers.

With the help of Equity Trust Inc., a Massachusetts-based organization that promotes property ownership reform, the Decaters gained ownership rights to the land in 1995—without having to pay the full value themselves. The couple purchased just its "agricultural use value," while Equity Trust, acting as a conservation land trust (a nonprofit institution that controls land for the benefit of current and future generations), purchased "easements," or deed restrictions, that were equal in value to the land's development rights. Together, the two payments amounted to the original asking price.

Agricultural easements are a good way for small farmers to gain ownership control over land when they're not looking to develop or sell it anyway, because they limit the property's market price to its working agricultural value, making it more affordable—while conserving it.

In transferring development rights to the conservation land trust, the Decaters forever forfeited their rights to subdivide or develop the land for anything other than farming; the terms cannot be changed unless both parties agree through a court process. The transaction unpacked the bundle of property rights associated with land ownership, dividing ownership between two entities and placing deliberate restrictions on how the land could be used in the future.

Ramped Up Land-Use Rules

This approach made sense for the Decaters, because they were interested in more than just owning the farm for themselves. "We wanted to have some sort of relationship where it wasn't merely privatized ownership," Gloria explains, "but a socially and economically responsible form of land tenure." They also wanted to make certain that the land would continue to be cultivated by resident farmers with sustainable methods well into the future.

WHAT ARE CONSERVATION LAND TRUSTS?

Conservation land trusts are nonprofit organizations designed to protect ecologically fragile environments, open space, or small farms. According to the 2003 National Land Trust Census, there are 1,537 local and national conservation land trusts in operation nationwide, protecting approximately 9 million acres of land, an area four times the size of Yellowstone National Park. This is twice the acreage protected by conservation land trusts just five years ago. New conservation land trusts are formed at the rate of two per week, according to the Land Trust Alliance. They exist in every state; California leads with 173 land trusts, followed by Massachusetts (154) and Connecticut (125). While land trusts protect land in a variety of ways, two of the most common approaches are acquiring land and acquiring conservation easements, legal agreements that permanently restrict the use of land, shielding it from development to ensure its conservation.

For more information on land trusts, see: Land Trust Alliance <www.lta.org>, Equity Trust, Inc. <www.equitytrust.org>, and Vermont Land Trust <www.vlt.org>.

Their vision for the farm was secured by designing easement provisions that went beyond any existing precedent. For example, most easements on farmland define agriculture rather loosely. As Equity Trust's Ellie Kastanopoulos notes, "anyone willing to put a few cows on their property and call it a farm" could exploit many agricultural easements. The Decaters and Equity Trust built in a "ramped up" agriculture requirement: Live Power Community Farm must be farmed continually by resident farmers and remain organic or "biodynamic" (a farming philosophy that treats the land as a balanced and sustainable unit and uses the rhythms of nature to maintain the health of the farm).

The Decaters' other major concern was the affordability of their land for future farmers. They see a lot of young farmers for whom "one of the biggest stumbling blocks is getting access to land," Gloria says. While traditional conservation easements ban developers, they do not curb the upward pressure on the price of the land from individual home or estate buyers. Steve worried that when he and Gloria were ready to pass on the land, market forces could "spike the cost of the land so high that any farmer would be bid clear out of the picture." To prevent this, the Decaters and Equity Trust crafted limitations on the resale price of the land into the easement.

Today, Live Power is an active 40-acre horse-powered community supported agriculture (CSA) farm, thriving amidst encroaching development and the huge corporate farms that dominate California agriculture. Not only do the Decaters own their land, but their unique conservation easement ensures that it will permanently remain an affordable, active, and ecologically sustainable farm. The Decaters are true stewards of the land, and the land trust's easement provisions reflect their commitment.

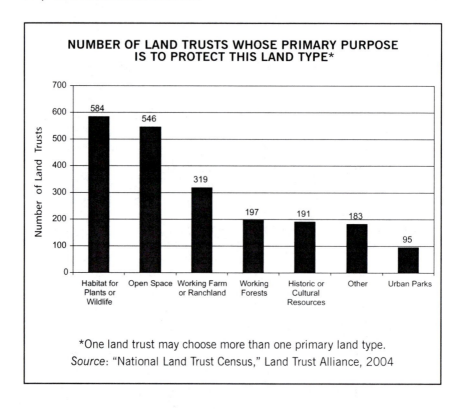

NUMBER OF LAND TRUSTS WHOSE PRIMARY PURPOSE IS TO PROTECT THIS LAND TYPE*

One land trust may choose more than one primary land type.
Source: "National Land Trust Census," Land Trust Alliance, 2004

New Ways of Looking at Land Ownership

In addition to conservation land trusts, Equity Trust and others have implemented a second land trust model. So-called "community land trusts" usually focus on low-income housing in urban areas (see "Burlington Bursts the Affordable Housing Debate," p. 19), but have in some cases included agricultural interests. They operate by purchasing tracts of land and then leasing them on a long-term basis to tenants who agree to a detailed land-use agreement. Although a farmer who enters into such a relationship would not own the land, he or she would have agricultural control and would own any improvements made to the land. In the tenant contract, the land trust would retain a purchase option for those improvements so that when the farmer was ready to move on, the land trust could ensure the lands remained affordable for new farmers. The land-use agreement could also include provisions to ensure the land remains in production. This option works well in areas where land is exorbitantly expensive, prohibiting the farmer from purchasing even restricted land, or when easements are not available.

In both land trust models, Equity Trust stresses, there is flexibility in how the relationship between the land trust and farmer is defined. Key to the definition is the land use agreement, which can be tailored for the particular situation according to either party's wishes. Kastanopolous notes that these are complex arrangements and "there is no black and white way of doing things." Indeed, one of Equity Trust's missions is to "change the way people think about and hold property." Their goal is to provide models that can be replicated and adapted to varied situations

These partnerships and new ways of looking at land ownership acknowledge that there are diverse interests in a piece of land. The farmers, the community, the environment, and future users are all considered. Steven Decater is excited by the prospect of agricultural land trusts catching on. "We'll have permanent farms," he says, "and they're going to be needed." He's right about that. Farm real estate values have risen by 70% in the last 20 years (see figure). Across the country, massive mechanized and chemically sustained corporate-controlled farms are rapidly replacing small-time farmers.

The most vulnerable small farmers are ones who sink tremendous energy and resources into improving their soil but are unable to afford the market value of the land they work. Their lack of ownership control puts their land, and their investment, in jeopardy. This is a particularly common experience for operators of CSA farms, in which producers sell "shares" directly to consumers who receive regular harvest portions during the growing season. According to an informal survey conducted by Equity Trust in the late 1990s, 70% of CSA farms operated on rented land.

Land trusts allow small tenant farms to access land, resist rising property values, and conserve small agricultural tracts. They provide an alternative to unchecked development and farm consolidation, while helping to preserve communities, shield the environment from development, and protect the livelihoods of small farmers. But they are underutilized—in part because the strategy poses certain challenges. It requires:

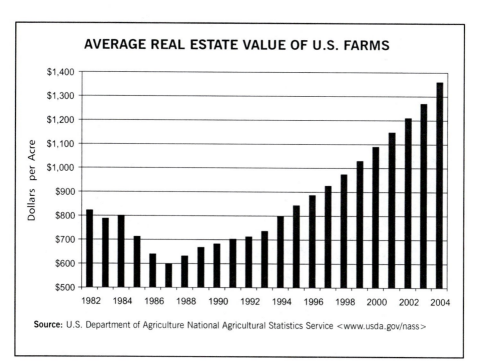

AVERAGE REAL ESTATE VALUE OF U.S. FARMS

Dollars per Acre

Source: U.S. Department of Agriculture National Agricultural Statistics Service <www.usda.gov/nass>

- resources to purchase the agricultural value of the land,
- willingness by current landowners to sell or donate the land to a land trust,
- technical expertise, and
- in the conservation land trust model, the presence of a conservation land trust with enough resources to pay for easements—which has become more difficult with skyrocketing property values.

Yet thanks to the hard work of the Decaters, Equity Trust, and other organizations including the Vermont Land Trust (VLT) and the Institute of Community Economics (ICE), this innovative approach to land ownership has taken hold in several parts of the country (see "What Are Conservation Land Trusts?"). The VLT oversees many similar transactions every year; it has worked with more than 1,000 landowners and conserved more than 400 farms. Although the group has not quite figured out how to meet the high demand for affordable land as demand pressure drives land prices up across the state, it is nevertheless successfully managing to preserve large areas of farmland in Vermont—and writing affordability restrictions into their easements wherever possible.

Steve Getz, a dairy farmer assisted by the VLT through an easement purchase, says, "We would not have been able to afford the land without the VLT." He and his wife Karen say they respect how the land trust model challenges the "it's my land and I'll do whatever I please with it" mantra that reflects the dominant conception of private land ownership in this country. They now own a successful pasture-based dairy farm in Bridport that will be forever preserved. ❑

CHAPTER 2:

COST-BENEFIT ANALYSIS AND CLIMATE CHANGE

Article 1.2.1

KATRINA HITS CANCER ALLEY

A Dollars & Sense *Interview with Environmental Justice Activist Monique Harden*

March/April 2006

The environmental, economic justice, and antiracism movements have not always been on the same page. A growing number of activists in all three, however, have begun to recognize that comprehensive analyses and strategies that address ecological devastation and economic and racial injustice together are indispensable. No one better embodies that crucial advance than Monique Harden. Harden is codirector of Advocates for Environmental Human Rights, a nonprofit, public interest law firm in New Orleans that she cofounded with attorney Nathalie Walker in 2002. Harden also coordinates international coalitions of community organizations advocating for human rights and environmental justice. Here are excerpts from Dollars & Sense *collective member Ben Greenberg's interview with Harden in New Orleans.* —Eds.

D&S: Let's start with the immediate environmental impacts of Katrina. What kinds of hazardous substances did the storm release?

MONIQUE HARDEN: It's important to understand the significant number of industrial facilities operating in Louisiana and the massive amount of toxic pollution that these industries release into our air, water, and land. Between New Orleans and Baton Rouge, an area known as "Cancer Alley," there are approximately 130 oil refineries and petrochemical facilities. When you are aware of the industrial pollution all around us, you can understand the toxic impact of forceful hurricane winds pushing onto communities the water and sediment that have received industrial discharges for many decades.

Our organization, Advocates for Environmental Human Rights, has been working with several groups to take samples of the sediment left behind after the flood waters were drained. We didn't want a replay of what EPA did in New York after 9/11—claiming that air quality was good when in fact it was very unhealthy. So, early on, Wilma Subra, a chemist in Louisiana, began taking sediment samples and analyzing them for our organizations. Both her sampling analysis and the tests that EPA conducted revealed high levels of contaminants in the sediment covering yards, streets, and sidewalks in flooded communities. Arsenic and diesel fuel substances are the most prevalent but not the only contaminants. However, EPA concluded that only more retesting and analysis was needed. We saw it very differently and have been demanding that the agency take action to immediately clean up the sediment.

The problem here is that EPA has not established a standard for cleaning up toxic sediment or soil; instead the agency has only established standards for further assessment. But we have looked at various Superfund sites and found that EPA has set, on a case-by-case basis, requirements for cleaning up these sites that should, at the very least, apply to our Gulf Coast communities. For example, in the PAB Oil & Chemical Services site in Louisiana, EPA required that arsenic in the soil be cleaned up so that no more than 10 milligrams per kilogram of arsenic remains in the soil on this site. In neighborhoods that were flooded in New Orleans, there are sediment-arsenic concentrations that are over 70 milligrams per kilogram. EPA's inaction threatens the health of residents who have returned to communities with contaminated sediment. Children, the elderly, and other people with poor health are particularly vulnerable to the toxins that EPA refuses to clean up.

After Hurricane Katrina, federal and state health agencies posted notices advising people to wear protective gear, such as Tyvek suits, respirator masks, gloves, and shoe covers, but not one government agency provides this protective gear to people returning to the area. Instead, a few nonprofit organizations have raised funds to deliver protective gear and health information to people. But these efforts are a drop in the bucket. For example, on December 1st, when a section of the Lower Ninth Ward was opened to residents, our organizations ran out of Tyvek suits—we had 1,000—and all the other protective gear in the first two and a half hours. Many more people needed this protective gear, but we couldn't help them. I felt terrible that our help was not enough and that our government could care less about protecting our health. In response to our requests, the city of New Orleans submitted an application to FEMA for protective gear, but there has been no response.

D&S: Tell me about the work that Advocates for Environmental Human Rights was doing before Katrina.

MH: Our mission is to advance and defend the human right to a healthy environment. We provide litigation, public advocacy, and community organizing support—all with the aim of reforming severe flaws in the U.S. environmental regulatory system that allow fundamental human rights to life, health, and racial equality to be violated. The failure of EPA to clean up contaminated sediment in Gulf Coast communities is part of a systemic problem; it underscores just how irrelevant human health protection is to the environmental regulatory system, notwithstanding the volumes of environmental laws and regulations established by our government.

D&S: **So your approach is to work on local issues but affect national policy?**

MH: That's correct. In March 2005, AEHR filed the first-ever human rights legal challenge against the United States for its failed environmental regulatory system. We prepared that litigation on behalf of Mossville, a historic African-American community in the southwest corner of Louisiana. In this petition, we sought specific health and environmental remedies for Mossville residents, as well as reform of the U.S. environmental regulatory system. We filed the petition with the Inter-American Commission on Human Rights of the Organization of American States.

D&S: **What company or companies were in violation of those residents' human rights and what were the specific environmental problems?**

MH: First of all, let me clarify: we are not charging the companies; we are charging the U.S. government for violating the human rights of Mossville residents. The government has authorized corporations that own fourteen toxic facilities in and around Mossville to endanger the lives of Mossville residents, harm their health, and burden this African-American community with millions of pounds of toxic chemicals that have made the air unhealthy, poisoned fish in local waters, and contaminated the soil.

What's more, a federal agency, the Agency for Toxic Substances and Disease Registry, has conducted dioxin testing of Mossville residents' blood, showing average dioxin concentrations that are three times higher than the national average. Dioxin can cause cancer and other serious health problems. However, this agency has resisted assisting the community in its demands for medical monitoring and health care.

Notwithstanding years of work by Mossville Environmental Action Now, our federal and state environmental and health agencies have not taken any meaningful action that protects the health of people living in Mossville. Instead these agencies issue more and more permits that allow the industrial facilities to increase pollution.

Demanding human rights protection is critical to ending this injustice, which is why Mossville Environmental Action Now and AEHR filed the legal petition with the Inter-American Commission on Human Rights. This commission, like so many other human rights judicial bodies, has determined that a government's failure to adequately protect the environment can violate human rights. In Mossville, and many other people of color and poor communities, fundamental human rights to life, health, and racial equality are trampled on by the U.S. system of so-called "environmental protection."

D&S: **Can you give a little background on Mossville?**

MH: Mossville was founded in the 1790s by emancipated Blacks. It was a place where people could go and raise their families in a safe haven from the racial hostility that was all around them. There's some history written on Mossville—elder Mossville residents will tell you that in the past the community was able to thrive because of its rich natural resources. Folks were able to farm, hunt, and fish; businesses were able to develop from those natural resources.

However, Mossville was never incorporated and did not have governance authority. Zoning and other decisions were made by the parish [county], state, and federal governments. Remember, when industrial facilities were getting their foothold in Mossville and other parts of Louisiana, the 1930s through the 1950s, African Americans in the South did not have the right to vote and were oppressed and discriminated against by Jim Crow laws. So when industrial facilities began popping up in Louisiana, Mossville residents had no say in where they would locate, and this became an area that was targeted for industrial development. People in Mossville were not able to challenge, much less resist, the industrialization of their community.

Today, in and around Mossville, there are an oil refinery complex owned by Conoco Phillips, a coal-fired power plant owned by Entergy, five vinyl production facilities—the largest of which are PPG Industries and Georgia Gulf—and six other petrochemical facilities. All of these facilities are operating and spewing pollution within a quarter-mile of the community. Several have reported that Mossville residents would be killed if there was a catastrophic leak of chlorine gas or an explosion of petroleum-based products. You would think that with such hazards these facilities would operate safely, but they have frequent industrial accidents.

D&S: **How large a community is Mossville?**

MH: It's a community of approximately 1,000 residents.

D&S: **Listening to you speak about Mossville, it's staggering to understand just how directly the situation there is the outgrowth of U.S. racism. It's a very direct relationship.**

MH: Absolutely, and Mossville shares many commonalities with other communities—whether the residents are African American, Latino, Asian American, Native American, or poor whites. When you're dealing with environmental justice there are very strong historical ties to political and economic systems that have marginalized and exploited people of color and the poor.

D&S: **Can you talk about how economic policies have contributed to environmental racism in Louisiana?**

MH: Sure. You have to understand that Louisiana has only known two forms of economic development: slave plantations and heavy industry. In fact, many of the industrial facilities are located on former slave plantations, and a few companies have applied the names of these plantations to their facilities. It's no accident that many of these facilities are located in close proximity to communities with mostly African-American residents.

Seventy years or so after the Civil War, investment in industrial manufacturing began to pick up in the state because of its natural resources, especially oil and navigable waters. The state government lured companies by enacting a statewide tax exemption in 1936. Under the Industrial Property Tax Exemption, as it's called, new facilities are exempt from paying property taxes on their facilities for up to 10 years.

Then, if a company puts new capital investment into an existing facility, its exemption is renewed; this can go on into perpetuity.

The problem with the industrial tax exemption, of course, is that it has become a form of corporate welfare for companies like Exxon and Shell that are now wealthier than many countries. The largesse that these companies have acquired has also made them politically powerful in the legislature and allowed them to run roughshod over environmental and worker-safety laws. So, we now have aging and accident-prone industrial facilities largely dumping pollution in African-American communities like Mossville. And a prevailing political and economic climate in Louisiana and the United States in which these industrial corporations set the agenda.

One result is poverty. Dr. Paul Templet, a professor at Louisiana State University, has correlated pollution and poverty. In a nutshell, his research shows that the more industrial pollution a state has, the more poverty that state has. In Louisiana, we have one of the highest rates both of poverty and of industrial pollution. His analysis shows that stricter environmental standards that reduce industrial pollution require more jobs, which means more economic investment in the state and in the people in the state. A thriving economy requires good environmental conditions.

D&S: Can you talk about where Katrina fits in?

MH: Katrina hit a state that has encouraged oil companies to install a broad network of oil pipelines that have destroyed coastal wetlands. If they were still intact, these wetlands would have absorbed some of the hurricane's force and reduced its damage. At the same time, our state embraces industries whose increasing emissions contribute to the global warming effect of hurricanes becoming more intense. And our state has provided these companies with a man-made canal—the Mississippi River Gulf Outlet—that not only damaged wetlands, but actually served to funnel Katrina's storm surge into our communities in St. Bernard and Orleans parishes.

D&S: New Orleans obviously faces a crisis now in terms of rebuilding a viable economy. What are the roles of these companies in creating the new economic life of the area?

MH: I want to be clear that before Hurricane Katrina, neither New Orleans nor the state of Louisiana had what could be called a viable economy. Basic things like public school education and health care have been underfunded for years. It's now a struggle for all of us just to get back to having poor and inadequate public school and health care systems.

Instead of figuring out how we can do it better, much of the focus has been on planning ways to keep poor and mostly African-American people out of the state. The people who suffered the most from the failed levee systems and outrageous governmental neglect in the days following Katrina are now being targeted with governmental plans and actions that block their return home. I guess the thinking is that if you lock out poor people, the economy will improve.

Millions of our taxpayer dollars have gone to restoring oil company pipelines and other infrastructure that has devastated our environment and made us more vulnerable to hurricanes. In contrast, hurricane-damaged communities have not been restored. Another glimpse into how oil companies and the economy may intersect after Katrina is the announcement that Shell will cosponsor, for the first time, the New Orleans Jazz Fest. The company has been lauded as a savior of this cultural event; this view completely ignores how Shell has contributed to the disastrous consequences of Hurricane Katrina.

D&S: Could you give a breakdown of some of the specific communities in New Orleans and the environmental problems they face?

MH: Gert Town is an African-American neighborhood in New Orleans where the Thompson Hayward Company mixed pesticides, herbicides, and dry cleaning agents across the street from residents' homes and churches for approximately 40 years. This plant was shut down in the 1980s when it was discovered to be illegally dumping chemicals into the city's drainage system. That triggered enforcement that amounted to nothing more than a "cooperative agreement" between the state Department of Environmental Quality (DEQ) and the company owners for cleaning up waste contaminated with DDT and other banned chemicals. The agreement set out a series of cleanup steps and a schedule of 90 days or less for each step. However, nearly 20 years later, four million pounds of contaminated waste have yet to be removed.

Days before Hurricane Katrina struck, the community, organized as Gert Town Revival Initiative, and AEHR had compelled DEQ to allow the community to participate in the design of the cleanup plan. Then the hurricane came, causing four feet of flooding in Gert Town. Sediment sampling now shows the presence of DDT and other chemicals from Thompson Hayward, in addition to the arsenic and diesel fuel substances. This means that the storm moved pesticides and other chemicals from the site into the community.

D&S: And there are other communities with similar problems?

MH: Yes. There's the Agriculture Street community. This subdivision was built in the 1960s and 1970s and marketed to African Americans. People who bought these houses or moved into the rental units had no idea their homes were built on top of a toxic landfill. It was only after residents began to realize that they and their neighbors suffered serious health problems, including cancer, that they learned about the toxic landfill underneath them. A study by a state agency showed that Agriculture Street residents had the highest incidence of breast cancer statewide for both women and men.

In 1994 the community was designated a Superfund site. EPA provided a ridiculous cleanup that involved removing one to two feet of contaminated soil from yards that have 17 feet of soil contaminated with over 150 toxic chemicals and heavy metals. And EPA refused to temporarily relocate residents who were exposed to toxins during over a year of excavation.

Residents have had to sue federal and state housing agencies and other responsible government agencies for building their subdivision on top a toxic landfill. A few weeks ago, residents won their lawsuit in a state court, but the government defendants are expected to appeal.

D&S: How has the situation been compounded since Katrina?

MH: People have no homes! During Katrina, the failure of the levees flooded this neighborhood with water as high as nine feet. Homes are covered in toxic mold and many have extensive structural damage. Many of the hazardous contaminants that triggered EPA's Superfund site designation and were supposed to be trapped underground are now present in the sediment. Residents are wrestling with insurance companies and mortgage companies. Some have been able to secure homes elsewhere, but not others.

D&S: What are some of the challenges facing New Orleans residents who want to return home to environmentally safe neighborhoods?

MH: Sediment contamination is a representative problem. EPA is not cleaning up the sediment because reconstruction money is being spent on everything except for enabling people to return and rebuild their communities. Federal spending on Hurricane Katrina is a boondoggle for contractors and government agencies. For example, $3 million of hurricane relief spending went to the Department of Defense for the purchase of ammunition. This is outrageous! Meanwhile, six months after Katrina, we still have communities that look like the hurricane passed yesterday.

In October 2004, the federal government instituted the so-called "Assistance to Internally Displaced Persons Policy," which states what our government is committed to do in order to protect the human rights of people displaced from their communities by natural disasters. This policy commits our government to providing comprehensive assistance, from immediate disaster response through long-term development support. Even though this policy was developed by the U.S. Agency for International Development and, presumably, directed to internally displaced persons in foreign countries, we believe that our government should, at a minimum, exercise the same care and commitment to protecting the human rights of people in our country who are still in need of the humanitarian assistance, the return and transition assistance, and the long-term development assistance that are articulated in this policy.

D&S: A lot of the organizing in New Orleans now involves local groups allied with national ones. Can you talk about the role of people and nonprofits outside of New Orleans?

MH: Post-Hurricane Katrina, there are national and local organizations that are doing a great job of working together for justice. There are also groups that are exploiting Hurricane Katrina for their own benefit. People who couldn't find the Ninth Ward or Chalmette on a map are now working in the position of "Katrina Policy Chief"—I'm not making this up, it's an actual position—in organizations that have no relationship with local communities.

In my organizing experience, the formula for success is working in service of communities that are directly harmed by injustice. The formula for failure is creating coalitions that do not respect the need for communities to be organized and self-determined. Social transformation can only be achieved through community organizing. Without organized communities speaking for themselves and guiding the work of coalitions, you just have a bunch of groups trying to feel important.

D&S: Last September you said on the radio show "Living On Earth" that you were optimistic, that "this is an opportunity for us to transform in a progressive and positive way the lives of people in New Orleans and along the Gulf Coast of the United States." Five months later, are you still feeling optimistic?

MH: I'll go to my grave feeling optimistic about achieving social justice. And I say that because I know that the seed for achieving a just world is community organizing, and I know from experience that when communities are organized there's nothing that they can't achieve. ❑

Article 1.2.2

CAR TROUBLE
The automobile as an environmental and health disaster

BY ALEJANDRO REUSS
March/April 2003

(Scene: Los Angeles, the 1940s)

Eddie Valiant: A freeway? What the hell's a freeway?

Judge Doom: Eight lanes of shimmering cement running from here to Pasadena. Smooth, straight, fast. Traffic jams will be a thing of the past.... I see a place where people get off and on the freeway. On and off. Off and on. All day, all night. Soon where Toontown once stood will be a string of gas stations. Inexpensive motels. Restaurants that serve rapidly prepared food. Tire salons. Automobile dealerships. And wonderful, wonderful billboards reaching as far as the eye can see.... My god, it'll be beautiful.

Eddie Valiant: Come on. Nobody's gonna drive this lousy freeway when they can take the Red Car [trolley] for a nickel.

Judge Doom: Oh, they'll drive. They'll have to. You see, I bought the Red Car so I could dismantle it.

—Who Framed Roger Rabbit? (1988)

At the end of *Roger Rabbit*, a speeding train saves the day, destroying the solvent-spraying juggernaut that is set to level the fictitious Toontown for the freeway. In other words, the movie is a fairy tale about how the modern American city did *not* come into existence. In reality, Los Angeles came to represent the awful extreme of U.S. car culture. Auto companies *did* buy up the city's Red Car trolley and dismantle it. The landscape became just the cluttered wasteland of highways, fast-food joints, filling stations, and billboards dreamed by the villainous Judge Doom.

The federal government rolled out an asphalt carpet for the automobile: It built the interstate highways that fueled "white flight" to the new suburban sprawl, and carried the new "middle class" on its summer vacations. Soon, freeways criss-crossed American cities, slicing through low-income neighborhoods and consigning commuters to the twice-daily ordeal of gridlock. Roads and highways (along with the military, for which the interstates were originally intended) were politically acceptable objects of public spending even in the postwar United States. And why not? They represented an enormous subsidy to the private industries at the heart of U.S. capitalism—oil, steel, and cars.

The car effectively privatized a wide swath of the public arena. In place of the city square, it created the four-way intersection. Instead of walking or riding a trolley, the motorists sealed themselves inside their individual steel cocoons. Cars offered convenience—for grocery shopping, trips to the mall, chauffeuring the kids to school and practice, etc.—to those who got them. Their real triumph, however, was to manufacture inconvenience for those who didn't. People who could not afford cars had such unenviable choices as navigating the brave new world of speeding traffic on foot or waiting for the bus. A genuine political commitment to public transportation might have lessened the class and race divide. Most public transportation funding, however, has gone to road and highway construction geared to the motorist, and much of what remains for mass transit has been devoted to commuter trains serving the suburban middle class. Low-income city residents have largely been abandoned to an infrequent and polluting diesel bus.

As it turned out, life inside the car was not all it was cracked up to be either—especially when traffic on the freeway slowed to a crawl. In gridlock, you can practically see the steam coming out of drivers' ears. As odious as much of the time spent in cars might be, however, Americans have learned, or been convinced, to "love the car." It has become a fetish object—a symbol of freedom and individualism, power and sex appeal. The commercials always seem to show a carefree motorist speeding through the countryside or climbing a secluded mountain to gaze on the landscape below. Fortunately, not too many SUV owners actually spend their time tearing up the wilderness. Unfortunately, they spend much of it spewing exhaust into the city air.

The SUV certainly ranks among the more absurd expressions of American over-consumption (General Motors' Yukon XL Denali, to cite an extreme example, is over 18 feet long and weighs about three tons). But it is too easy to condemn this overgrown behemoth and then hop self-satisfied back into a midsize sedan. Most of what is wrong with the SUV—the resources it swallows, the dangers it poses, and the blight it creates—is wrong with the automobile system as a whole. Automobiles pollute the oceans and the air, overheat cities and the earth, devour land and time, produce waste and noise, and cause injury and illness.

Here, in more detail, is an indictment of the car as an environmental and public-health menace:

The Bill of Particulars

Oil Pollution

Transportation accounts for over two-thirds of U.S. oil consumption, according to the Department of Energy. The problem of oil pollution, therefore, lands squarely at the doorstep of a transportation system based on internal combustion. Oil tanker spills are the most visible scourge of the world's oceans. According to the National Research Council study Oil in the Sea, tankers spew 400 million tons of oil into the world's oceans each year. Technologies to prevent or contain oil spills, however, cannot solve the problem of marine oil pollution, since the main cause is not spills, but the consumption of oil. Urban consumption, including runoff from roads and used motor oil just poured down the drain, accounts for more than half of the ocean pollution, over one billion tons of oil annually. That does not count, of course, oil that does not make it to the seas, that stains roadways, contaminates the land, or spoils fresh water supplies.

Air Pollution

Automotive emissions are a major source of ozone and carbon monoxide pollution. "[I]n numerous cities across the country," according to the Environmental Protection Agency (EPA), "the personal automobile is the single greatest polluter." Ozone, a major component of urban smog, is formed by unburned fuel reacting with other compounds in the atmosphere. It causes irritation of the eyes and lungs, aggravates respiratory problems, and can damage lung tissue. Researchers at the Centers for Disease Control in Atlanta took advantage of temporary traffic reduction during the 1996 Olympic Games to observe the effects of automotive emissions on asthma attacks. Their study, published in the *Journal of the American Medical Association*, showed a 28% reduction of peak ozone levels and an 11–44% drop in the number of children requiring acute asthma care (depending on the sample). Carbon monoxide, formed by incomplete burning of fuel, impairs the oxygen-carrying ability of the blood. According to the EPA, "In urban areas, the motor vehicle contribution to carbon monoxide pollution can exceed 90 percent." A 2002 study published in the journal *Circulation* showed a link between automotive exhaust and heart attacks, and Harvard Medical School researchers called exhaust an "insidious contributor to heart disease."

Climate Change

Automotive exhaust also contains carbon dioxide, a "greenhouse gas" and the principal culprit in climate change (or "global warming"). It is produced, in the words of the EPA, by the "perfect combustion" of hydrocarbons. Internal combustion engines generate this greenhouse gas no matter how efficient or well-tuned they may be. In the United States, the country with the world's highest per capita carbon dioxide emissions, transportation accounts for over 30% of total emissions, according to a 1998 report of the United Nations Framework Convention on Climate Change. More than half that amount, reports the EPA, is due to personal transportation. As average fuel efficiency gets worse (it declined by nearly 7% between 1987 and 1997) and U.S. motorists rack up more vehicle miles (they increased by a third over the same period), the automobile contributes more and more to global warming.

Heat Islands

The temperature in a major city on a summer day can be as much as 8°F higher than that of surrounding rural areas, according to the Berkeley National Laboratory's Heat Island Group. The automobile contributes to "heat islands" mainly through increased demand for roads and parking. The asphalt and concrete used for these surfaces are among the most heat-absorbent materials in the urban environment. Paving also contributes to the loss of trees, which provide shade and dissipate heat. In the 1930s, when orchards dotted Los Angeles, summer temperatures peaked at 97°F, according to the Heat Island Group. Since then L.A. has become one of the country's worst heat islands, with summer temperatures reaching over 105°F. This does not just make the city less pleasant in the summertime. Heat islands cause increased energy use for cooling and increased ozone formation. Researchers estimate a 2% increase in Los Angeles's total power use and a 3% increase in smog for every 1°F increase in the city's daily high temperature.

Land Use

Cars occupy a huge amount of space. Paved roads occupy over 13,000 square miles of land area across the United States—nearly 750 square meters per U.S. motor vehicle—and parking occupies another 3,000 square miles, according to a report by Todd Litman of the Victoria Transport Policy Institute. In urban areas, roads and parking take up 20-30% of the total surface area; in commercial districts, 50-60%. When moving, vehicles require a "buffer zone" that varies with size and speed. Litman calculates, for example, that a pedestrian walking at 3 miles per hour (m.p.h.) requires 20 square feet of space. A cyclist riding at 10 m.p.h. needs 50 square feet. At full occupancy, a bus traveling at 30 m.p.h. requires 75 square feet per passenger. Meanwhile, a car traveling at 30 m.p.h. demands 1,500 square feet. In short, much of the road space is not required by on-road transportation as such, but by the private car. The same goes for parking space. A parked car requires twenty times the space as a parked bicycle, and eighty times the space as a person.

Materials

In the words of the EPA, "Vehicles require a lot of energy and materials to make, consume a lot of energy when used, and present unique waste disposal challenges at end-of-life." The auto industry uses nearly two thirds of the rubber, over one third of the iron, and over one fourth of the aluminum produced in the United States. Over ten million cars, moreover, are junked in the United States each year. About three fourths of the average car's weight—including the vast majority of the steel—is recycled. The rest crowds garbage dumps and contributes to toxic pollution. About 270 million tires (about 3.4 million tons) are scrapped in the United States annually. While nearly half are burned for energy, about 500 million tires now swell U.S. junk piles, where they "act as breeding grounds for rats and mosquitoes," according to the EPA, and periodically erupt into toxic tire fires. The U.S. cars scrapped each year also contain upwards of 8 tons of mercury. Meanwhile, polyvinyl chloride from scrap cars produces dioxins and other toxic pollutants. The study *End-of-Life Vehicles: A Threat to the Environment* concludes that the cars scrapped in Europe each year (75-85% as many as in the United States) produce 2 million tons of hazardous waste, about one tenth of the EU's total hazardous waste production.

Time

Car travel swallows more and more time as commutes grow longer and congestion more severe. The 2002 Urban Mobility Report from the Texas Transportation Institute calculated, on the basis of data from 75 U.S. cities, that the average motorist wasted 62 hours per year sitting in rush-hour traffic. (That's just the difference between rush-hour travel time and the normal time required to make the same trip.) In Los Angeles, the figure reached 136 hours. All told, over one third of the average rush-hour trip in the very large cities surveyed was wasted on traffic congestion. How is that an environmental or health issue? According to report Transport, Environment, and Health, issued by the World Health Organization (WHO) Regional Office for Europe, studies have connected traffic congestion with increased stress and blood pressure, as well as "aggressive behavior and increased likelihood of involvement in a crash."

Activity

Lack of exercise contributes to coronary heart disease, hypertension, some cancers, osteoporosis, poor coordination and stamina, and low self-esteem. The WHO Regional Office for Europe argues that "walking and cycling as part of daily activities should become a major pillar" of public-health strategy, and that daily travel offers the most promise to "integrate physical activities into daily schedules." Car dependence, instead, extends the sedentary lifestyle even to mobility. Half of all car trips in Europe, according to the WHO Regional Office, are under 5 km, distances most people can cover by bicycle in less than 20 minutes and on foot in well under one hour. High levels of automotive traffic, moreover, may deter people from walking or cycling—due to the unpleasantness of auto exhaust, the fear of crossing fast-moving traffic, or the dangers of riding a bicycle surrounded by cars. Some people may substitute car trips, but those without access to cars (especially children and elderly people) may simply venture outside less frequently, contributing to social isolation (another health risk factor).

Noise

Noise pollution is no mere nuisance. Researchers are beginning to document the damage that noise, even at relatively low levels, can do to human health. A 2001 study by Gary Evans of Cornell University, for example, has shown that children chronically exposed to low-level traffic noise suffer elevated blood pressure, increased changes in heart rate when stressed, and higher overall levels of stress-related hormones. In a separate study, on children exposed to low-level noise from aircraft flight patterns, Evans also documented negative effects of noise pollution on children's attention spans and learning abilities.

Collisions

Finally, the car crash ranks among the leading causes of death and injury in the United States. The statistics for 2001, compiled by the National Highway Traffic Safety Administration, were typical: over 42,000 people killed, over 360,000 people suffering incapacitating injuries, and over 3 million people injured overall. Over the last 25 years, the number of people killed per vehicle mile has declined by over 50%—undoubtedly thanks to such factors as increased availability and use of safety belts and airbags, improved vehicle design, and improved trauma care. The absolute number of deaths, however, has decreased by less than 20% (using the benchmark of 51,000 in 1980), as total vehicle miles traveled have more than doubled. Overall, the U.S. death toll from car crashes over the last quarter century is over one million people. During just the last decade, the total number of people injured in U.S. car crashes has topped 32 million.

The Path of Redemption

The environmental and public-health problems associated with the automobile have often inspired well-meaning exhortations to car-pool, drive less, or drive smaller cars, as well as dreams of "cars of the future" requiring less material or burning cleaner fuels. On the whole, however, the problems are neither individual nor technological—but social. So no individual nor technological solution will do. A comprehensive solution requires turning the "machine space" built for and dominated by the car back into human space: In the place of sprawl, compact development with work, school, stores, and recreation nearby and reachable without a car. In the place of the private car, reliable, clean, and accessible public transportation (along with small, efficient, nonpolluting vehicles for those who need them). In the place of internal combustion, the cyclist and the pedestrian—no longer marginalized and endangered, but respected as integral parts of a new, sustainable transportation system.

Cuba and China are the world's leading countries in bicycle use. Even in the rich capitalist counties, however, there are islands of sanity where public and human-powered transportation exist at least on a par with the automobile. Groningen, the Netherlands' sixth-largest city, suggests the possibilities: low speed limits reduce the dangers of urban traffic to cyclists and pedestrians; cars are not permitted on some streets, while bicycles can travel on any public way (including bike-only lanes and paths); parking for cars is restricted to garages, while secure bicycle parking facilities are plentiful (especially near train stations); cars are excluded from all squares in the city center, while careful city planning ensures that places of work and commerce are accessible to public transportation, cyclists, and pedestrians. As a result, Groningen residents now make nearly half of all in-city trips by bicycle; less than one third by car. The Dutch city of Delft, and the German cities of Freiburg and Muenster, are similar harbingers of a possible sustainable future.

The sustainable-transportation movement has shown encouraging worldwide growth in recent years. Transportation activists in the United Kingdom have carried out direct-action "street takings," closing off roads and highways and prompting spontaneous street fairs, to show what a car-free future might look like. The "Critical Mass" movement, starting in San Francisco in 1992 but quickly spreading to other cities, has brought together cyclists for rolling protest "marches" against auto hegemony. Activists have promoted worldwide car-free days, in which residents of hundreds of cities have participated. Bogotá, Colombia, a city of 7 million, held its first annual car-free day in 2000, complete with fines for any motorists caught within the city limits. Its popularity among city residents has bolstered long-term plans to exclude cars from the city, on a permanent basis, during peak morning and afternoon travel hours. In 2002, Seattle became the first U.S. city to officially host a car-free day.

With greater struggle, a more thorough-going transportation reform might be possible even within the confines of capitalism. This would require, however, a colossal economic shift—away the production of private automobiles, gasoline, and roads, and toward the reconstruction of public transportation and public space in general. It's highly unlikely, considering the ruin of former auto production centers like Detroit and Flint, that the "free market" could manage such a shift without imposing a wrenching dislocation on individuals and communities dependent on auto production. Moreover, it's virtually unimaginable, considering the trends toward privatization and commodification rampant in contemporary capitalism, that it would carry out such a transformation spontaneously. ❑

Article 1.2.3

EXTINCTION IS FOREVER
Debating Dams and Dollars in the Northwest Salmon Crisis

BY JAN CLAUSEN
May/June 2000

An unlikely combination of business executives, grassroots environmentalists, Pacific Northwest tribal leaders, and state and federal bureaucrats came together last September to sign the death warrant on a dam. The setting was impeccably corporate:the Hilton Hotel in downtown Portland, Oregon. Attire ranged from suits and ties to a whimsical t-shirt depicting hands raised in tribute to a soaring salmon with the caption "Fish Worship: Is It Wrong?" A man from a group called Wild Salmon Nation arrived lugging a huge model fish with detachable scales. Yakama Nation tribal chair William Yallup opened the proceedings with a traditional prayer. Next up were industry flacks and government bureaucrats mouthing upbeat clichés. In closing, the assembly joined in singing a version of the Neil Young tune "Long May You Run," with lyrics extolling free-flowing rivers.

The ceremony marked the signing of an agreement to remove Condit Dam, a small hydroelectric facility near the mouth of Washington State's White Salmon River, a tributary of the Columbia. Since its construction in 1913, Condit has blocked salmon and steelhead trout from reaching historic spawning grounds. Fish advocates view the agreement as one small step toward resolving a massive environmental crisis that has wiped out Pacific Northwest salmon in almost 40% of the rivers where they spawn and put the salmon at risk of extinction in close to half of the remaining streams. The salmon's problems stem from a complex series of environmental changes brought by a rapidly developing industrial economy. Overfishing, increasing demand on water supplies, and the impact of careless logging and agricultural practices all play a role. But one of the biggest fish killers in the Columbia River Basin is the gauntlet of hydroelectric dams that anadromous fish including salmon must run. Anadromous fish are born and die in fresh water but spend much of their lives in the ocean. In order to reproduce, they must survive the dams twice—once when they are juveniles, or smolts, making their journey to the ocean, and again when they return to spawn and die precisely where their lives began.

Although Condit is small potatoes as Northwest dams go, it is the tallest of the nation's dams currently slated for demolition, and the symbolism of the removal agreement is significant in a region furiously embroiled in the politics of fish rescue. Much of the politicking centers on practical economic concerns, but under the guise of disagreements over bottom-line issues the protagonists also are skirmishing over competing models of economic well-being. Fundamentally, they are debating the appropriate relationship between people and nature, and revealing the limits of a conceptual system that ignores forms of wealth not reducible to dollars.

Confronting the Killing Fields

Ground zero in the debate over the costs and benefits of saving salmon is a proposal to remove four federally owned and operated hydroelectric dams on the lower Snake River in eastern Washington. The Snake River, the mighty Columbia's largest tributary, was once the breeding ground for about half of the anadromous fish in the four-state Columbia Basin. After the Ice Harbor, Lower Monumental, Little Goose, and Lower Granite dams were built in the 1960s and '70s, fish populations declined alarmingly. Over the past three decades, the Snake has lost nearly 90% of its wild anadromous fish. Snake River coho salmon were declared extinct in 1986. In 1991, Snake River sockeye became the first variety of Pacific salmon to be listed under the Endangered Species Act.

The four dams on the lower river have created what Alaska Governor Tony Knowles recently dubbed "killing fields." Expensive efforts to mitigate the impact have failed utterly. And most scientists concur that taking out the dams would offer the best chance for fish recovery.

Yet their sheer size and economic importance far exceeds that of other dams considered for demolition, making their removal a far from simple matter. Together, the four facilities generate about 5% of the Northwest's electricity and create a sluggish channel allowing shipping on a 140-mile stretch of the Snake River between Pasco, Washington, and Lewiston, Idaho.

Driving much of the official urgency to save the fish is the Endangered Species Act. Treaties giving local tribes the right to harvest fish also play an important role. In addition, a broad segment of the general public shares the alarm expressed in the environmentalist's slogan: Extinction is forever. Love for salmon isn't confined to tree-hugging types; people who regard "environmentalists" as a slur often revel in sports fishing and savor barbecued salmon, giving anadromous fish a cachet that has eluded less-beloved yet no-less-endangered species like the spotted owl.

The Native American community became an early advocate of lower Snake dam removal. In 1995, The Columbia River Inter-Tribal Fish Commission, which represents four tribes with fishing rights in the Columbia system, proposed returning the Snake River to its natural flow. As the idea gathered support, it brought expressions of dismay from the region's politicians. Nevertheless, the dams operator, the U.S. Army Corps of Engineers, has spent the last three years studying whether to retire the four dams by breaching their earthen portions, allowing the river to flow around the remaining concrete structures. ("Breaching" involves partial removal of the dam to allow fish passage, without removing the concrete.) The Corps has been joined by a bewildering array of government agencies presided over by the National Marine Fisheries Service, whose mission it is to interpret Endangered Species Act provisions. Should the agencies recommend that the dams be decommissioned, Congress would still have to approve the plan.

The debate over removing the Snake River dams will test not only the region's, but the nation's willingness to discard the old notion that any free-flowing river is a "wasted" resource. That notion has deep roots in frontier history, which can be described as a lengthy series of schemes for extracting wealth from nature. In the

Northwest, it received a big boost from the New Deal initiative to create massive federal dam projects for popular purposes. Explaining the passion with which many defend the dams, policy analyst Steve Weiss of the Northwest Energy Coalition, a Seattle based environmental group, points to an impending paradigm shift: "It's a culture clash over, 'Do we dominate the environment or do we live in it? Can we do techno fixes, or must nature do it?'"

The Challenge From Native Americans

No group has challenged the mainstream paradigm more radically than Pacific Northwest tribes for whom salmon figures as both a crucial economic resource and a central element of spiritual and ceremonial life. Tribal fish advocates are calling into question both the measurement of wealth exclusively in dollars and the assumption that economic benefit requires the technological manipulation of nature. The short shrift given the tribes' interests provides a vivid example of social bias masquerading as pragmatic economic calculation. As Steve Weiss sees it, dams have widespread backing because they symbolize "white men taming the Wild West," while tribes and nontribal fisherfolk lack sufficient "iconic status" to have their stake in the fate of salmon taken seriously.

"Everyone talks about what farmers will lose or what other groups will lose if we take out the dams, but nobody talks about what Indians will lose if the fish go extinct," says Donald Sampson, executive director of the Columbia River Inter Tribal Fish Commission. Sampson, who's in his late thirties, is a university-trained fisheries biologist and former chair of the Umatilla Confederated Tribes. He can be refreshingly irreverent, savoring jokes about ingenious ways of eliminating dam-favoring politicians and mocking federal bureaucrats for their "paralysis by analysis." But there's no mistaking his gravity when he describes tribal successes in restoring naturally reproducing salmon runs on the Umatilla River or explains how tradition- al ceremonies strengthen the bonds between salmon and tribal people. Even tribal members who fish commercially, he says, have respect for the fish, such that "you never hear an Indian talk about 'that critter,' 'that dumb critter,' the way non-Indians do." Historically, he maintains, tribal people recognized their responsibility to manage their relationship to the land not just for the group's immediate benefit but for coming generations.

Clearly, Sampson is talking about a concept of material well-being that is at odds with the prevailing bottom-line mentality. But even when making bottom-line calculations, much could be done to correct built-in biases in the very terms that typically structure economic analyses of "improvements" to the natural order. A recent article in the journal Environmental Law making the legal case for dam breaching draws attention to this problem: "Frequently ... the perceived benefits of dams are fully quantified and overstated, while the costs are greatly understated and ignored. Traditional cost-benefit analysis did not calculate true social costs, such as environmental damage ... and support subsidies."

Putting a Dollar Value on Salmon

In an attempt to fill in some of these gaps, the U.S. Army Corps of Engineers estimated the "existence value" of salmon in an evaluation of various conservation measures. This move has been controversial.

Many people doubt the reliability of answers given to the question, "What would you pay to know that salmon exist?" Enviros often feel uneasy about the pressure to express even the value of nature as a monetary calculation, yet the salmon's urgent plight draws them into the game of putting a price tag on 10 million years of evolution (the amount of time the close anadromous relatives of today's Pacific salmon have been around). Taking a different approach, the Columbia River treaty tribes have refused to calculate the dollar value of the species whose survival they see as integrally connected to their own identity and the well being of the Earth.

In effect, they are refusing to separate spiritual values from material interests, thereby challenging the cherished European-American concept of "the economy" as a law unto itself. I asked Charles Hudson, the tribal fish commission's public information manager, to explain this stand. "In our minds," he responded, "you only begin the argument with tens of billions of dollars. If it came to extinction, how would you ever put a dollar amount on the institutional racism involved? Treaty rights are not a negotiable item."

Yet Hudson also stresses that, for tribal members on reservations where jobs are scarce, fishing often constitutes the only "homegrown and traditional" source of income. He speaks angrily of the unjust "wealth transfer" in both the 19th and 20thcenturies: the resource that created the tribes' pretreaty prosperity was decimated so that rivers could generate income for settlers. The tribes possessed real wealth even though they didn't subscribe to Western concepts of private property. Hudson's analysis of wealth transfer reveals how the poverty now so widespread among indigenous people stems from economic choices made by settlers and their heirs. By reminding us that there recently existed on North American soil a functioning model of the good life that had nothing to do with capitalist relations of production (or even a cash economy), the tribes powerfully contradict the deadly force of TINA, the disabling suspicion that There Is No Alternative to existing economic arrangements. They nudge us to look beyond the restrictive framework that equates all "real" material values with marketplace transactions.

Dollar Costs and Benefits

While the tribes push the mainstream cultural envelope by insisting on their treaty rights, nontribal enviros work hard to show how removing the dams can work in today's economy. The dams' defenders, led by powerful Washington Republican Senator Slade Gorton, have loudly forecast economic disaster ever since the plan was first aired, and thus far no one in the Northwest's congressional delegation has had the courage to come out in favor of breaching. (Oregon's Democratic governor, John Kitzhaber, did take a strong stand in favor of the removal plan this past February). The politicians' preference for the status quo is unsurprising given that cheap hydroelectric power has long been the backbone of the Northwest's industrial economy.

Industrialists with no direct stake in the four lower Snake dams apparently subscribe to a sort of economic domino theory, fearing that even a localized move to prioritize salmon might encourage public scrutiny of the high environmental costs of present patterns of river usage. Such fears surfaced during negotiations over the Condit Dam removal agreement, with Condit's private owner, PacifiCorp, insisting that the agreement not be construed as setting any precedents.

Economic Enfranchisement Through Dams By no means do all the dams' champions hail from the corridors of power. East of the Cascade Mountains—the range the divides the Northwest's rainy coastal region from the dry interior—many families of modest means have long relied on federal subsidies rooted in FDR's Depression era vision of vast public works that would create opportunities for the dispossessed. That dependence can turn support for dams into a quasi-theological principle. Blaine Harden, an eastern Washington native who calls himself "a legatee of the conquered river," writes of the dam-related "federal dollars that rained for decades [giving] me and my family work, water, electricity, and pride in ourselves."

For some, dams are literally a theological matter, to judge from a diatribe posted on the website saveourdams.com. The author denounces "the 'New Age Religion'" whose followers "believe in earth first and want to return the earth to the way it was before man set foot upon it. They believe in the created above the creator and they want to do this at any cost."

Like Governor Kitzhaber, he and other activists stress the importance of planning for effective ways to cushion localized negative effects. In fact, monetary costs and benefits of breaching are roughly in balance, according to a recent analysis by the Northwest Energy Coalition drawing on government-sponsored studies. The real problem is that the change would disadvantage certain groups while benefiting others. As Governor Kitzhaber of Oregon points out, the challenge thus becomes "to develop an ecosystem recovery strategy that spreads the costs as broadly as possible," including the costs of mitigating negative economic impacts.

Despite the difficult political climate, Bill Arthur, Northwest Regional Director of the Sierra Club, believes that the dam-removal debate is beginning to follow the trajectory of the region's ancient forest controversy, with doomsday predictions gradually giving way to a narrower focus on real problems and manageable solutions. Like Governor Kitzhaber, he and other activists stress the importance of planning for effective ways to cushion negative economic impacts. According to Tim Stearns of Save Our Wild Salmon, "We [environmentalists] have done most of the economic transition stuff that the administration should have done."

For example, American Rivers commissioned a retired Army Corps of Engineers official to examine ways to restructure the region's transportation system in anticipation of the day when farmers will no longer be able to ship their crops by barge on the Snake River between Lewiston, Idaho and Pasco, Washington. He found uncompetitive pricing among shippers and hidden taxpayer subsidies of about $30 million a year to operate the lower Snake waterway. Given appropriate investment in transportation infrastructure, enviros argue, shipping farm goods by road or rail instead of by water could actually strengthen the agricultural economy. Senator Gorton blasted the study as "more voodoo economics from another D.C.-based special interest group." Those most likely to benefit from dam removal in bottom-line terms include tribes, rail and trucking firms, the nontribal commercial fishing industry, private power companies, and the recreation industry. One knowledge-able enviro told me that official projections of the dollar benefits of dam removal to the recreation industry got revised drastically downward before the findings were released. The original estimate, which seems to have scared the feds, indicated a net yearly increase of $1 billion in recreation-related activity with a free-flowing river.

In addition to higher transportation costs, the potential economic downside of breaching includes loss of jobs related to operating the dams and the river ports they create; diminished irrigation opportunities; higher electrical rates throughout the Northwest; and the actual costs of the bypassing operation, which have been esti-mated between $800 million and $1.1 billion. Economists propose a buyout of the 13 corporate farms that rely on Ice Harbor Dam for irrigation water.

The cost of the breaching would amount to about $25 million per year above the current operating budget of the Bonneville Power Administration (BPA), which sells electricity from a complex of federally owned dams including those on the lower Snake. Its customers would probably absorb most of this cost. (By comparison, the BPA's customers still pay $500 million annually on the enormous debt left over from a disastrous nuclear-power venture that collapsed in the 1980s.) Dismantling the four lower Snake dams would cause electrical rates to rise moderately, though the Northwest would continue to enjoy the cheapest power in the nation. The BPA's worst case estimate shows a 10% increase for ratepayers whose bills are currently 40% below the national average.

While the lost electricity could readily be replaced on the open energy mar-ket, where power often comes from "dirty" coal- and oil-fired plants or somewhat cleaner gas, enviros are pushing for a combination of conservation (to reduce energy demand)and power from renewable sources such as wind, solar, or geothermal power. Opponents of dam removal appear to hope that the need for unpleasant change will simply go away if they scuttle the breaching plan. But the cautious Oregonian, whose editorial page routinely insists that the dams can coexist with the salmon recovery, recently concluded that no credible effort to improve fish survival will be any cheaper than partial removal. For instance, Idaho would face a severe drop in irrigation water if stream flows increased to aid fish. The lost irrigation could elimi-nate as many as 6,500 jobs and $430 million in income, according to Rob Masonis of American Rivers. The region as a whole would have to cope with unpopular restrictions on logging, farming, and development. And nontribal economists have calculated that extinction of the Snake River's anadromous stocks—more likely if dams remain—could cost U.S. taxpayers $12 billion or more in compensation to tribes with treaty fishing rights. Given such considerations, Governor Kitzhaber argues that breaching will distribute the economic burden of saving salmon more equitably than other credible fish-recovery plans.

National Implications

Recently, environmental groups and tribes have taken the debate over the salmon crisis to the national level, running ads in The *New York Times* aimed at prod-ding Al Gore to justify his "green" reputation by making dam removal an issue in his presidential campaign. The word is out to members of eastern and midwestern Congressional delegations that the Northwest's cherished energy price advantage must not continue at the cost of decimating endangered species and that the best available scientific studies forecast extinction of Snake River salmon by 2017 absent effective intervention.

With Gore unresponsive and the National Marine Fisheries Service evidently prepared literally to study the fish to death rather than make politically difficult decisions, Tim Stearns of Save Our Wild Salmon inquires with more than a touch of xasperation, "If they don't like dam removal, what do they like?"

His question reverberates with national implications. In reporting on the agreement o remove Condit Dam, the local and national press noted a widespread uestioning of the historic assumption that "harnessing" rivers for energy and irrigation is always beneficial. The press connected the Condit story to the case of Edwards Dam, a 24-foot-high hydropower facility on Maine's Kennebec River. This dam was recently demolished at the behest of the Federal Energy Regulatory Commission to restore native fish.

Big dams still look like progress to a lot of people but every day more of us are recognizing that healthy environments need free-flowing water. In the process, we are rethinking the appropriate role of human beings in modifying natural systems. Assessing the stakes in the Snake River debate, Northwest Energy Coalition policy analyst Steve Weiss sums up, "It's one battle [over] a huge paradigm of 'how do we live on this planet?' Whatever happens will change the playing field." ❑

Article 1.2.4

PRICING THE PRICELESS
Inside the Strange World of Cost-Benefit Analysis

BY LIZ HEINZERLING AND FRANK ACKERMAN
March/April 2003

How strictly should we regulate arsenic in drinking water? Or carbon dioxide in the atmosphere? Or pesticides in our food? Or oil drilling in scenic places? The list of environmental harms and potential regulatory remedies often appears to be endless. In evaluating a proposed new initiative, how do we know if it is worth doing or not? Is there an objective way to decide how to proceed? Cost-benefit analysis promises to provide the solution—to add up the benefits of a public policy and compare them to the costs.

The costs of protecting health and the environment through pollution control devices and other approaches are, by their very nature, measured in dollars. The other side of the balance, calculating the benefits of life, health, and nature in dollars and cents, is far more problematic. Since there are no natural prices for a healthy environment, cost-benefit analysis creates artificial ones. Researchers, for example, may ask a cross-section of the affected population how much they would pay to preserve or protect something that can't be bought in a store. The average American household is supposedly willing to pay $257 to prevent the extinction of bald eagles, $208 to protect humpback whales, and $80 to protect gray wolves.

Costs and benefits of a policy, however, frequently fall at different times. When the analysis spans a number of years, future costs and benefits are *discounted,* or treated as equivalent to smaller amounts of money in today's dollars. The case for discounting begins with the observation that money received today is worth a little more than money received in the future. (For example, if the interest rate is 3%, you only need to deposit about $97 today to get $100 next year. Economists would say that, at a *3% discount rate,* $100 next year has a *present value* of $97.) For longer periods of time, or higher discount rates, the effect is magnified. The important issue for environmental policy is whether this logic also applies to outcomes far in the future, and to opportunities—like long life and good health—that are not naturally stated in dollar terms.

Why Cost-Benefit Analysis Doesn't Work

The case for cost-benefit analysis of environmental protection is, at best, wildly optimistic and, at worst, demonstrably wrong. The method simply does not offer the policy-making panacea its adherents promise. In practice, cost-benefit analysis frequently produces false and misleading results. Moreover, there is no quick fix, because these failures are intrinsic to the methodology, appearing whenever it is applied to any complex environmental problem.

It puts dollar figures on values that are not commodities, and have no price.
Artificial prices have been estimated for many benefits of environmental regulation. Preventing retardation due to childhood lead poisoning comes in at about $9,000 per lost IQ point. Saving a life is ostensibly worth $6.3 million. But what can it mean to say that one life is worth $6.3 million? You cannot buy the right to kill someone for $6.3 million, nor for any other price. If analysts calculated the value of life itself by asking people what it is worth to them (the most common method of valuation of other environmental benefits), the answer would be infinite. The standard response is that a value like $6.3 million is not actually a price on an individual's life or death. Rather, it is a way of expressing the value of small risks of death. If people are willing to pay $6.30 to avoid a one in a million increase in the risk of death, then the "value of a statistical life" is $6.3 million.

It ignores the collective choice presented to society by most public health and environmental problems.
Under the cost-benefit approach, valuation of environmental benefits is based on individuals' private decisions as consumers or workers, not on their public values as citizens. However, policies that protect the environment are often public goods, and are not available for purchase in individual portions. In a classic example of this distinction, the philosopher Mark Sagoff found that his students, in their role as citizens, opposed commercial ski development in a nearby wilderness area, but, in their role as consumers, would plan to go skiing there if the development was built. There is no contradiction between these two views: as individual consumers, the students would have no way to express their collective preference for wilderness preservation. Their individual willingness to pay for skiing would send a misleading signal about their views as citizens.

It is often impossible to arrive at a meaningful social valuation by adding up the willingness to pay expressed by individuals. What could it mean to ask how much you personally are willing to pay to clean up a major oil spill? If no one else contributes, the clean-up won't happen regardless of your decision. As the Nobel Prize-winning economist Amartya Sen has pointed out, if your willingness to pay for a large-scale public initiative is independent of what others are paying, then you probably have not understood the nature of the problem.

It systematically downgrades the importance of the future.
One of the great triumphs of environmental law is that it seeks to avert harms to people and to natural resources in the future, and not only within this generation, but in future generations as well. Indeed, one of the primary objectives of the National Environmental Policy Act, which has been called our basic charter of environmental protection, is to nudge the nation into "fulfill[ing] the responsibilities of each generation as trustee of the environment for succeeding generations."

The time periods involved in protecting the environment are often enormous—even many centuries, in such cases as climate change, radioactive waste, etc. With time spans this long, any discounting will make even global catastrophes seem trivial. At a discount rate of 5%, for example, the deaths of a billion people 500 years from now become less serious than the death of one person today. Seen in this way, discounting looks like a fancy justification for foisting our problems off onto the people who come after us.

It ignores considerations of distribution and fairness.
Cost-benefit analysis adds up all the costs of a policy, adds up all the benefits, and compares the totals. Implicit in this innocuous-sounding procedure is the assumption that it doesn't matter who gets the benefits and who pays the costs. Yet isn't there is an important difference between spending state tax revenues, say, to improve the parks in rich communities, and spending the same revenues to clean up pollution in poor communities?

The problem of equity runs even deeper. Benefits are typically measured by willingness to pay for environmental improvement, and the rich are able and willing to pay for more than the poor. Imagine a cost-benefit analysis of locating an undesirable facility, such as a landfill or incinerator. Wealthy communities are willing to pay more for the benefit of not having the facility in their backyards; thus, under the logic of cost-benefit analysis, the net benefits to society will be maximized by putting the facility in a low-income area. In reality, pollution is typically dumped on the poor without waiting for formal analysis. Still, cost-benefit analysis rationalizes and reinforces the problem, allowing environmental burdens to flow downhill along the income slopes of an unequal society.

Conclusion

There is nothing objective about the basic premises of cost-benefit analysis. Treating individuals solely as consumers, rather than as citizens with a sense of moral responsibility, represents a distinct and highly questionable worldview. Likewise, discounting reflects judgments about the nature of environmental risks and citizens' responsibilities toward future generations.

These assumptions beg fundamental questions about ethics and equity, and one cannot decide whether to embrace them without thinking through the whole range of moral issues they raise. Yet once one has thought through these issues, there is no need then to collapse the complex moral inquiry into a series of numbers. Pricing the priceless just translates our inquiry into a different language, one with a painfully impoverished vocabulary. ❏

This article is a condensed version of the report Pricing the Priceless, *published by the Georgetown Environmental Law and Policy Institute at Georgetown University Law Center. The full report is available on-line at www. ase.tufts.edu/gdae. See also Ackerman and Heinzerling's book on these and related issues,* Priceless: Human Health, the Environment, and the Limits of the Market, *The New Press, January 2004.*

Article 1.2.5

CLIMATE ECONOMICS IN FOUR EASY PIECES

Conventional cost-benefit models cannot inform our decisions about how to address the threat of climate change.

FRANK ACKERMAN
November/December 2008

Once upon a time, debates about climate policy were primarily about the science. An inordinate amount of attention was focused on the handful of "climate skeptics" who challenged the scientific understanding of climate change. The influence of the skeptics, however, is rapidly fading; few people were swayed by their arguments, and doubt about the major results of climate science is no longer important in shaping public policy.

As the climate *science* debate is reaching closure, the climate *economics* debate is heating up. The controversial issue now is the fear that overly ambitious climate initiatives could hurt the economy. Mainstream economists emphasizing that fear have, in effect, replaced the climate skeptics as the intellectual enablers of inaction.

For example, William Nordhaus, the U.S. economist best known for his work on climate change, pays lip service to scientists' calls for decisive action. He finds, however, that the "optimal" policy is a very small carbon tax that would reduce greenhouse gas emissions only 25% below "business-as-usual" levels by 2050—that would, in other words, allow emissions to rise well above current levels by mid-century. Richard Tol, a European economist who has written widely on climate change, favors an even smaller carbon tax of just $2 per ton of carbon dioxide. That would amount to all of $0.02 per gallon of gasoline, a microscopic "incentive" for change that consumers would never notice.

There are other voices in the climate economics debate; in particular, the British government's Stern Review offers a different perspective. Economist Nicholas Stern's analysis is much less wrong than the traditional Nordhaus-Tol approach, but even Stern has not challenged the conventional view enough.

What will it take to build a better economics of climate change, one that is consistent with the urgency expressed by the latest climate science? The issues that matter are big, non-technical principles, capable of being expressed in bumper-sticker format. Here are the four bumper stickers for a better climate economics:

- Our grandchildren's lives are important.

- We need to buy insurance for the planet.

- Climate damages are too valuable to have prices.

- Some costs are better than others.

1. Our grandchildren's lives are important.

The most widely debated challenge of climate economics is the valuation of the very long run. For ordinary loans and investments, both the costs today and the resulting future benefits typically occur within a single lifetime. In such cases, it makes sense to think in terms of the same person experiencing and comparing the costs and the benefits.

In the case of climate change, the time spans involved are well beyond those encountered in most areas of economics. The most important consequences of today's choices will be felt by generations to come, long after all of us making those choices have passed away. As a result, the costs of reducing emissions today and the benefits in the far future will not be experienced by the same people. The economics of climate change is centrally concerned with our relationship to our descendants whom we will never meet. As a bridge to that unknowable future, consider our grandchildren—the last generation most of us will ever know.

Suppose that you want your grandchildren to receive $100 (in today's dollars, corrected for inflation), 60 years from now. How much would you have to put in a bank account today, to ensure that the $100 will be there 60 years from now? The answer is $55 at 1% interest, or just over $5 at 5%.

In parallel fashion, economists routinely deal with future costs and benefits by "discounting" them, or converting them to "present values"—a process that is simply compound interest in reverse. In the standard jargon, the *present value* of $100, to be received 60 years from now, is $55 at a 1% *discount rate*, or about $5 at a 5% discount rate. As this example shows, a higher discount rate implies a smaller present value.

The central problem of climate economics, in a cost-benefit framework, is deciding how much to spend today on preventing future harms. What should we spend to prevent $100 of climate damages 60 years from now? The standard answer is, no more than the present value of that future loss: $55 at a discount rate of 1%, or $5 at 5%. The higher the discount rate, the less it is "worth" spending today on protecting our grandchildren.

The effect of a change in the discount rate becomes much more pronounced as the time period lengthens. Damages of $1 million occurring 200 years from now have a present value of only about $60 at a 5% discount rate, versus more than $130,000 at a 1% discount rate. The choice of the discount rate is all-important to our stance toward the far future: should we spend as much as $130,000, or as little as $60, to avoid one million dollars of climate damages in the early twenty-third century?

For financial transactions within a single lifetime, it makes sense to use market interest rates as the discount rate. Climate change, however, involves public policy decisions with impacts spanning centuries; there is no market in which public resources are traded from one century to the next. The choice of an intergenerational discount rate is a matter of ethics and policy, not a market-determined result.

Economists commonly identify two separate aspects of long-term discounting, each contributing to the discount rate.

One component of the discount rate is based on the assumption of an upward trend in income and wealth. If future generations will be richer than we are, they will need less help from us, and they will get less benefit from an additional dollar of income than we do. So we can discount benefits that will flow to our wealthier descendants, at a rate based on the expected growth of per capita incomes. Among economists, the income-related motive for discounting may be the least controversial part of the picture.

Setting aside changes in per capita income from one generation to the next, there may still be a reason to discount a sum many years in the future. This component of the discount rate, known as "pure time preference," is the subject of longstanding ethical, philosophical, and economic debate. On the one hand, there are reasons to think that pure time preference is greater than zero: both psychological experiments and common sense suggest that people are impatient, and prefer money now to money later. On the other hand, a pure time preference of zero expresses the equal worth of people of all generations, and the equal importance of reducing climate impacts and other burdens on them (assuming that all generations have equal incomes).

The Stern Review provides an excellent discussion of the debate, explaining Stern's assumption of pure time preference close to zero and an overall discount rate of 1.4%. This discount rate alone is sufficient to explain Stern's support for a substantial program of climate protection: at the higher discount rates used in more traditional analyses, the Stern program would look "inefficient," since the costs would outweigh the present value of the benefits.

2. We need to buy insurance for the planet.

Does climate science predict that things are certain to get worse? Or does it tell us that we are uncertain about what will happen next? Unfortunately, the answer seems to be yes to both questions. For example, the most likely level of sea level rise in this century, according to the latest Intergovernmental Panel on Climate Change reports, is no more than one meter or so—a real threat to low-lying coastal areas and islands that will face increasing storm damages, but survivable, with some adaptation efforts, for most of the world. On the other hand, there is a worst-case risk of an abrupt loss of the Greenland ice sheet, or perhaps of a large portion of the West Antarctic ice sheet. Either one could cause an eventual seven-meter rise in sea level—a catastrophic impact on coastal communities, economic activity, and infrastructure everywhere, and well beyond the range of plausible adaptation efforts in most places.

The evaluation of climate damages thus depends on whether we focus on the most likely outcomes or the credible worst-case risks; the latter, of course, are much larger.

Cost-benefit analysis conventionally rests on average or expected outcomes. But this is not the only way that people make decisions. When faced with uncertain, potentially large risks, people do not normally act on the basis of average outcomes; instead, they typically focus on protection against worst-case scenarios. When you go to the airport, do you leave just enough time for the average traffic delay (so that you would catch your plane, on average, half of the time)? Or do you allow time for some estimate of worst-case traffic jams? Once you get there, of course, you will experience additional delays due to security, which is all about worst cases: your *average* fellow passenger is not a threat to anyone's safety.

The very existence of the insurance industry is evidence of the desire to avoid or control worst-case scenarios. It is impossible for an insurance company to pay out in claims as much as its customers pay in premiums; if it did, there would be no money left to pay the costs of running the company, or the profits received by its owners. People who buy insurance are therefore guaranteed to get back less than they, on average, have paid; they (we) are paying for the security that insurance provides in case the worst should happen. This way of thinking does not apply to every decision: in casino games, people make bets based on averages and probabilities, and no one has any insurance against losing the next round. But life is not a casino, and public policy should not be a gamble.

Should climate policy be based on the most likely outcomes, or on the worst-case risks? Should we be investing in climate protection as if we expect sea level rise of one meter, or as if we are buying insurance to be sure of preventing a seven-meters rise?

In fact, the worst-case climate risks are even more unknown than the individual risks of fire and death that motivate insurance purchases. You do not know whether or not you will have a fire next year or die before the year is over, but you have very good information about the likelihood of these tragic events. So does the insurance industry, which is why they are willing to insure you. In contrast, there is no body of statistical information about the probability of Greenland-sized ice sheets collapsing at various temperatures; it's not an experiment that anyone can perform over and over again.

A recent analysis by Martin Weitzman argues that the probabilities of the worst outcomes are inescapably unknowable—and this deep uncertainty is more important than anything we do know in motivating concern about climate change. There is a technical sense in which the expected value of future climate damages can be infinite because we know so little about the probability of the worst, most damaging possibilities. The practical implication of infinite expected damages is that the most likely outcome is irrelevant; what matters is buying insurance for the planet, i.e., doing our best to understand and prevent the worst-case risks.

3. Climate damages are too valuable to have prices.

To decide whether climate protection is worthwhile, in cost-benefit terms, we would need to know the monetary value of everything important that is being protected. Even if we could price everything affected by climate change, the prices would conceal a critical form of international inequity. The emissions that cause climate change have come predominantly from rich countries, while the damages will be felt first and worst in some of the world's poorest, tropical countries (although no one will be immune from harm for long). There are, however, no meaningful prices for many of the benefits of health and environmental protection. What is the dollar value of a human life saved? How much is it worth to save an endangered species from extinction, or to preserve a unique location or ecosystem? Economists have made up price tags for such priceless values, but the results do not always pass the laugh test.

Is a human life worth $6.1 million, as estimated by the Clinton administration, based on small differences in the wages paid for more and less risky jobs? Or is it worth $3.7 million, as the (second) Bush administration concluded on the basis of questionnaires about people's willingness to pay for reducing small, hypothetical risks? Are lives of people in rich countries worth much more than those in poor countries, as some economists infamously argued in the IPCC's 1995 report? Can the value of an endangered species be determined by survey research on how much people would pay to protect it? If, as one study found, the U.S. population as a whole would pay $18 billion to protect the existence of humpback whales, would it be acceptable for someone to pay $36 billion for the right to hunt and kill the entire species?

The only sensible response to such nonsensical questions is that there are many crucially important values that do not have meaningful prices. This is not a new idea: as the eighteenth-century philosopher Immanuel Kant put it, some things have a price, or relative worth, while other things have a dignity, or inner worth. No price tag does justice to the dignity of human life or the natural world.

Since some of the most important benefits of climate protection are priceless, any monetary value for total benefits will necessarily be incomplete. The corollary is that preventive action may be justified even in the absence of a complete monetary measure of the benefits of doing so.

4. Some costs are better than others.

The language of cost-benefit analysis embodies a clear normative slant: benefits are good, costs are bad. The goal is always to have larger benefits and smaller costs. In some respects, measurement and monetary valuation are easier for costs than for benefits: implementing pollution control measures typically involves changes in such areas as manufacturing, construction, and fuel use, all of which have well-defined prices. Yet conventional economic theory distorts the interpretation of costs

---

AVERAGE RISKS OR WORST-CASE SCENARIOS?

You don't have to look far to find situations in which the sensible policy is to address worst-case outcomes rather than average outcomes. The annual number of residential fires in the United States is about 0.4% of the number of housing units. This means that a fire occurs, on average, about once every 250 years in each home—not even close to once per lifetime. By far the most likely number of fires a homeowner will experience next year, or even in a lifetime, is zero. Why don't these statistics inspire you to cancel your fire insurance? Unless you are extremely wealthy, the loss of your home in a fire would be a devastating financial blow; despite the low probability, you cannot afford to take any chances on it.

What are the chances of the ultimate loss? The probability that you will die next year is under 0.1% if you are in your twenties, under 0.2% in your thirties, under 0.4% in your forties. It is not until age 61 that you have as much as a 1% chance of death within the coming year. Yet most U.S. families with dependent children buy life insurance. Without it, the risk to children of losing their parents' income would be too great—even though the parents are, on average, extraordinarily likely to survive.

in ways that exaggerate the burdens of environmental protection and hide the positive features of some of the "costs."

For instance, empirical studies of energy use and carbon emissions repeatedly find significant opportunities for emissions reduction at zero or negative net cost—the so-called "no regrets" options.

According to a longstanding tradition in economic theory, however, cost-free energy savings are impossible. The textbook theory of competitive markets assumes that every resource is productively employed in its most valuable use—in other words, that every no-regrets option must already have been taken. As the saying goes, there are no free lunches; there cannot be any $20 bills on the sidewalk because someone would have picked them up already. Any new emissions reduction measures, then, must have positive costs. This leads to greater estimates of climate policy costs than the bottom-up studies that reveal extensive opportunities for costless savings.

In the medium term, we will need to move beyond the no-regrets options; how much will it cost to finish the job of climate protection? Again, there are rival interpretations of the costs based on rival assumptions about the economy. The same economic theory that proclaimed the absence of $20 bills on the sidewalk is responsible for the idea that all costs are bad. Since the free market lets everyone spend their money in whatever way they choose, any new cost must represent a loss: it leaves people with less to spend on whatever purchases they had previously selected to maximize their satisfaction in life. Climate damages are one source of loss, and spending on climate protection is another; both reduce the resources available for the desirable things in life.

But are the two kinds of costs really comparable? Is it really a matter of indifference whether we spend $1 billion on bigger and better levees or lose $1 billion to storm damages? In the real-world economy, money spent on building levees creates jobs and incomes. The construction workers buy groceries, clothing, and so on, indirectly creating other jobs. With more people working, tax revenues increase while unemployment compensation payments decrease.

None of this happens if the levees are not built and the storm damages are allowed to occur. The costs of prevention are good costs, with numerous indirect benefits; the costs of climate damages are bad costs, representing pure physical destruction. One worthwhile goal is to keep total costs as low as possible; another is to have as much as possible of good costs rather than bad costs. Think of it as the cholesterol theory of climate costs.

In the long run, the deep reductions in carbon emissions needed for climate stabilization will require new technologies that have not yet been invented, or at best exist only in small, expensive prototypes. How much will it cost to invent, develop, and implement the low-carbon technologies of the future?

Lacking a rigorous theory of innovation, economists modeling climate change have often assumed that new technologies simply appear, making the economy inexorably more efficient over time. A more realistic view observes that the costs of producing a new product typically decline as industry gains more experience with it, in a pattern called "learning by doing" or the "learning curve" effect. Public investment is often necessary to support the innovation process in its early, expensive stages. Wind power is now relatively cheap and competitive, in suitable locations; this is a direct result of decades of public investment in the United States and Europe, starting when wind turbines were still quite expensive. The costs of climate policy, in the long run, will include doing the same for other promising new technologies, investing public resources in jump-starting a set of slightly different industries than we might have chosen in the absence of climate change. If this is a cost, many communities would be better off with more of it.

A widely publicized, conventional economic analysis recommends inaction on climate change, claiming that the costs currently outweigh the benefits for anything more than the smallest steps toward reducing carbon emissions. Put our "four easy pieces" together, and we have the outline of an economics that complements the science of climate change and endorses active, large-scale climate protection.

How realistic is it to expect that the world will shake off its inertia and act boldly and rapidly enough to make a difference? This may be the last generation that will have a real chance at protecting the earth's climate. Projections from the latest IPCC reports, the Stern Review, and other sources suggest that it is still possible to save the planet—if we start at once. ❑

Sources: Frank Ackerman, *Can We Afford the Future? Economics for a Warming World,* Zed Books, 2008; Frank Ackerman, *Poisoned for Pennies: The Economics of Toxics and Precaution,* Island Press, 2008; Frank Ackerman and Lisa Heinzerling, *Priceless: On Knowing the Price of Everything and the Value of Nothing,* The New Press, 2004; J. Creyts, A. Derkach, S. Nyquist, K. Ostrowski and J. Stephenson, *Reducing U.S. Greenhouse Gas Emissions: How Much at What Cost?,* McKinsey & Co., 2007; P.-A. Enkvist, T. Naucler and J. Rosander, "A Cost Curve for Greenhouse Gas Reduction," *The McKinsey Quarterly,* 2007; Immanuel Kant, *Groundwork for the Metaphysics of Morals,* translated by Thomas K. Abbot, with revisions by Lara Denis, Broadview Press, 2005 [1785]; B. Lomborg, *Cool It: The Skeptical Environmentalist's Guide to Global Warming,* Alfred A. Knopf, 2007; W.D. Nordhaus, *A Question of Balance: Economic Modeling of Global Warming,* Yale University Press, 2008; F.P. Ramsey, "A mathematical theory of saving," *The Economic Journal* 138(152): 543-59, 1928; Nicholas Stern *et al.,* *The Stern Review: The Economics of Climate Change,* HM Treasury, 2006; U.S. Census Bureau, "Statistical Abstract of the United States." 127th edition. 2008; M.L. Weitzman, "On Modeling and Interpreting the Economics of Catastrophic Climate Change," December 5, 2007 version, www. economics.harvard.edu/faculty/weitzman/files/modeling.pdf.

Article 1.2.6

THE COSTS OF EXTREME WEATHER

Climate inaction is expensive—and inequitable.

BY HEIDI GARRETT-PELTIER
November/December 2011

Two thousand eleven has already been a record-setting year. The number of weather disasters in the United States whose costs exceed $1 billion—ten—is the highest ever. August witnessed one of the ten most expensive catastrophes in U.S. history, Tropical Storm Irene. An initial estimate put the damages from Irene at between $7 billion and $13 billion. In this one storm alone, eight million businesses and homes lost power, roads collapsed, buildings flooded, and dozens of people lost their lives. Meanwhile, Texas is experiencing its hottest year in recorded history: millions of acres in the state have burned, over 1,550 homes have been lost to wildfires as of early September, and tens of thousands of people have had to evacuate their homes. The devastation caused by the storms and droughts has left individuals and businesses wondering how they'll recover, and has left cash-strapped towns wondering how they'll pay for road and infrastructure repairs.

Extreme weather events like these are expected to become more frequent and more intense over the next century. That's just one of the impacts of climate change, which, according to the consensus of scientists and research organizations from around the world, is occurring with both natural and human causes, but mainly from the burning of fossil fuels. According to NASA, since 1950 the number of record high-temperature days has been rising while the number of record low-temperature days has been falling. The number of intense rainfall events has also increased in the past six decades. At the same time, droughts and heat waves have also become more frequent, as warmer conditions in drier areas have led to faster evaporation. This is why in the same month we had wildfires in Texas (resulting from more rapid evaporation and drought) and flooding in the Northeast (since warmer air holds more moisture and results in more intense precipitation).

In response to these dramatic weather changes, the courses of action available to us are *mitigation, adaptation*, and *reparation*. *Mitigation* refers to efforts to prevent or reduce climate change, for example, cutting fossil fuel use by increasing energy efficiency and using more renewable energy. *Adaptation* refers to changing our behaviors, technologies, institutions, and infrastructure to cope with the damages that climate change creates—building levees near flood-prone areas or relocating homes further inland, for example. And as the term implies, *reparation* means repairing or rebuilding the roads, bridges, homes, and communities that are damaged by floods, winds, heat, and other weather-related events.

Of these, mitigation is the one strategy whose costs and benefits can both be shared globally. Moving toward a more sustainable economy less reliant on the burning of fossil fuels for its energy would slow the rise in average global temperatures and make extreme weather events less likely. Mitigation will have the greatest impact with a shared worldwide commitment, but even without binding international agreements, countries can take steps to reduce their use of coal, oil, and natural gas.

According to the Intergovernmental Panel on Climate Change, even the most stringent mitigation efforts cannot prevent further impacts of climate change in the next few decades. We will still need to adapt and repair—all the more in the absence of such efforts. But the costs and burdens of adaptation and reparation are spread unevenly across different populations and in many cases the communities most affected by climate change will be those least able to afford to build retaining walls or relocate to new homes. Farmers who can afford to will change their planting and harvesting techniques and schedules, but others will have unusable land and will be unable to sustain themselves. Roads that are washed away will be more quickly rebuilt in richer towns, while poorer towns will take longer to rebuild if they can at all. The divide between rich and poor will only grow.

Given the high cost of damages we've already faced just this year, mitigation may very well be sound economic planning. But it is also the most humane and equitable approach to solving our climate problem. ❑

Sources: NOAA/NESDIS/NCDC, "Billion Dollar U.S. Weather/Climate Disasters 1980-August 2011"; Michael Cooper, "Hurricane Cost Seen as Ranking Among Top Ten," *New York Times*, August 30, 2011; "Hurricane Irene Damage: Storm Likely Cost $7 Billion to $13 Billion," *International Business Times*, August 29, 2011; Intergovernmental Panel on Climate Change, *Fourth Assessment Report: Climate Change 2007*, Working Group II ch. 19; NASA, "Global Climate Change: Vital Signs of the Planet—Evidence"; U.S. EPA, "Climate Change—Health and Environmental Effects, Extreme Events."

Article 1.2.7

A GREATER THREAT?
Federal Spending on the Military vs. Climate Change

BY AMY GLUCKMAN
September/October 2009

I t's not surprising that it took some time for the world's largest single consumer of oil to start taking climate change seriously. But the U.S. military has finally begun to do so. Intelligence agencies and the Defense Department "for the first time are taking a serious look at the national security implications of climate change," the *New York Times* reported in August, noting that the Pentagon's next Quadrennial Defense Review, due in 2010, will include a section on climate change for the first time.

The discovery of a grave new threat to national security usually means more money for the Defense Department. But the Pentagon is not the locus of U.S. government climate-change policy. Passing legislation to cut greenhouse-gas emissions via a cap-and-trade program or a carbon tax is widely viewed as the most important step the federal government must take—a politically difficult step but not one requiring large government expenditures.

Federal spending also forms an important component of climate change policy, however. For one thing, the government is itself a major greenhouse-gas emitter and must make clean-energy and energy-efficiency investments for its own facilities and

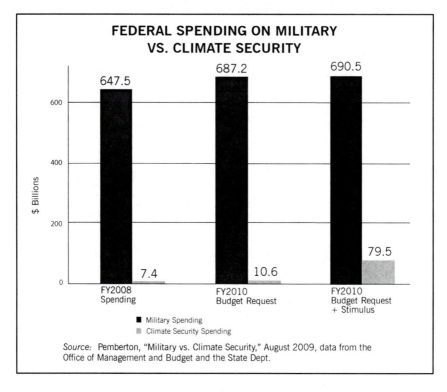

FEDERAL SPENDING ON MILITARY VS. CLIMATE SECURITY

647.5 — 687.2 — 690.5
600
400
200
0
7.4 — 10.6 — 79.5

$ Billions

FY2008 Spending | FY2010 Budget Request | FY2010 Budget Request + Stimulus

■ Military Spending
▨ Climate Security Spending

Source: Pemberton, "Military vs. Climate Security," August 2009, data from the Office of Management and Budget and the State Dept.

vehicle fleets. Government-funded research and development can facilitate and speed up the larger transition to a low-carbon economy. U.S. foreign aid dollars can help poorer countries to make that transition and to prepare for climate-change damages that are on the way. And tax expenditures—revenue the government forgoes when it creates special tax incentives—can channel personal and business spending in low-carbon directions.

	MILITARY VS. CLIMATE CHANGE SPENDING IN U.S. FOREIGN AID ($ BILLIONS)	
	FY 2008	FY 2010
Climate Change	0.21	0.72
Military	10.17	11.89

Source: Pemberton, "Military vs. Climate Security," August 2009, data from the Office of Management and Budget and the State Dept.

So how does federal spending on climate change compare to spending on traditional military force? Is climate-change spending rising in line with its new status as a serious security threat?

A new Institute for Policy Studies/Foreign Policy in Focus report by Miriam Pemberton tackles this question. Pemberton combed carefully through the FY 2008 budget, the Obama administration's FY 2010 budget request, and the stimulus package passed last February. Her analysis shows that spending to address climate change will be dramatically higher in FY 2010 compared to FY 2008—but that most of that improvement comes from the stimulus package, a one-time shot in the arm. And federal spending on climate change is still just a drop compared to the barrels of money going to reinforce U.S. military power.

In FY 2008, military spending exceeded climate-change spending by a ratio of 88 to1. In FY 2010, that ratio will be down to around 9 to 1, mostly thanks to the stimulus package. Excluding the stimulus money leaves the military-to-climate-change spending ratio at 65 to 1 for FY 2010. (The actual budget figures are shown in the figure above.)

The Obama administration plans to hike spending on helping foreign countries tackle climate change more than three-fold in FY 2010 compared to FY 2008. With that increase, the U.S. government will be spending about $20 on foreign military assistance for every $1 on foreign climate-change assistance, down from $50 for every $1 in FY 2008 (see the table above).

Sources: Miriam Pemberton, "Military vs. Climate Security: Mapping the Shift from the Bush Years to the Obama Era," Institute for Policy Studies/Foreign Policy in Focus, August 2009; John Broder, "Climate Change Seen as Threat to U.S. Security," *New York Times*, August 9, 2009; Jeff Brady, "Military's Oil Needs Not Deterred by Price Spike," NPR, Nov. 14, 2007.

Article 1.2.8

CLIMATE CHANGE AND ECOSOCIALISM

AN INTERVIEW WITH JOEL KOVEL
March/April 2009

Joel Kovel is co-editor of the journal Capitalism Nature Socialism, *author of* Enemy of Nature *(Zed Books, 2007), and co-producer of the 2007 video "A Really Inconvenient Truth."* D&S *collective member Larry Peterson interviewed Kovel in October 2009.*
—*Eds.*

DOLLARS & SENSE: **Many people are confused by the range of estimates of the extent of the problem of climate change. In your view, how dire is the threat, and how much time do we have to confront the problem in a serious way?**

JOEL KOVEL: To me, the overall problem—not simply of climate change, but the whole ecological crisis of which climate change comprises a major part—is the gravest threat ever faced by humanity. We had better learn to recognize that the world as it has been known has been fundamentally changed, and act accordingly. Even if the tendencies that have given rise to this are reversed tomorrow—actually quite inconceivable—we will be suffering the consequences for generations. At the other end, my best guess is that we have ten years to begin to make basic changes. Otherwise, tipping points will be passed, and civilization will go downhill very rapidly.

The basic principle is that everything in nature exists interconnectedly, something that humanity in the modern era has largely forgotten. A sign of that forgetting is the habit of reducing everything to the costs of everything, i.e., economic reductionism. I would argue that this is a manifestation of our whole estrangement from nature.

D&S: **Some people claim that earlier predictions of environmental crisis have been shown to be remarkably wrongheaded. Couldn't emerging technology resolve the climate crisis, as it has seemed to head off ones people have predicted before?**

JK: First of all, those predictions were not "remarkably wrongheaded"; they were only somewhat premature. Today, virtually all of the major predictions are being borne out. Julian Simon, a flamboyant believer in the sustainability of our society (he predicted that it could last seven billion years!) crowed in the '70s and '80s about winning bets that prices of raw materials would drop over time. You don't see people making that claim any more, especially in the energy sector. Here a positive feedback loop emerges, as the perception of "peak oil" drives warfare, social unrest, and intensified ravaging of the environment: see what's happening in Northern Alberta to the oil sands; or what Chevron is doing in Ecuador; or the story in Niger, with uranium extraction, and so on. And the most comprehensive study, the U.N.'s "Millennium Assessment Report" of 2005, concluded that the majority of planet Earth's ecosystems were in rapid decay.

The point about technology pulling us out of this dilemma deserves special emphasis. Of course we can always benefit from better technology; but that doesn't mean that the technology now available is inadequate to address this problem. What's missing are the social conditions for contending with ecological crisis. I'm afraid that speaking of state and market as leading the way is all too often a reshuffling of the same old deck. We need to confront the really salient issue. Consider this: since 1957, society has tripled its output of atmospheric carbon. In the same period population has increased by a factor of 2.3—a serious problem, to be sure, but a substantially lesser one; from another angle, we can say that the average person is "responsible" for 1.3 times as much carbon per capita as was the case fifty years ago. Clearly, the responsibility for the increase lies with the economic system; indeed, it would take two billion more people consuming at 1957 rates to throw the same amount of carbon into the atmosphere as we do today. So the question is, really, what induces the insane and uncontrollable "growth complex" of material goods, which by any rational assessment is driving this crisis? And this points us in the direction of the capitalist system.

D&S: **So will living standards have to fall? Will dyed-in-the-wool consumerist societies—not to mention resource-hungry developing ones—be able to make such a rapid and thorough transformation?**

JK: We cannot begin to approach this question except through a confrontation with capitalism, since consumerism is strictly the reflex of capitalist overproduction. We need to change the "need structures" that are induced through mass culture and undergird consumerist addiction. In addition, ever-growing inequalities of wealth introduce widespread envy and material cravings into society. All of these tendencies of capitalism make it impossible for society to respect ecological limits.

Living standards as now constructed in the industrial countries will have to fall. However, the notion of "living standard" is relative to one's worldview and mode of social existence. From the earliest days people have been able to live remarkably integral and spiritually advanced lives with a drastically lower level of "things" than now obtains in the so-called advanced societies. And it should not be forgotten that we are spending more and more just to reverse the effects of previous consumption and its associated waste. Our challenge is to see if lives can be reconstructed within the context of overcoming ecological crisis. This is why I argue that building toward a society beyond capitalism is the necessary condition for sustainability.

D&S: **How have you and others at *Capitalism Nature Socialism* developed an ecologically conscious version of Marxism?**

JK: Jim O'Connor's idea of the Second Contradiction made an "Eco-Marxism" possible by allowing the categories of Marxism to be applied in a rigorous way to our interactions with the external, natural world. Following Karl Polanyi, Jim integrated these with traditional crisis theory, showing both the essential unity of all forms of capitalist exploitation, and also their crisis-ridden character. The Second Contradiction postulated that the drive toward surplus value and profit caused capital to discount, hence degrade, the "conditions of production," which were defined by Jim as nature, the workers themselves, and infrastructure. An unintended yet necessary consequence of this was to depress the rate of profit, just as exploitation of workers reduced their ability to buy the commodities they made.

My focus has been on the expansive dynamic of capital, which accounts for its unsustainability, and immediately for the phenomena of climate change. I see this as rooted, first of all, in the fundamental shift outlined by Marx between an economy centered about use values, and the capitalist alternative centered in exchange value. People in pre-capitalist markets sell commodities for money in order to obtain other commodities they can use. Those in capitalist markets advance money to produce commodities to exchange for more money. Marx makes the profound observation that the second circuit has no limit, because money, as pure number, has no limit, in contrast to commodities produced for use—a person can consume only so much. Hence the capitalist economy is disconnected from nature at its root, and is "free" to mutilate the ecosphere. That this concretely happens is due to associated features of capitalism, such as competition driven by private ownership of the means of production, the complicity of the capitalist state, and the lawless character of a society grounded in exploitation.

Capitalism Nature Socialism also gives major emphasis to ecofeminist work because of the centrality of gender in our relations with nature; and finally, to an openness to radical and ecologically rational alternatives to capitalism: ecosocialism.

D&S: What about the international geopolitical realities? How can we expect Western governments, with all their historical baggage regarding pollution (and so much else), to seriously engage with the developing world, much of which is ruled by authoritarian governments, and beholden to foreign and domestic elites?

JK: The international dimension is crucial insofar as the ecological crisis is manifestly planetary, in both its causes and its effects. The rate of change of key ecosystems quite precisely follows the path of what has been called "globalization," one of the chief features of which is expansion in trade. While capitalism is the root problem, the present neoliberal period of capitalism, which began in the 1970s, is the setting for the heightened and globalized exploitation of nature (and also of labor) that surfaces as ecological crisis, with climate change as a principal but by no means exclusive manifestation.

What we call "imperialism" is deeply implicated in the ecological crisis. Throughout history, ecological events, at times catastrophic as in pandemics, have been interwoven with the rest of the fabric. The epoch of Western domination was ushered in by the spread of European diseases that eliminated 90% of the indigenous population of the Americas. Hence the uneven distribution of ecologically induced suffering is anything but new. Nor should it be read as absolute, since what characterizes the current ecological crisis is the "globalization" of hazards as well as of finance and trade—that is to say, if the seas rise six meters, a great deal of very valuable property will be destroyed along with that of commoners.

One of the most ominous implications of the present crisis is a survivalist mentality, manifest from gated communities, to vicious crackdowns on "illegal aliens," to fundamentalist wars. Anything that severs the interconnections of an ecosystem hastens its disintegration; this is bound to be the fate of a humanity disintegrating into fragments according to the logic of imperialism and its associated splittings.

But the ecological crisis affords another path as well, which increasing numbers of people are taking. This involves finding and adopting a universalist ethic stemming from perception of our common fate and our unity with nature. It requires overcoming all forms of chauvinism, including those that hold the human species over the rest of nature. Its practical foundation, however, is in anti-imperialist politics.

D&S: **A few months back the senior science advisor to the British government claimed that he would "lose credibility" with the very government that—with much fanfare—commissioned his group's study if he insisted that the government commit itself to acknowledging its policy implications. Is this emblematic of the politics of climate change worldwide?**

JK: Unfortunately, yes. There are of course even more lurid stories that came out of the Bush administration, where climate officials circulated in and out of Exxon-Mobil, and reputable scientists were routinely threatened and punished for speaking the truth about climate change.

There is a basic lesson to be learned: The ecological crisis poses a bigger threat to humanity than fascism. During World War II, in Britain and the United States, the ruling classes and the state collaborated in the biggest mobilization in human history to defeat the Axis. In that case the capitalists could see that a degree of suspension of the normal operations of the market, as through planning, rationing, price controls, etc., would gain them the prized control over the global economy once the war crisis was over; from another angle, they could see their way clear of the seemingly intractable depression that had haunted the 1930s.

In this case, resolution of climate change (not to mention the other features of ecological crisis) will require such deep and permanent cuts in the processes of accumulation as to bring the capitalist era to a close. For example, a young economist, Minqi Li, has recently demonstrated ["Climate Change, Limits to Growth, and the Imperative for Socialism," *Monthly Review*, July/August 2008] that all scenarios that hold down global warming below the threshold of positive feedback loops that accelerate climate change will require sustained contractions in world domestic product—in other words, an end to "growth," which means the end of capitalism. The big bourgeoisie knows this, which is why they act irresponsibly, typically sacrificing the future to the accumulation of wealth. If they behaved differently, they wouldn't have control over accumulation, and others would step forward to take control. As Marx wrote, the capitalist is the personification of capital.

D&S: **What about the coverage of the issue in the media? More of the same?**

JK: Absolutely the same principle holds for the corporate media, which have during the neoliberal era become absorbed into ever-greater conglomerations of capital. This has necessarily stifled the independent voices of the press, as we see in reporting of political races, the war in Iraq, and much else. Here, once more, the context is a threat to the capitalist system itself, and therefore the behavior is more extreme. Watch the Weather Channel or the robotic weather correspondents on news programs. Will they ever, in reporting the increasingly bizarre weather patterns that accompany climate change, suggest that these correspond to an ever-gathering crisis, much less suggest that there might be a structural dynamic driving that crisis?

Virtually every sane adult (and many more children than one would suspect) knows that something very fishy is going on in the sphere of climate. People tend to be understandably worried about this. Imagine what a threat to the system would result if they became at all enlightened, which is to say, able to recognize just how profound is the threat to their future and even more, to the future of their children—and also that there is a coherent explanation as to why this is happening, one implicating the very centers of capitalist power.

To secure capital's rule, it is necessary to keep people in the dark, or to be more exact, confused, distracted, and vaguely reassured. The media tends, therefore, to meet people halfway, then move them in the wrong direction. False prophets like Al Gore are praised for calling attention to the threat posed by the carbon economy, and the fact that Gore does not attend to the role played by the accumulation of capital is never brought forward. At the same time, the corporate image machine is geared up for greenwashing.

Unhappily, the job of mass deception is relatively easy, since with the stakes so high and given the inherent complexities and level of fear, it takes only a little uncertainty to slow down necessary action. The media system is very effective in doing this.

D&S: **What about carbon trading/taxes, the switch to renewables, and nuclear power? Can they help even in the short term?**

JK: There is a simple and effective touchstone for evaluating proposed solutions to the climate change crisis: do not look at the technical details but at the class forces in play, and always act so as to weaken the forces of capital. From this standpoint, some schemes are doomed from their inception, while the fate of others depends on the politics of their implementation.

In the first category belongs emissions trading, including the Kyoto Protocols and their so-called "Clean Development Mechanisms" in which projects in the Global South are used, like Papal indulgences, to permit the industrial North to keep putting CO_2 into the atmosphere. This sounds odd, and it is. To be blunt: Kyoto is set up to fail, except from the standpoint of a "success" that is also a failure, namely, the making of money from the licensing of pollution credits (because such money becomes capital, which must be invested to make more capital, which is to say, made to enter a fresh cycle of throwing carbon into the atmosphere). What dooms Kyoto is transparently that of being the scheme of climate control entrusted to capital. I am not sure whether capitalists know consciously that an effective program of containing climate change will bring down their system, but they certainly act on this basis.

(When I refer to "Kyoto," I follow a common practice of including both the formal documents and the mass of practices undertaken in their wake. The written protocol is vague about a lot of details and implications. However, the total regime signified by Kyoto is one in which the actors are exclusively allied with capital. Hence everything is interpreted to create credits rather than taxes and to allow these to become subject to new forms of wealth generation through speculation. The architects of the Kyoto Protocols rationalized this as necessary to induce capitalists to get on board. They have done so—on a vessel headed toward the rocks.)

Carbon taxes belong to the second category. In principle they have the potential to reduce carbon emissions. In practice, this depends on how they are written, who is made to pay, and who stands behind them. As is pretty much the case for all kinds of taxation, politics are the decisive factor.

Alternative energy is an absolute necessity, and also a political football. The reader had better disabuse her or himself of the notion that nuclear power will solve this crisis, despite all the cheerleading for it. Intractably dangerous, enormously destructive, and expensive to build and operate, nuclear power is also basically inadequate. An MIT report from 2003 [S. Ansolabehere et al., "The Future of Nuclear Power," Massachusetts Institute of Technology, July 2003] says that 1,000 to 1,500 new 1,000-megawatt reactors would have to be built by 2050 just to displace 15–25% of the expected growth in carbon emissions from electricity generation over that time.

Similar considerations hold for genuinely renewable energies like solar, wind, geothermal, tidal, etc., despite their clear superiority from an ecological perspective. The point deserves the utmost emphasis: there is no technological or administrative fix for the ecological crisis. An effective resolution requires social transformation, one overriding criterion of which must be to keep carbon in the ground in the first place, and whose overall goals include reducing the burden of society on nature and promoting the healing and restoration of damaged ecosystems.

This requires radically anti-capitalist ecopolitics, some goals of which in the case of climate would be:

• solidarity with popular struggles to block the extraction of carbon and uranium; these occur worldwide, from Nigeria to Ecuador to Australia to California, and they need to be coordinated as well as extended;

• free and universal public transportation (just like schools and health care);

• nationalization of the oil, coal, and gas industries;

• total mobilization to force worthy climate protocols in Copenhagen in December 2009, by direct action if necessary—as is almost certainly going to be the case. This may require as many as a million people in the streets.

These measures can be seen as the prefiguration of the World Social Forum movement's slogan, "Another world is possible."

D&S: How can we deal with other environmental issues—nanotechnology, and pollution of the oceans and of space, for example—when all our efforts would seem to have to be focused on climate change?

JK: We need the notion of an ecological crisis to grasp that there are a number of ecosystemic crises, each of which can wreak major havoc and all of which are interrelated and share the same susceptibility to the accumulative pressure of capital. This is why, by the way, it is better to think in terms of ecology than environment, since the notion of an environment does not carry an assumption that its parts are interrelated. Within an ecological way of looking at things, things are differentiated but internally related. The climate crisis is one cause of the increasingly grave and lethal water crisis, just as terrestrial water flows shape climate. The same goes for increasing food crises, where the diversion of crops for biofuel production is causing incipient famine, while biotechnology becomes a potentially deadly instrument of capital by recklessly interfering with the evolved checks and balances by means of which nature introduces a degree of stability and equilibrium.

The ecological perspective requires that we see ourselves as part of nature, including as organic bodies subject to disease. Pandemics are themselves ecological events, co-determined by pollution-induced immune system disturbances, and increasingly likely. This perspective demands a complete rethinking of human existence. It cannot be grasped by a purely economic analysis.

D&S: What if a socialist movement becomes viable—perhaps due in part to the social and economic breakdown that would inevitably accompany the rapid climate change some are forecasting only a few decades hence—and takes power only to find itself unable to meet basic needs due to the effects of climate change?

JK: Today, any viable socialist movement has to be ecologically rooted, or else it is irrelevant. I would define ecosocialism as the movement toward a society of freely associated labor animated by ecocentric values, that is, by an ethic that foregrounds the healing of nature. In contrast to earlier socialisms, which often sought to perfect capitalism while redistributing the social product, ecosocialism advances the notion of limits on growth, not as a restriction upon life but as the flourishing of ecosystems in a state of balance and vibrant evolution.

Any actual socialist movement that comes to a degree of power in the interim would obviously be only a partial realization of this goal. There is no use in lamenting this prospect. One simply does the best one can and accepts the result stoically. Of course a degree of coercion would be required, especially of residual capitalist class forces. At some point, for example, the government will just have to decree strict rationing, or redirect production by fiat, without letting "market forces" do it. This is what happened in the World Wars, and the ecological crisis is their equivalent in terms of emergency. That's what states are for, and in any predictable scenario short of complete chaos, we will not be able to immediately dispense with state power. Everything here depends on how deeply ecosocialist principles have been internalized, that is, on how democratic/nonviolent means and ends have been integrated.

Rosa Luxemburg said a century ago that the real choice was between "socialism and barbarism." This remains the choice, except that socialism has become ecosocialism; while barbarism now comes into focus as ecocatastrophe, fascism, and endless war, with the nuclear option stronger than ever. That is simply the history into which we have been thrown, and we have no option except to make the best of it. ❏

PART 2

IS GOVERNMENT UP TO THE JOB?

Article 2.1

WAR ON THE EARTH

BY BOB FELDMAN
March/April 2003

In this era of "permanent war," the U.S. war machine bombards civilians in places like Serbia, Afghanistan, and Iraq. It also makes "war on the earth," both at home and abroad. The U.S. Department of Defense is, in fact, the world's largest polluter, producing more hazardous waste per year than the five largest U.S. chemical companies combined. Washington's Fairchild Air Force Base, the number one producer of hazardous waste among domestic military bases, generated over 13 million pounds of waste in 1997 (more than the weight of the Eiffel Tower's iron structure). Oklahoma's Tinker Air Force Base, the top toxic waste emitter, released over 600,000 pounds in the same year (the same amount of water would cover an entire football field about two inches deep).

Just about every U.S. military base and nuclear arms facility emits toxics into the environment. At many U.S. military target ranges, petroleum products and heavy metals used in bombs and bullets contaminate the soil and groundwater. And since the Pentagon operates its bases as "federal reservations," they are usually beyond the reach of local and state environmental regulations. Local and state authorities often do not find out the extent of the toxic contamination until after a base is closed down.

Active and abandoned military bases have released toxic pollution from Cape Cod to San Diego, Alaska to Hawaii. In June 2001, the Military Toxics Project and the Environmental Health Coalition released the report "Defend Our Health: A People's Report to Congress," detailing the Pentagon's "war on the earth" in the United States and Puerto Rico. (See map.) The contaminants emitted from military bases include pesticides, solvents, petroleum, lead, mercury, and uranium. The health effects for the surrounding communities are devastating: miscarriages, low birth weights, birth defects, kidney disease, and cancer.

Even the Defense Department itself now acknowledges some of the environmental destruction wrought by the U.S. military worldwide. The Pentagon's own Inspector General documented, in a 1999 report, pollution at U.S. bases in Canada, Germany, Great Britain, Greenland, Iceland, Italy, Panama, the Philippines, South Korea, Spain, and Turkey. Again, since even U.S. military bases abroad are treated as U.S. territory, the installations typically remain exempt from the environmental authority of the host country.

Activists worldwide have called attention to the scourge of toxic pollution, target- range bombardment, noise pollution, abandoned munitions, and radioactive waste unleashed by U.S. bases. (See map.) The International Grassroots Summit on Military Bases Cleanup in 1999 brought together 70 representatives of citizen groups affected by U.S. military contamination. The gathering adopted an "Environmental Bill of Rights for Persons, Indigenous Peoples, Communities and Nations Hosting Foreign and Colonial Military Bases," declaring that past and present military bases "threaten health, welfare, and the environment, [as well as] future generations." The document emphasizes that the burden of environmental destruction has fallen disproportionately on "economically disadvantaged communities, women, children, people of color and indigenous people." And it demands that the "foreign and colonial" armed forces responsible for the contamination bear the costs the cleanup."

Yet until the era of "permanent war" and global U.S. militarism gives way to an era of world peace, the U.S. military machine will likely remain above the law. And the Pentagon will continue its "war on the earth." ❑

FIGURE 1: THE AMERICAS

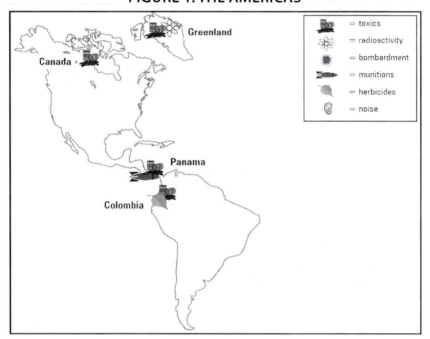

CANADA: The U.S. military built a network of radar sites in Northern Canada between 1953 and 1958. Cancer-causing agents were used in the construction and maintenance of the sites, which are now contaminated.

GREENLAND: In 1968, a B-52 carrying four nuclear bombs crashed near the Pentagon's Thule Air Force base in northern Greenland, causing severe plutonium contamination of the area.

PANAMA: The U.S. military left firing ranges in the Panama Canal Zone littered with thousands of unexploded rounds. A July 1998 Pentagon report found that the U.S. Army Corps of Engineers dumped tons of soil from a project to widen the canal onto 92 acres in Panama's Empire Range, damaging the rainforest ecosystem. A 1997 study for the U.S. Army also discovered the carcinogen TCI in the ground water at Fort Koblhe—at twenty times the level acceptable under U.S. federal law. COLOMBIA: Large-scale herbicide spraying under the "Plan Colombia"—ostensibly for coca eradication—has caused "serious human health effects; large-scale destruction of food crops; and severe environmental impacts in sensitive tropical ecosystems," according to a 2002 report of the *Aerial Spraying Review*, an environmental publication. There is also evidence that the Pentagon-sponsored fumigation campaign has caused a "loss of agricultural resources, including fish kills and sickness and death of livestock." Border areas of Ecuador have also been contaminated.

FIGURE 2: THE UNITED STATES

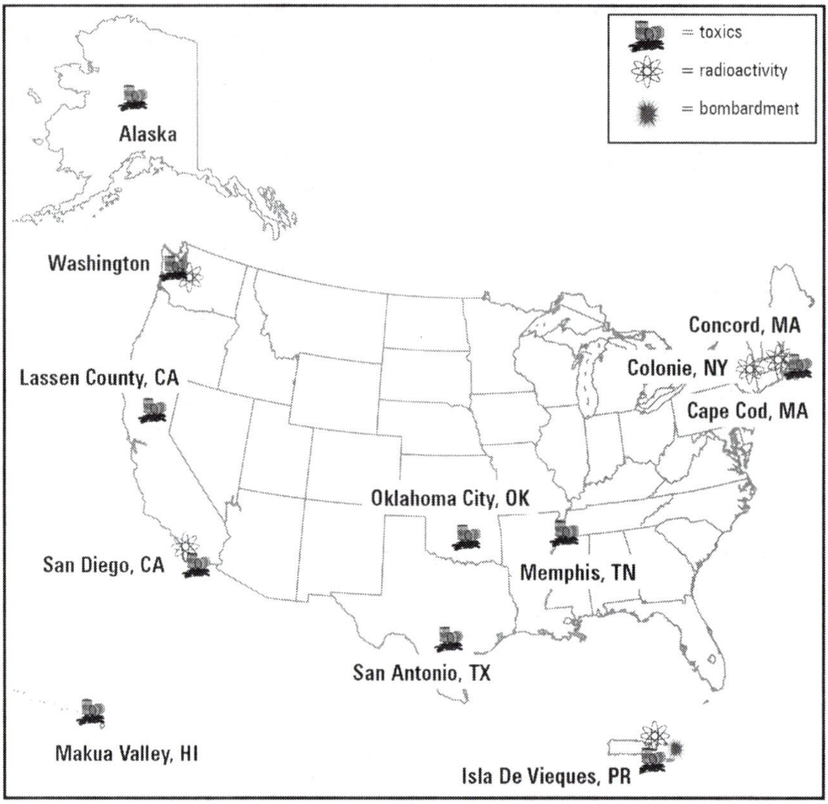

MAKUA VALLEY, HI: In the Makua Valley, the U.S. Army's live-fire assault training has caused fires and erosion and introduced alien plants and animals. These activities have threatened over 40 endangered plant and animal species, including the elpano bird. Homes and churches have also been destroyed by the fires and erosion. In addition, heavy metals and other pollutants from the base have contaminated the soil and groundwater.

ALASKA : U.S. military land fills, drum storage areas, fuel spill areas, and leaking underground storage tanks have polluted communities surrounding Cape Romanzof Long Range Radar station in Hooper Bay, Alaska. While fishing near Fort Greeley, Alaska, members of local indigenous tribes have found canisters of mustard gas left over from the 1950s and 1960s—when the U.S. military tested biological and chemical weapons at the site.

WASHINGTON: The U.S. Navy is the leading cause of oil spills off the Washington coast. The Navy spilled over 10,000 gallons of oil into Puget Sound in 1998. It also tests depleted uranium weapons in prime fishing waters nearby.

LASSEN COUNTY, CA: The Sierra Army Depot—where the military burns and detonates munitions— ranked as California's top source of air pollution in 1999, releasing 17% of all the toxic air emissions for the entire state. Increased cancer rates have been reported in both the surrounding county and the nearby Pyramid Lake Indian Reservation in Nevada.

SAN DIEGO, CA: The largest polluter in San Diego is the U.S. Navy, which has created 100 toxic and radioactive waste sites in San Diego Bay over the last eighty years. The National Oceanic and Atmospheric Administration found that the bay had the country's second-most-toxic estuary sediments, with the pollution concentrated around Navy and Navy-contractor sites. Fish in San Diego Bay contain high levels of mercury and radioactive compounds. The Navy also spilled over 11,000 gallons of oil into the bay in 1998.

OKLAHOMA CITY, OK: The Agency for Toxic Substance and Disease Registry found the average birth weight in the Kimsey neighborhood near Tinker Air Force Base to be about two ounces lower than in other Oklahoma City neighborhoods. It attributed the low birth weights to Kimsey residents' greater exposure to chemicals released from the base.

MEMPHIS, TN: The Pentagon's Defense Distribution Depot began operating as a chemical-weapons dump in the heart of Memphis' African-American community in 1942—and didn't warn residents of the danger. The depot contaminated the soil and groundwater. People who live nearby suffer a disproportionate number of miscarriages, birth defects, childhood cancers, and kidney ailments.

SAN ANTONIO, TX: Kelly Air Force Base ranked as the county's fifth-largest air polluter before its 2001 closing. Metals, solvents. and fuel from the base also contaminated the local groundwater. Over 70former Kelly Air Force Base workers have developed Lou Gehrig's Disease in recent years. The U.S. Agency for Toxic Substance and Disease Registry found elevated levels of cancer, low birth weight, and birth defects in the San Antonio neighborhood closest to the base.

COLONIE, NY: A plant which manufactured 30mm depleted uranium rounds for the U.S. military contaminated a nearby residential community, where the soil was found to contain 500 times more uranium than normal.

CONCORD, MA: Starmet, a company that manufactured depleted uranium ammunition for the U.S. military, contaminated Concord's groundwater and soil with uranium. Local residents have contracted some cancers at rates up to twice those of other Massachusetts residents.

CAPE COD, MA: Toxic pollution from the Massachusetts Military Reservation, former site of Otis Military Base, has contaminated drinking water in the nearby town of Falmouth. Over the years, the military "recycled" old ammunition and hazardous wastes at Otis by openly burning them. It also dumped 6 million gallons of aviation fuel directly on the ground. By 1986, Falmouth's cancer rate was 38% higher than the state average.

ISLA DE VIEQUES, PUERTO RICO: After fifty years of U.S. Navy target practice, Isla de Vieques has more craters per square kilometer than the moon. The Navy's use of bombs, depleted uranium, and Agent Orange on Vieques has produced a cancer rate 26% higher than in the rest of Puerto Rico. Vieques's children also show high levels of mercury and lead. The Navy, which occupies 26,000 of the island's 33,000 acres, has also contaminated the soil, destroyed its coral reefs, and emitted toxic heavy metals into the marine environment.

FIGURE 3: THE MIDDLE EAST AND ASIA

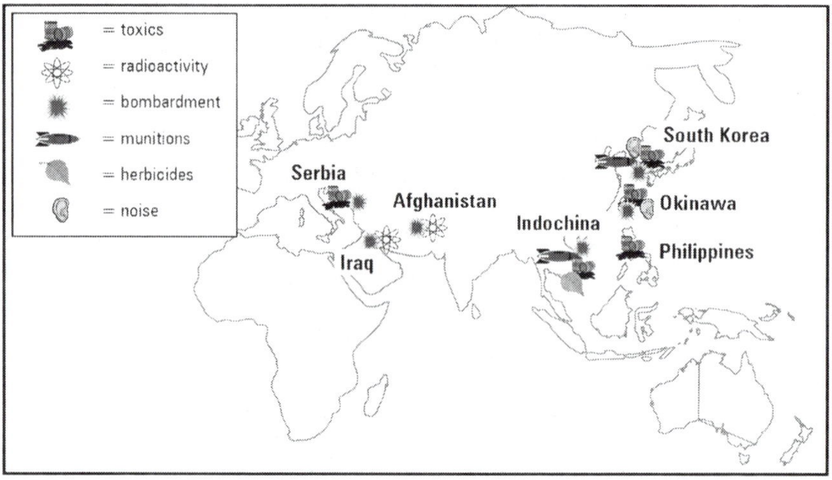

SERBIA: After the U.S. military bombed a petrochemical complex in the suburbs of Belgrade in 1999, the destroyed plastics factory and ammonia production unit released toxins such as chlorine into the air.

IRAQ: U.S. bombing of oil facilities in January 1991 caused spills of 6 to 8 million barrels of crude oil, killing about 30,000 marine birds. For nearly a year afterwards, oil well fires spewed toxic soot. The bombing also poisoned Iraqi water supplies. In addition, according to Iraq's Ministry of Health, depleted uranium from U.S. weapons has contaminated the soil and plants in southern Iraq, causing cancers and deformities associated with uranium exposure.

AFGHANISTAN: Following the Pentagon's 2001-2002 military campaign in Afghanistan, the Uranium Medical Research Center (UMRC) sent two scientific teams to Afghanistan to examine the effects of U.S. bombing on Kabul. Many residents, the UMRC teams found, had symptoms consistent with uranium exposure (joint pains, flu-like illnesses, bleeding mucous membranes, etc.). One fourth of the Kabul newborns examined had health problems consistent with uranium, including lethargy, skin rashes, and enlarged heads.

INDOCHINA: Nearly thirty years after the end of the U.S. war in Southeast Asia, many of the affected ecosystems have still not recovered, according to the Environmental Conference on Cambodia, Laos and Vietnam (Stockholm, 2002). Ten percent of southern Vietnam's forests (including one-third of the coastal mangoes, which play a vital role in the coastal ecosystem and fish habitats) were destroyed by the 72 million liters of herbicide the U.S. military dropped during the Vietnam War era. Arsenic and dioxin in the herbicides are expected to pose a health threat long into the future. Since 1975, 50,000 civilians have been killed by the landmines and other weapons the U.S. military left behind. The U.S.'s vast bombing campaign also left millions of large bomb craters.

SOUTH KOREA: Oil from the Yongsan 8th garrison's base has contaminated the soil and water. Asbestos has been found around the Camp Indian base. In May 1998, a ruptured pipeline at the Mt. Rackun military base polluted a large section of a South Korean forest conservancy area. U.S. military drills and maneuvers have also damaged farmlands and destroyed crops. Oil discharged by the U.S. Army has polluted the Sankogos River, contaminated farmland, and destroyed crops. Off the coast of South Korea, the U.S. military has used small islands as bombing ranges, creating noise pollution for nearby villages. The ammunition left behind has also injured residents.

OKINAWA: U.S. military exercises with live artillery have caused forest fires, soil erosion, and earth tremors—leaving sections of Okinawa barren and shell-ridden. Toxins emitted by the U.S. military have infiltrated Okinawa's land, water and air, and have been linked to low birth weights and elevated rates of leukemia and other cancers. Noise pollution at Kadena Air Base may also be a cause of low birth weights.

PHILIPPINES: The former site of Clark Air Base has contaminated the groundwater. The U.S. military also dumped hazardous waste in a municipal landfill in a residential area of Mabalacat. The power plant at the Subic Bay Naval Base emitted untreated pollutants directly into the air. Toxic waste from the destruction of excess bombs and ammunition were poured into local streams. In addition, most of the sewage generated at the Subic Bay base was discharged each day, untreated, directly into the bay.

Resources: Safety Forum Research/Safetyforum. com <www.safetyforum.com>; Military Toxics Project and Environmental Health Coalition, "Defend Our Health: A People's Report to Congress," (June 2001); Greenpeace <www.greenpeace.org>; East Asia/U.S. Women's Network Against Militarism <www.apcjp. org/womens_ network/skorea.htm>; Okinawan Peace Network of Los Angeles <www. uchinanchu.org>; Organization for the Prohibition of Chemical Weapons Technical Assistance Visit, Final Report, 8/14/01; Financial Times, 9/7/01 Ecocompass/IslandPress; Fellowship of Reconciliation Panama Campaign <www. forusa.org/program/panama>; Coastal Post newsmonthly <www.coastalpost.com>

Article 2.2

INDUSTRY ATTACKS ON DISSENT, FROM RACHEL CARSON TO OPRAH

Forty years after the publication of Rachel Carson's groundbreaking book Silent Spring, *corporations are still producing poisons—and still trying to keep critics from fighting back.*

BY LAURA ORLANDO
March/April 2002

In March 1996, the British government announced that ten people had died after eating beef from cattle sick with "mad cow disease." A month later, financier, movie actress, and talk-show host Oprah Winfrey discussed the topic on national television. While interviewing guest Howard Lyman of the Humane Society about his belief that American cattle might be at risk for the disease, Winfrey told her audience, "It has just stopped me cold from eating another burger." A group of Texas cattle ranchers sued Winfrey and Lyman for libeling cattle. Four years and over $1 million later, the two were vindicated in court.

Winfrey and Lyman were sued under the Texas False Disparagement of Perishable Food Products Act. Food disparagement laws are a new tool in an old bag of tricks used by corporations to protect their own economic interests at the expense of public discussion. Silencing public debate with frivolous, time-consuming, and costly lawsuits has become so commonplace that the technique has its own name: strategic lawsuits against public participation, or SLAPP suits. Winfrey and Lyman won in lower federal court because the judge ruled that cattle were not "perishable food products." The cattlemen pursued the matter in appellate court. A three-judge panel eventually ruled against the Texas ranchers. But the SLAPP suit achieved its objective by forcing Winfrey and Lyman to spend an enormous amount of time and money defending themselves—and by serving as a warning to the rest of us that saying what we believe to be true may cost us more than we can bear.

Lawsuits, and the threat of lawsuits, are not the only means industry uses to stifle dissent. Industry routinely buys the science that suits its needs (tobacco is a good example) and according to Sheldon Rampton, editor of the newsletter *PR Watch*, spends at least $10 billion every year on "public relations."

Industry's use of half-truths and intimidation to defend its toxic assault on life is nothing new. But until 40 years ago, when Rachel Carson's book *Silent Spring* was published, one could argue that we—the people—didn't know what was going on. *Silent Spring* woke up the nation, creating a national consciousness about the health and environmental consequences of pesticide use. Industry woke up too. Bruce Johnson, a Seattle lawyer, told the *New York Times* in 1999, "If [food disparagement laws] had been in place in the 1960s, Rachel Carson might not have found a publisher willing to print *Silent Spring*."

Trying to Silence *Silent Spring*

Before World War I, about half of the industrial products in the United States were made from renewable resources, such as plant-, wood-, and animal-based materials. In the 1920s and 1930s, oil and chemical companies like Union Carbide, Shell, and Dow expanded their interest in petrochemical manufacturing. The petrochemical industry, strengthened immensely by World War II, replaced renewable materials with synthetic organic compounds made from the by-products of oil and natural gas: for instance, synthetic rubber replaced natural rubber, chemical detergents replaced animal- based soaps, and polyester replaced cotton. In the 1950s and 1960s, the thriving plastics industry accelerated the shift even more. Today, 92% of the materials used for U.S. products and production processes are nonrenewable.

In many cases, the processes used to manufacture synthetic products created toxic wastes, and often the products themselves—either intact or when dissipated into the environment—were harmful to life. Among the most lethal of these products were synthetic pesticides. Before 1940, most pesticides were made from plants; a few were made from toxic metals like arsenic and mercury. But the synthetic chemicals created for chemical warfare during World War II were found to be highly effective weed and insect killers. So in 1945, with strong government backing, these poisons entered commercial markets. Within ten years, synthetic pesticides had captured 90% of the agricultural pest-control market. Pesticides such as dichloro diphenyl trichloroethane (DDT), dieldrin, and aldrin were dropped from planes like bombs over Dresden. State and federal government agencies blanketed neighborhoods with poisons in an attempt to eradicate pests like gypsy moths and Japanese beetles. Farmers used DDT and other synthetic insecticides on a variety of crops, including cotton, peanuts, and soybeans. Suburbanites embraced the new chemicals in their war against perceived nuisances like crab grass and dandelions.

Few people understood the dangers to life that these new chemicals presented. Sickness and death among chemical manufacturing workers were sometimes the first indication that the materials they worked with were toxic. But most people believed that you had to be an industrial worker to get sick. Rachel Carson's *Silent Spring* was the first widely read publication to say that everybody was being poisoned. *Silent Spring* was serialized by *The New Yorker* in June 1962 and came out in book form that same year. The book was—and still is—a devastating testament to the mortal dangers of synthetic chemical poisons. Carson, a wildlife biologist with two best sellers and a National Book Award under her belt, wrote, "We allow the chemical death rain to fall as though there were no alternative, whereas in fact there are many, and our ingenuity could soon discover many more if given opportunity."

Silent Spring was written before big business politics and sophistry were so well versed at setting the terms of discourse about environmental issues. Still, during the four years that Carson spent writing the book, she was well aware that it would unleash the wrath of the chemical industry. Deeply concerned about potential industry attacks and lawsuits, she did what she could to protect herself. Carson and her literary agent Marie Rodell asked lawyers from Houghton Mifflin, her publisher, to review the manuscript. Carson made sure Houghton Mifflin had libel insurance and she renegotiated a contract with them that put a monetary limit on her personal liability. And building the best defense of all, she meticulously checked her facts and diligently worked on a list of principal sources to document her conclusions.

Carson's concerns were well founded. After *The New Yorker* serialized parts of the book, the *New York Times* ran an article with the headline, " '*Silent Spring*' Is Now Noisy Summer: Pesticide Industry Up In Arms Over a New Book." The story began, "The $300,000,000 pesticides industry has been highly irritated by a quiet woman author whose previous works on science have been praised for the beauty and precision of the writing." It quoted the president of the Montrose Chemical Corporation —a major manufacturer of DDT, a pesticide that Carson discussed at length—as saying that Carson wrote not "as a scientist but rather as a fanatic defender of the cult of the balance of nature."

Some of the criticism seems laughable now. After the second installment from *Silent Spring* appeared in *The New Yorker,* a man from California wrote to the magazine:

> Miss Rachel Carson's reference to the selfishness of insecticide manufacturers probably reflects her Communist sympathies, like a lot of our writers these days. We can live without birds and animals, but, as the current market slump shows, we cannot live without business. As for insects, isn't it just like a woman to be scared to death of a few little bugs! As long as we have the H-bomb everything will be O.K. P.S. She's probably a peace-nut too.

But industry's attack on Rachel Carson was swift and vicious. The chemical companies banded together and hired a public relations firm to malign the book and attack Carson's credibility. The pesticide industry trade group, the National Agricultural Chemicals Association, spent over $250,000 (equivalent to $1.4 million today) to denigrate the book and its author. The company that manufactured and sold the pesticides chlordane and heptachlor, the Velsicol Chemical Company of Chicago, threatened to sue Houghton Mifflin.

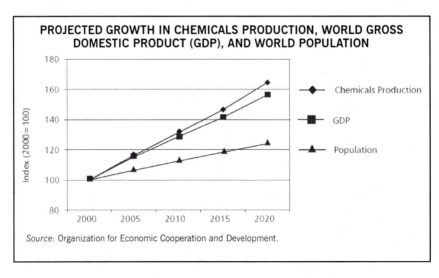

PROJECTED GROWTH IN CHEMICALS PRODUCTION, WORLD GROSS DOMESTIC PRODUCT (GDP), AND WORLD POPULATION

Source: Organization for Economic Cooperation and Development.

Milton Greenstein, legal counsel and vice president of *The New Yorker*, was called by at least one chemical company and told that the magazine would be sued if it didn't pull the last installment it planned to run of Carson's book. Greenstein responded, "Everything in those articles has been checked and is true. Go ahead and sue." John Vosburgh, editor of Audubon Magazine, which published excerpts from *Silent Spring*, said pretty much the same thing when Audubon was threatened. According to Carson biographer Linda Lear, Velsicol's lawyers suggested to Vosburgh that printing "a muckraking article containing unwarranted assertions about Velsicol pesticides" might "jeopardize [the] financial security" of magazine employees and their families. Vosburgh was so incensed that he wrote an editorial that appeared with the book excerpts, criticizing the chemical industry's response.

Industry threats did not stop the publication of *Silent Spring*, nor did the attacks prevent the book from becoming wildly successful. Carson was a popular writer who had the support of her editors, her publisher, and even President Kennedy, who cited *Silent Spring* as a reason to examine the health effects of pesticides. After the book was published, Carson was interviewed by Eric Severeid on national television and she testified before Congress about chemical poisons. She was profiled in *Life* magazine and featured in the *New York Times* and the *Washington Post*. In a review for the Book-of-the-Month Club, Supreme Court Justice William O. Douglas wrote that *Silent Spring* "is a call for immediate action and for effective control of all merchants of poison," and called the book "the most important chronicle of this century for the human race."

Carson effectively got her message across in part because what she had to say was radically new to the public, because her facts were unassailable, and because industry, though quite capable of attacking her and the publications that featured her work, had not yet learned how to overload the media—and by extension the people—with its own point of view.

Today's Targets

Rachel Carson understood the forces at work in government and industry. Having served on the staff of the U.S. Fish and Wildlife Service for 16 years, she was well aware of government's role in promoting and defending chemical poisons. "The crusade to create a chemically sterile, insect-free world," Carson wrote, "seems to have engendered a fanatic zeal on the part of many specialists and most of the so-called control agencies." We were living, she said, in an era "dominated by industry, in which the right to make a dollar at whatever cost is seldom challenged. When the public protests, confronted with some obvious evidence of damaging results of pesticide applications, it is fed little tranquilizing pills of half truth. We urgently need an end to these false assurances, to the sugar coating of unpalatable facts."

This language is too mild to describe what is happening today. Not only has the production of chemical poisons continued, but the chemical industry has become much more skillful at manipulating the media for its own ends. Now we are fed bigpills of outright lies, prevarication, and deception. We do not need to see industry's press releases; we hear the corporate viewpoint every day, all the time. Forty years after Rachel Carson tripped the alarm bell, we have been largely conditioned by industry to accept that which is harmful to us and to reject the warning signs of environmental devastation. We have been made ready to believe that a conservation ethic is incompatible with prosperity and that with creature comforts come sacrifices. Many of us want the sugar coating because, to a great extent, we are consumer junkies who believe that, if we demand that industry change its behavior, we will have to change our own

But of course not everyone wants the sugar coating, and some people are writing and talking about environmental issues in ways that are as compelling as *Silent Spring*. It is just harder to hear them now, harder to unpeel the layers of deception created by corporations and regulators. And when dissenting voices are heard, industry is quick to strike back.

For example, two recent books, *Living Downstream* and *Our Stolen Future*, are filled with the kind of critical thinking and meticulous research found in Carson's *Silent Spring*. Both deal with the chemical causes and consequences of health and environmental degradation. Both take industry to task. Both were attacked. Sandra Steingraber's 1997 book, *Living Downstream: An Ecologist Looks at Cancer and the Environment*, is the *Silent Spring* of the post-baby boom generation. Viewing cancer through several lenses—as biologist, cancer survivor, poet, and activist—Steingraber shows the links between cancer and environmental degradation. The book is beautifully written and powerfully frank. Reviewer Nancy Evans wrote: "The author describes the many kinds of silence that surround cancer issues, personal and political, individual and collective. The silence of scientists who fear loss of funding, the silence that fear imposes on people with cancer and those at risk. She suggests that *Silent Spring* shows us 'how one kind of silence breeds another, how the secrecies of government beget a weirdly quiet and lifeless world.' "

Living Downstream was also reviewed in the *New England Journal of Medicine* in November 1998. The negative review was signed "Jerry H. Berke, M.D., M.P.H." Trouble is, the journal failed to note Berke's affiliation with the W.R. Grace Company, a notorious environmental polluter.

Berke, director of toxicology for W.R. Grace, began his review with an attack on all environmentalists: "An older colleague of mine once suggested that the work product of an environmentalist is controversy. Fear and the threat of unseen, unchosen hazards enhance fund-raising for environmental political organizations and fund environmental research, he suggested." Berke called Steingraber's book "biased" and "obsessed with environmental pollution." And like a loyal industry toxicologist, he wrote, "The focus on environmental pollution and agricultural chemicals to explain human cancer has simply not been fruitful nor given rise to useful preventive strategies."

The mainstream media essentially ignored *Living Downstream*. No one can say exactly why, but one can guess that the book didn't win any points in the corporate controlled media by eloquently pressing for prevention and suggesting that people change the way they think about chemicals. The book calls for a "human rights approach," which would recognize that the "current system of regulating the use, release, and disposal of known and suspected carcinogens—rather than preventing their generation in the first place—is intolerable."

Like *Living Downstream, Our Stolen Future*—a book about endocrine disrupters (synthetic chemicals that disrupt hormones)—has also come under fire. When it was published in 1996, *Our Stolen Future* caused an immediate stir. Using a new way to examine the effects of chemical contamination, authors Theo Colborn, Dianne Dumanoski, and John Peterson Myers provide evidence that endocrine disruptors are widespread in the environment and are making people sick. A staggering list of synthetic chemicals, they tell us, interferes with hormones in humans and wildlife. These chemicals are common in the manufacture of pesticides, herbicides, and petrochemicals: they are found in soaps and detergents, flame retardants, and the dioxins produced in pulp and paper mills. In humans, the presence of endocrine disruptors can result in, among other things, severe reproductive tract deformities, declines in sperm count, elevated risk of cancer, and even behavioral changes. Our Stolen Future makes a powerful case for caution when using these chemicals.

But industry was having none of it. As Sheldon Rampton and John Stauber point out in *Trust Us, We're Experts!*, industry's attack on the book was "instant and vicious." The industry-funded Advancement of Sound Science Coalition held a press conference at which no fewer than ten scientists labeled the book as "fiction." And another industry-financed group, the American Council on Science and Health, "obtained a copy of the book in galley form months before publication and prepared an 11-page attack on it before it even hit the bookstores." Not surprisingly, the *Wall Street Journal* referred to *Our Stolen Future* as an "environmental 'hype machine.'" One chemical industry leader, the Monsanto Company, has a long record of going after its critics. Monsanto manufactured DDT and polychlorinated biphenyls (PCBs) before they were banned by the U.S. Environmental Protection Agency in the 1970s. It still makes a long list of synthetic chemicals and aggressively markets genetically engineered products like bovine growth hormone (Posilac) and genetically modified seeds. A billion-dollar company when *Silent Spring* first appeared, it published a parody of Carson's work, called "The Desolate Year," in the October 1962 issue of *Monsanto Magazine*. Since then, Monsanto has become a corporate role model in sugar-coating unpalatable facts and silencing dissent.

For example, *Against the Grain: Biotechnology and the Corporate Takeover of Your Food*, a book by Dr. Marc Lappé and Britt Bailey, was originally supposed to be published by Vital Health. But the company cancelled publication after receiving a threatening letter from a Monsanto lawyer, who said he believed the manuscript contained false statements about Monsanto's biggest money maker, the herbicide RoundUp. Common Courage Press picked up the book and published it in 1998. That same year, *The Ecologist* magazine published a special issue, "The Monsanto Files," which took a critical look at the chemical/biotechnology giant. But *The Ecologist*'s printer, Penwells of Saltash Cornwall (with whom *The Ecologist* had worked for 29 years), destroyed the 14,000 copy print run without even notifying the magazine. Penwells refused to comment on its decision and Monsanto denied any responsibility for the action, prompting *The Ecologist*'s editor, Zac Goldsmith, to say, "The fact that Monsanto had nothing to do with the decision to pulp is, if anything, more scary than if they had made some kind of legal threat. It goes to show what a powerful force a reputation can be." The magazine was able to line up another printer for the Monsanto issue.

In both cases, Monsanto's critics managed to find other venues for getting their information out to the public. But, like the SLAPP suit waged against Oprah Winfrey and Howard Lyman, the chemical company's actions—or maybe only its reputation for doing damage—caused serious disruption along the way. It's all part of a sophisticated set of techniques that industry uses to take the legs out from under dissent.

The Obligation to Act

Forty years ago, Rachel Carson wrote, "We have fallen into a mesmerized state that makes us accept as inevitable that which is inferior or detrimental, as though having lost the will or the vision to demand that which is good?" (Perhaps the question mark expresses Carson's wish to be hopeful.) Today, we are up against an immensely more organized, coordinated, and powerful corporate PR machine than Carson or the early environmentalists faced. Although some people have woken up, it is hard not to feel numb when faced with yet another story about environmental degradation and chemical poisoning.

The facts about chemical production today are sobering. The world uses five billion pounds of pesticides every year, with almost half used in the United States. According to the Federal Emergency Management Agency, as many as 500,000 U.S. products pose physical or health hazards and can be defined as "hazardous chemicals." U.S. industry uses 70,000 different chemical substances, but there is little or no attempt to assess their health or environmental impacts. Each year, over 1,000 new synthetic chemicals are introduced in the United States. But only a small fraction of these are tested for carcinogenity or endocrine disruption, and there is little understanding of how they interact with each other. The list of known poisons is long and troubling. It is as if we have forgotten, or have never known, "that which is good."

It is hard to be hopeful. In a chapter entitled "To the Ends of the Earth," *Our Stolen Future* follows a PCB molecule from its creation in a Monsanto chemical plant near Anniston, Alabama, to its entry into a polar bear in the Arctic. That chemical has now made its way to court, in the blood of thousands of Anniston residents who are suing Monsanto for knowingly dumping PCBs in their community. In January 2002, during opening arguments, a Monsanto lawyer carried on the company's long tradition of denial and deceit: "We would all rather live in a pristine world. We are all going to be exposed to things on a daily basis. Our bodies can deal with it."

We can't address the environmental crisis without going right to industry's door. A good first step is to hold industries accountable for the pollution they generate and the harm they cause. In places like Anniston, people are trying. But the greatest impact will come from fundamentally changing what corporations produce and how. This could be done by making laws based on, for example, the Precautionary Principle, which says that if there is reasonable suspicion that a technology, process, or chemical could be harmful, its application should be altered or it should be stopped altogether—even if some cause-and-effect relationships have not been fully established scientifically. Moreover, the burden of proof lies with the activity's proponents and not with the general public. This is not a "fringe" idea. The European

Commission (the executive body of the European Union responsible for implementing and managing policy) and some nations, such as Sweden and Germany, have adopted the Precautionary Principle as part of a structured approach to risk analysis. In 1997, the state of Massachusetts enacted a law that uses the Precautionary Principle as a guide for preventing toxic pollution.

Carson wrote, "The obligation to endure gives us the right to know." We know much more now than we did 40 years ago. If we are to endure, then we are also obligated to act. Human ingenuity has in it immense resources for good: by making good choices, we can live well without destroying life.

Resources: Resources: Rachel Carson, *Silent Spring* (Houghton Mifflin, 1962); Theo Colborn, Dianne Dumanoski, and John Peterson Myers, Our Stolen Future (Dutton, 1996) <www. ourstolenfuture.com>; Linda Lear, Rachel Carson: Witness for Nature (Henry Holt, 1997); Sheldon Rampton and John Stauber, Trust Us, We're Experts! How Industry Manipulates Science and Gambles with Your Future (Jeremy P. Tarcher/Putnam, 2001) <www.prwatch.org>; Sandra Steingraber, Living Downstream: An Ecologist Looks at Cancer and the Environment (Addison-Wesley, 1997) <www..steingraber.com>.

Article 2.3

WAY BEYOND GREENWASHING
Have corporations captured "Big Conservation"?

BY JONATHAN LATHAM
March/April 2012

Imagine an international mega-deal. The global organic food industry agrees to support international agribusiness in clearing as much tropical rainforest as they want for farming. In return, agribusiness agrees to farm the now-deforested land using organic methods, and the organic industry encourages its supporters to buy the resulting timber and food under the newly devised "Rainforest Plus" label. There would surely be an international outcry.

Virtually unnoticed, however, even by their own membership, the world's biggest wildlife conservation groups have agreed to exactly such a scenario, only in reverse. Led by the World Wide Fund for Nature (WWF, still known as the World Wildlife Fund in the United States), many of the biggest conservation nonprofits including Conservation International and the Nature Conservancy have already agreed to a series of global bargains with international agribusiness. In exchange for vague promises of habitat protection, sustainability, and social justice, these conservation groups are offering to greenwash industrial commodity agriculture.

The big conservation nonprofits don't see it that way, of course. According to WWF's "Vice President for Market Transformation" Jason Clay, the new conservation strategy arose from two fundamental realizations.

The first was that agriculture and food production are the key drivers of almost every environmental concern. From issues as diverse as habitat destruction to over-use of water, from climate change to ocean dead zones, agriculture and food production are globally the primary culprits. To take one example, 80-90% of all fresh water extracted by humans is for agriculture, according to the UN Food and Agriculture Organization's "State of the World's Land and Water" report.

This point was emphasized once again in an analysis published in the scientific journal *Nature* in October 2011. The lead author of this study was Professor Jonathan Foley. Not only is Foley the director of the University of Minnesota-based Institute on the Environment, but he is also a science board member of the Nature Conservancy.

The second crucial realization for WWF was that forest destroyers typically are not peasants with machetes but national and international agribusinesses with bulldozers. It is the latter who deforest tens of thousands of acres at a time. Land clearance on this scale is an ecological disaster, but Claire Robinson of Earth Open Source points out it is also "incredibly socially destructive," as peasants are driven off their land and communities are destroyed. According to the UN Permanent Forum on Indigenous Issues, 60 million people worldwide risk losing their land and means of subsistence from palm plantations.

By about 2004, WWF had come to recognize the true impacts of industrial agriculture. Instead of informing their membership and initiating protests and boycotts, however, they embarked on a partnership strategy they call "market transformation."

Market Transformation

With WWF leading the way, the conservation nonprofits have negotiated approval schemes for "Responsible" and "Sustainable" farmed commodity crops. According to WWF's Clay, the plan is to have agribusinesses sign up to reduce the 4-6 most serious negative impacts of each commodity crop by 70-80%. And if enough growers and suppliers sign up, then the Indonesian rainforests or the Brazilian Cerrado will be saved.

The ambition of market transformation is on a grand scale. There are schemes for palm oil (the Roundtable on Sustainable Palm Oil; RSPO), soybeans (the Round Table on Responsible Soy; RTRS), biofuels (the Roundtable on Sustainable Biofuels), Sugar (Bonsucro) and also for cotton, shrimp, cocoa and farmed salmon. These are markets each worth many billions of dollars annually and the intention is for these new "Responsible" and "Sustainable" certified products to dominate them.

The reward for producers and supermarkets will be that, reinforced on every shopping trip, "Responsible" and "Sustainable" logos and marketing can be expected to have major effects on public perception of the global food supply chain. And the ultimate goal is that, if these schemes are successful, human rights, critical habitats, and global sustainability will receive a huge and globally significant boost.

The role of WWF and other nonprofits in these schemes is to offer their knowledge to negotiate standards, to provide credibility, and to lubricate entry of certified products into international markets. On its UK website, for example, WWF offers its members the chance to "Save the Cerrado" by emailing supermarkets to buy "Responsible Soy." What WWF argues will be a major leap forward in environmental and social responsibility has already started. "Sustainable" and "Responsible" products are already entering global supply chains.

Reputational Risk

For conservation nonprofits these plans entail risk, one of which is simple guilt by association. The Round Table on Responsible Soy (RTRS) scheme is typical of these certification schemes. Its membership includes WWF, Conservation International, Fauna and Flora International, the Nature Conservancy, and other prominent nonprofits. Corporate members include repeatedly vilified members of the industrial food chain. As of January 2012, there are 102 members, including Monsanto, Cargill, ADM, Nestle, BP, and UK supermarket ASDA.

That is not the only risk. Membership in the scheme, which includes signatures on press-releases and sometimes on labels, indicates approval for activities that are widely opposed. The RTRS, for example, certifies soybeans grown in large-scale chemical-intensive monocultures. They are usually GMOs. They are mostly fed to animals. And they originate in countries with hungry populations. When, according to an ABC News poll, 52% of Americans think GMOs are unsafe and 93% think genetically modified organisms (GMOs) ought to be labeled, for example, this is a risk most organizations dependent on their reputations probably would not consider.

The remedy for such reputational risk is high standards, rigorous certification, and watertight traceability procedures. Only credibility at every step can deflect the seemingly obvious suspicion that the conservation nonprofits have been hood-winked or have somehow "sold out."

So, which one is it? Are "Responsible" and "Sustainable" certifications indicative of a genuine strategic success by WWF and its fellows, or are the schemes nothing more than business as usual with industrial-scale greenwashing and a social-justice varnish?

Low and Ambiguous Standards

The first place to look is the standards themselves. The language from the RTRS standards (see sidebar), to stick with the case of soy, illustrates the tone of the RTRS principles and guidance.

There are two ways to read these standards. The generous interpretation is to recognize that the sentiments expressed are higher than what is actually practiced in many countries where soybeans are grown, in that the standards broadly follow common practice in Europe or North America. Nevertheless, they are far lower than organic or fair-trade standards; for example, they don't require crop rotation, or prohibit pesticides. Even a generous reading also needs to acknowledge the crucial point that adherence to similar requirements in Europe and North America has contaminated wells, depleted aquifers, degraded rivers, eroded the soil, polluted the oceans, driven species to extinction, and depopulated the countryside—to mention only a few well-documented downsides.

There is also a less generous interpretation of the standards. Much of the content is either in the form of statements, or it is merely advice. Thus section 4.2 reads: "Pollution is minimized and production waste is managed responsibly." Imperatives, such as: "must," "may never," "will," etc., are mostly lacking from the document. Worse, key terms such as "pollution," "minimized," "responsible," and "timely" (see sidebar) are left undefined. This chronic vagueness means that both certifiers and producers possess effectively infinite latitude to implement or judge the standards. They could never be enforced, in or out of court.

THE ROUNTABLE ON RESPONSIBLE SOY STANDARDS

RTRS standards (version 1, June 2010) cover five "principles." Principle 1: Legal Compliance and Good Business Practices. Principle 2: Responsible Labour Conditions. Principle 3: Responsible Community Relations. Principle 4: Environmental Responsibility. Principle 5: Good Agricultural Practice.

Language typical of the standards includes, under Principle 2 (Responsible Labour Conditions), section 2.1.1 states: "No forced, compulsory, bonded, trafficked, or otherwise involuntary labor is used at any stage of production," while section 2.4.4 states, "Workers are not hindered from interacting with external parties outside working hours."

Under Principle 3 (Responsible Community Relations), section 3.3.3 states: "Any complaints and grievances received are dealt with in a timely manner."

Under Principle 4 (Environmental Responsibility), section 4.2 states: "Pollution is minimized and production waste is managed responsibly," and section 4.4 states: "Expansion of soy cultivation is responsible."

Under Principle 5 (Good Agricultural Practice), Section 5.9 states: "Appropriate measures are implemented to prevent the drift of agrochemicals to neighboring areas."

Dubious Verification and Enforcement

Unfortunately, the flaws of RTRS certification do not end there. They include the use of an internal verification system. The RTRS uses professional certifiers, but only those who are members of RTRS. This means that the conservation nonprofits are relying on third parties for compliance information. It also means that only RTRS members can judge whether a principle was adhered to. Even if they consider it was not, there is nothing they can do, since the RTRS has no legal status or sanctions.

The "culture" of deforestation is also important to the standards. Rainforest clearance is often questionably legal, or actively illegal, and usually requires removing existing occupants from the land. It is a world of private armies and bribery. This operating environment makes very relevant the irony under which RTRS members, under Principle 1, volunteer to obey the law. The concept of volunteering to obey the law invites more than a few questions. If an organization is not already obeying the law, what makes WWF suppose that a voluntary code of conduct will persuade it? And does obeying the law meaningfully contribute to a marketing campaign based on responsibility?

Of equal concern is the absence of a clear certification trail. Under the "Mass Balance" system offered by RTRS, soybeans (or derived products) can be sold as "Responsible" that were never grown under the system. Mass Balance means vendors can transfer the certification quantity purchased, to non-RTRS soybeans. Such an opportunity raises the inherent difficulties of traceability and verification to new levels.

How Will Certification Save Wild Habitats?

A key stated goal of WWF is to halt deforestation through the use of maps identifying priority habitat areas that are off-limits to RTRS members. There are crucial questions over these maps, however. First, even though soybeans are already being traded, the maps have yet to be drawn up. Secondly, the maps are to be drawn up by RTRS members themselves. Thirdly, RTRS maps can be periodically redrawn. Fourthly, RTRS members need not certify all of their production acreage. This means they can certify part of their acreage as "Responsible," but still sell (as "Irresponsible"?) soybeans from formerly virgin habitat. This means WWF's target for year 2020 of 25% coverage globally and 75% in WWF's "priority areas" would still allow 25% of the Brazilian soybean harvest to come from newly deforested land. And of course, the scheme cannot prevent non-members, or even non-certified subsidiaries, from specializing in deforestation.

These are certification schemes, therefore, with low standards, no methods of enforcement, and enormous loopholes. Pete Riley of UK GM Freeze dubs their instigator the "World Wide Fund for naïveté" and believes "the chances of Responsible soy saving the Cerrado are zero." Claire Robinson of Earth Open Source agrees: "The RTRS standard will not protect the forests and other sensitive ecosystems. Additionally, it greenwashes soy that's genetically modified to survive being sprayed with quantities of herbicide that endanger human health and the environment." There is even a website (www.toxicsoy.org) dedicated to exposing the greenwashing of GMO soy.

Many other groups apparently share that view. More than 250 large and small sustainable farming, social justice, and rainforest preservation groups from all over the world signed a "Letter of Critical Opposition to the RTRS" in 2009. Signatories included the Global Forest Coalition, Friends of the Earth, Food First, the British Soil Association and the World Development Movement.

Other commodity certifications involving WWF have also received strong criticism. The Mangrove Action Project in 2008 published a "Public Declaration Against the Process of Certification of Industrial Shrimp Aquaculture" while the World Rainforest Movement issued "Declaration against the Roundtable on Sustainable Palm Oil (RSPO)," signed by 256 organizations in October 2008.

What Really Drives Commodity Certification?

Commodity certification is in many ways a strange departure for conservation nonprofits. In the first place the big conservation nonprofits are more normally active in acquiring and researching wild habitats. Secondly, these are membership organizations, yet it is hard to envisage these schemes energizing the membership. How many members of the Nature Conservancy will be pleased to find that their organization has been working with Monsanto to promote GM crops as "Responsible"? Indeed, one can argue that these programs are being actively concealed from their members, donors, and the public. From their advertising, their websites, and their educational materials, one would presume that poachers, population growth and ignorance are the chief threats to wildlife in developing countries. It is not true, however, and as WWF's Jason Clay and the very existence of these certification schemes make clear, senior management knows it well.

In public, the conservation nonprofits justify market transformation as cooperative; they wish to work with others, not against them. However, they have chosen to work preferentially with powerful and wealthy corporations. Why not cooperate instead with small farmers' movements, indigenous groups, and already successful standards, such as fair-trade, organic and non-GMO? These are causes that could use the help of big international organizations. Why not, with WWF help, embed into organic standards a rainforest conservation element? Why not cooperate with your membership to create engaged consumer power against habitat destruction, monoculture, and industrial farming? Instead, the new "Responsible" and "Sustainable" standards threaten organic, fair-trade, and local food systems—which are some of the environmental movement's biggest successes.

One clue to the enthusiasm for "market transformation" may be that financial rewards are available. According to Nina Holland of Corporate Europe Observatory, certification is "now a core business" for WWF. Indeed, WWF and the Dutch nonprofit Solidaridad are currently receiving millions of euros from the Dutch government (under its Sustainable Trade Action Plan) to support these schemes. According to the plan, 67 million euros have already been committed, and similar amounts are promised.

The Threat From the Food Movement

Commodity-certification schemes like RTRS can be seen as an inability of global conservation leadership to work constructively with the ordinary people who live in and around wild areas of the globe; or they can be seen as a disregard for fair-trade and organic labels; or as a lost opportunity to inform and energize members and potential members as to the true causes of habitat destruction; or even as a cynical moneymaking scheme. These are all plausible explanations of the enthusiasm for certification schemes and probably each plays a part. None, however, explains why conservation nonprofits would sign up to schemes whose standards and credibility are so low. Especially when, as never before, agribusiness is under pressure to change its destructive social and environmental practices.

The context of these schemes is that we live at an historic moment. Positive alternatives to industrial agriculture, such as fair trade, organic agriculture, agroecology, and the System of Rice Intensification, have shown they can feed the planet, without destroying it, even with a greater population. Consequently, there is now a substantial international consensus of informed opinion that industrial agriculture is a principal cause of the current environmental crisis and the chief obstacle to hunger eradication.

This consensus is one of several roots of the international food movement. As a powerful synergism of sustainability, social-justice, sustainability, food-quality, and environmental concerns, the food movement is a clear threat to the long-term existence of the industrial food system. Incidentally, this is why big multinationals have been buying up ethical brands.

Under these circumstances, evading the blame for the environmental devastation of the Amazon, Asia, and elsewhere, undermining organic and other genuine certification schemes, and splitting the environmental movement must be a dream come true for members of the industrial food system. A true cynic might surmise that the food industry could hardly have engineered it better had they planned it themselves.

Who Runs Big Conservation?

To guard against such possibilities, nonprofits are required to have boards of directors whose primary legal function is to guard the mission of the organization and to protect its good name. In practice, for conservation nonprofits this means overseeing potential financial conflicts and preventing the organization from lending its name to greenwashing.

So, who are the individuals guarding the mission of global conservation nonprofits? U.S.-WWF boasts (literally) that its new vice-chair was the last CEO of Coca-Cola, Inc. (a member of Bonsucro) and that another board member is Charles O. Holliday Jr., the current chairman of the board of Bank of America, who was formerly CEO of DuPont (owner of Pioneer Hi-Bred International, a major player in the GMO industry). The current chair of the executive board at Conservation International is Robert Walton, better known as chair of the board of Wal-Mart (which now sells "sustainably sourced" food and owns the supermarket chain ASDA). The boards of WWF and Conservation International do have more than a sprinkling of members with conservation-related careers. But they are heavily outnumbered by business representatives. On the board of Conservation International, for example, are GAP, Intel, Northrop Grumman, JP Morgan, Starbucks, and UPS, among others.

The Nature Conservancy's board of directors has only two members (out of 22) who list an active affiliation to a conservation organization in their board CV (Prof. Gretchen Daly and Cristian Samper, head of the U.S. Museum of Natural History). Only one other member even mentions among his qualifications an interest in the subject of conservation. The remaining members are like Shona Brown, who is an employee of Google and a board member of Pepsico, or Meg Whitman, the current president and CEO of Hewlett-Packard, or Muneer A. Satter, a managing director of Goldman Sachs.

So, was market transformation developed with the support of these boards or against their wishes? The latter is hardly likely. The key question then becomes: Did these boards in fact instigate market transformation? Did it come from the very top?

Never Ending

Leaving aside whether conservation was ever their true intention, it seems highly unlikely that WWF and its fellow conservation groups will leverage a positive transformation of the food system by bestowing "Sustainable" and "Responsible" standards on agribusiness. Instead, it appears much more likely that, by undermining existing standards and offering worthless standards of their own, habitat destruction and human misery will only increase.

Market transformation, as envisaged by WWF, nevertheless might have worked. However, WWF neglected to consider that successful certification schemes start from the ground up. Organic and fair-trade began with a large base of committed farmers determined to fashion a better food system. Producers willingly signed up to high standards and clear requirements because they believed in them. Indeed, many already were practicing high standards without certification. But when big players in the food industry have tried to climb on board, game the system and manipulate standards, problems have resulted, even with credible standards like fair-trade and organic. At some point big players will probably undermine these standards. They seem already to be well on the way, but if they succeed their efforts will only have proved that certification standards can never be a substitute for trust, commitment and individual integrity.

The only good news in this story is that it contradicts fundamentally the defeatist arguments of the WWF. Old-fashioned activist strategies, of shaming bad practice, boycotting products, and encouraging alternatives, do work. The market opportunity presently being exploited by WWF and company resulted from the success of these strategies, not their failure. Multinational corporations, we should conclude, really do fear activists, non-profits, informed consumers, and small producers all working together. ❏

Sources: Jonathan A. Foley et al. "Solutions for a Cultivated Planet" *Nature*, October 2011 (Nature.com); Jason Clay, "Economics, Behavior and Biodiversity Loss: Sustainability as a Pre-competitive Issue," March 25, 2011 (youtube.com); Food and Agriculture Organization of the United Nations, "Scarcity and degradation of land and water: growing threat to food security," November 28, 2011 (fao.org); State of the World's Land and Water Resources for Food and Agriculture (SOLAW), November 28, 2011 (fao.org); Mat McDermott, "More Dirty Deforestation: 55% of Indonesia's Logging Illegal + Cargill's Two Hidden Palm Oil Plantations," May 6, 2010 (treehugger.com); Earth Open Source (earthopensource.org); United Nations (UN; un.org); Roundtable on Sustainable Palm Oil (RSPO; rspo.org); Round Table on Responsible Soy (RTRS; responsiblesoy.org); Roundtable on Sustainable Biofuels (rsb.epfl.ch); Bonsucro (Bonsucro.com); WWF, "Save the Cerrado: What's happening in the Cerrado?" (wwf.org. uk); Gary Langer, "Behind the Label, Many Skeptical of Bio-engineered Food," June 19, 2001 (abcnews.com); Round Table on Responsible Soy, "Why certifying under the RTST Standard?" (responsiblesoy.org); Natural Resources Defense Council, "Atrazine: Poisoning the Well," May 2010 (nrdc.org); The *Capital-Journal* Editorial Board, "Time for action on rural depopulation," July 28, 2011 (cjonline.com); "State of the World's Indigenous Peoples Report, Chapter 7: Emerging Issues," January 2010 (un.org); "A Brief History of Rubber" (rainforests.mongabay.com); "Letter of critical opposition to the Round Table on Responsible Soy," April 2009 (bangmfood. org); Global Forest Coalition (globalforestcoalition.org); Public Declaration Against the Process of Certification of Industrial Shrimp Aquaculture, November 3, 2008 (mangroveactionproject. org); World Rainforest Movement, "Declarations against the Roundtable on Sustainable Palm Oil (RSPO) in Defence of Human Rights, Food Sovereignty," September 2008 (wrm.org); System of Rice Intensification (SRI-Rice; sri.ciifad.cornell.edu); Sarah Hills, "Coca-Cola snaps up first Bonsucro certified sugarcane," June 22, 2011 (foodnavigator.com); "Wal-Mart Unveils Global Sustainable Agriculture Goal," October 14, 2010 (walmartstores.com); "Largest Corporate Dairy, Biotech Firm and USDA Accused of Conspiring to Corrupt Rulemaking and Pollute Organics," January 23, 2012 (cornucopia.org); Dutch Ministry of Agriculture, "Nature and Food Quality Sustainable Food: Public Summary of Policy Document" (government.nl); Jonathan Latham and Allison Wilson, "How the Science Media Failed the IAASTD," April 7, 2008 (independentsciencenews.org).

Article 2.4

BANKRUPTCY AS CORPORATE MAKEOVER
ASARCO demonstrates how to evade environmental responsibility.

BY ANNE FISCHEL, MARA KARDAS-NELSON, AND LIN NELSON
May/June 2010

> *"At around noon [every] July and August ... our folks would bring us into the*
> *house, because the smoke, the pollution, the sulfur, would settle into our commu-*
> *nity for about two or three hours ... when there was no breeze to take that away.*
> *When we would breathe that, we could not be outside because we were constantly*
> *coughing. So nobody can tell me that there was no ill effect on the majority of the*
> *folks that lived in Smeltertown."*
>
> —Daniel Solis, resident of Smeltertown, a Mexican-American neighborhood
> in El Paso, Texas, located next to an ASARCO smelter

After five long years in court, the bankruptcy of the American Smelting and Refining Company, or ASARCO, has finally been determined.

Hailed as one of the earliest and largest multinational corporations and responsible for the employment of hundreds of thousands, ASARCO has a long history of polluting both the environment and the workplace. After racking up billions in environmental damages, the company filed for bankruptcy in 2005.

It is billed as the largest environmental bankruptcy in United States history; 90 communities from 21 states will share a $1.79 billion settlement to cover the costs of environmental monitoring and cleanup and limited compensation to some of its workers. This figure, however, represents less than one percent of the funds originally identified as needed by claimants.

The ASARCO case emerged in the context of a diminished and disabled "Superfund," as the federal environmental program established to deal with hazardous waste sites is known. The fund was originally created by Congress to hold companies accountable for environmental damage and to ensure that communities are not left with large bills and no means to pay them. But years of corporate pressure on Capitol Hill has depleted Superfund, placing the financial burden of environmental cleanups on taxpayers, rather than on corporations.

This use of bankruptcies to avoid responsibility, coupled with a cash-strapped Superfund, offers a chilling glimpse into the world of corporate irresponsibility allowable under U.S. bankruptcy provisions and environmental policy. As the case closes, ASARCO is transforming from an aging corporation weighed down by shuttered factories and contaminated communities into a lean and profitable company. This is setting a precedent for how others can use legal loopholes to evade liability and undermine government protections.

Damaging Health and Environment, Yet Shaping Environmental Policy

ASARCO began operations in the late 1890s, mining, smelting, and refining essential ores (first lead, then copper) in order to provide base materials for industrial production. By the mid-20th century, the company had expanded to include holdings and operations in Latin America, Australia, Canada, Africa, and the Philippines. In 1914 company workers unionized through the Western Federation of Miners, which later became the Mine, Mill & Smelterworkers, eventually merging with the United Steelworkers in the 1960s. In its heyday, ASARCO operated in close to 90 U.S. communities in 22 states, employing thousands.

By the mid-1970s, employees and communities were growing concerned about environmental and public health risks resulting from company operations. Researchers, health departments, unions, and workers began tracking the impact of exposure to arsenic, lead, cadmium, and sulfur dioxide, all byproducts of the smelting process. In Tacoma, WA, site of one of ASARCO's largest smelting operations, dissident workers launched "The Smelterworker" newsletter, one of the first union-based occupational health efforts in the country. The Puget Sound Air Pollution Control Agency began to voice similar concerns when ASARCO's lobbying regarding federal laws and regulations successfully slowed development of a federal arsenic standard.

Health concerns also emerged in El Paso, Texas, site of a large ASARCO smelter that had polluted both sides of the U.S.-Mexico border. In 1970, following passage of the Clean Air Act, the City of El Paso sued ASARCO over its sulfur dioxide emissions. During the process of discovery, ASARCO submitted documentation of its emissions to the City for the first time. These reports showed that between 1969 and 1971, 1,012 metric tons of lead, 508 metric tons of zinc, eleven metric tons of cadmium, and one metric ton of arsenic had been released during operations.

By 1969 the city had a higher concentration of airborne lead than any other in the state. In the early 1970s a research team from the Centers for Disease Control (CDC), led by Dr. Philip Landrigan, confirmed a pattern of smelter-sourced lead threatening the children on the U.S. side.

The studies conducted by the CDC linked the high levels of lead in air, soil, and dust to the ASARCO smelter. They also linked the lead in soil and dust to elevated lead levels in children's blood. Landrigan's research team administered IQ tests and reaction time tests, and found significant differences in performance between lead-impacted children and those with lower blood levels. This pathbreaking research transformed scientific thinking about the impact of lead on children's development, and confirmed numerous dangers, even in children without obvious clinical symptoms.

At the time of research the threshold for lead in blood was 40 micrograms per deciliter. Today it is 10 micrograms per deciliter, and many health researchers and physicians want to see it set even lower. Yet some researchers had asserted that lead from smelters was not harmful to humans, and an El Paso pediatrician, in a study funded by an organization connected to the industry, claimed that levels of 40 to 80 micrograms were acceptable, as long as the children were properly nourished. As a result of the CDC studies, however, "it is now widely accepted in the scientific community that lead is toxic at extremely low levels," according to Landrigan.

Some of the affected children were treated with painful chelation therapy. Daniel Solis, a Smeltertown resident, recalls his siblings' reaction to the treatment:

> They would get hysterical because of how much the treatment would hurt, they would literally go underneath their cribs and they would hold on to the bottom of the bed. I would literally have to go underneath and drag them out… It was excruciating. My mom would cry to see… the pain that her kids would be going through. But we had no other choice, you know, my siblings were that infected with lead that they had to get that treatment.

In 1991, through its subsidiary Encycle, ASARCO received highly hazardous waste, sourced from a Department of Defense site at Rocky Mountain Arsenal in Colorado. Napalm, sarin nerve gas, cluster bombs, and white phosphorous had all been produced at this site, and private pesticide companies also rented space in the facility. At Encycle, hazardous waste labels were removed and materials were shipped to ASARCO facilities in El Paso and in East Helena, Mont. Neither facility was licensed to manage hazardous waste; it is possible that the waste was shipped to other sites as well. In El Paso, workers were not informed of the risks of such incineration and were not trained to deal with these hazardous materials. This lack of protection and withholding of information violates the federal right-to-know workplace law.

The Government Accountability Office (GAO) has verified that from 1991 to 1999, the El Paso and East Helena plants received and incinerated waste meant only for licensed hazardous waste facilities. This illegal disposal potentially exposed hundreds of workers and both communities. In 1998, the federal government fined ASARCO $50 million for these violations and problems at other ASARCO sites. The settlement did not include provisions for testing workers, soil, air, water, or community members for exposure to potential contaminants. The El Paso community was not informed about these illegal activities; the extent of knowledge in East Helena is unclear. The wrist-slap against the company—and the actions that provoked it—became public only through the investigative work of citizen activists in El Paso, leading to a *New York Times* exposé in 2006.

Although many communities endure severe health effects and environmental problems, ASARCO's ties to powerful politicians gave it substantial influence on public health policy. During the George W. Bush years, James Connaughton, one of ASARCO's key attorneys, served as head of the White House Council for Environmental Quality. A key ASARCO scientist was positioned for the federal Lead Advisory Board, while other prominent, independent scientists were pushed to the margins. ASARCO has also promoted the corporate "audit privilege," allowing companies to self-monitor hazards.

Superfund: Hope and Disappointment for Polluted Communities

ASARCO was hardly the only company polluting communities throughout the industrial boom of the 20th century. As research linked contamination to birth defects, higher cancer rates, and other serious illnesses, community advocates and municipal and state leaders took collective action. In 1980, in response to the discovery of hazardous waste at Love Canal, N.Y., Congress passed the Comprehensive Environmental Response, Compensation & Liability Act (CERCLA), better known as "Superfund." The Act made companies legally and financially responsible for environmental degradation that occurred as a result of their operations. Additionally, cleanup costs for "orphan sites" where specific companies could not be identified or held responsible would draw money from the Superfund, made of a series of corporate taxes, or "polluter-pays fees," and supported by government revenue. The legislation authorized the Environmental Protection Agency (EPA) to place heavily contaminated sites on the National Priorities List. If identified as a "Superfund site," a community qualified for enforced cleanup and funds. Since the inception of Superfund, the EPA has identified over 1,200 sites, including 20 ASARCO operations. One in four Americans lives within four miles of a Superfund site.

In 1995, under the watch of President Clinton and a Republican Congress, Superfund's polluter-pays fees expired, thus shifting most of the financial burden onto taxpayers. As of 2010, these fees have yet to be reinstated. By 2003, all corporate funds were exhausted and the Superfund now relies solely on taxpayer-funded government revenues. According to the U.S. Public Interest Research Group, in 1995 taxpayers paid only 18% ($300 million) of the Superfund, but by 2005, they contributed 100%—approximately $1.2 billion.

As a result of under-financing and lack of political will, the number of Superfund sites undergoing cleanup has diminished. While the EPA averaged 87 completed cleanups a year from 1997 to 2000, in 2008 only 30 sites were processed, representing a drop of over 50% in the pace of cleanups. Without polluter-pays fees and in light of the bankruptcy, the affected communities at ASARCO sites are left with few options to ensure comprehensive cleanup and reparations.

Penny Newman of the Center for Community Action & Environmental Justice calls the fund "impotent" without corporate contributions: "It's disingenuous to pretend a program exists without the funding." In spring 2009, the Obama administration directed $600 million in stimulus money to 50 Superfund sites—including the ASARCO site in Tacoma—that have shown significant progress in their cleanups. Obama and the EPA call this a "stopgap measure," setting the restoration of the polluter-pays tax as an important environmental health goal.

The Bankruptcy "Solution"

As environmental and community health concerns mounted, public pressure increased, and projected cleanup costs skyrocketed, ASARCO closed most of its operations. All of ASARCO's sites—operating, shuttered, or in remediation—were affected by the 2005 Chapter 11 bankruptcy filing. The company cited environmental liabilities as a primary explanation for the action.

The bankruptcy was not a last-minute act of desperation. On the contrary, the company had been rearranging itself for some time, shedding liabilities and cutting costs through sales and mergers. In 1999, ASARCO was "bought" by its major subsidiary, Grupo México, a Mexican-based company that is one of the largest metal producers in the world. This sale is significant because ASARCO's assets and records were shifted outside of the United States and therefore no longer under U.S. government jurisdiction; citizens requesting records and reme-diation from the company now had difficulty doing so. In 2002, ASARCO sold one of its most valuable mining complexes, Southern Peru Copper, to its new parent company, transferring even more valuable resources beyond national boundaries. Fearing a potential bankruptcy, the Department of Justice forced ASARCO to set up a $100 million trust to cover liabilities for impacted U.S. communities.

Chapter 11 of the U.S. Bankruptcy Code permits corporate reorganization and invokes "automatic stay," in which most litigation is put on hold until it can be resolved in court, with creditors ceasing collection attempts. This status allowed ASARCO to legally avoid paying for environmental damage at sites that required it for the duration of the bankruptcy. Additionally, pension payments and other monies owed to workers as negotiated by the United Steelworkers, which represents most employees, were threatened and delayed. As a result of the bankruptcy, the Steelworkers, a member of the bankruptcy creditors' committee, settled with a one-year extension of their collective bargaining agreement.

Complexities stemming from ASARCO's multinational status became more apparent during the 2005-2009 bankruptcy proceedings. During the case, Grupo México, by court ruling, was removed as the controlling agent of ASARCO. As such, Grupo México battled with another corporate suitor, India-based Sterilite/Vedanta Corporation, for control; Grupo México eventually prevailed. This competition pro-longed proceedings, as the judge assessed competing purchase offers and changing promises to affected communities and workers.

Through bankruptcy negotiations, ASARCO significantly reduced its debts to damaged communities. The *Tacoma News Tribune* reported that more than a dozen states and the federal government originally collectively filed $6 billion in environ-mental claims involving 20 ASARCO sites. Other estimates placed cleanup and liability costs as high as $25.2 billion. This figure was subsequently reduced to $3.6 billion in early bankruptcy court proceedings, which was later sliced to the final settlement of $1.79 billion.

In the days following the announcement of the settlement, government spokes-people and community members expressed a mix of relief and disappointment. According to U.S. Associate Attorney General Tom Perrelli, "The effort to recover this money was a collaborative and coordinated response by the states and federal government. Our combined efforts have resulted in the largest recovery of funds to pay for past and future cleanup of hazardous materials in the nation's history. Today is a historic day for the environment and the people affected across the country."

But activists and affected communities insist the ruling did not go far enough. In addition to paying less than originally projected, ASARCO's parent company, Grupo México, faces fewer responsibilities than it did before the bank-ruptcy. While the company had previously been pegged with penalty payments for the transfer of Southern Peru Copper, the bankruptcy decision, which rein-stated Grupo México control, nullified this.

The $1.79 billion settlement will also be unevenly split between affected com-munities. While Washington State celebrated the perseverance of their attorneys and coordinated work of departments, Texas, which had relatively little sustained support and attention by federal authorities, will not be as well served. The El Paso area has a modest $52 million to address complex and hazardous contamination.

ASARCO's Legacy and Communities' Call for Responsibility

Throughout the bankruptcy proceedings, U.S. Senator Maria Cantwell (D-WA) warned that ASARCO's use of bankruptcy will be imitated by other companies aiming to minimize their liability for environmental and health damages. The *Tacoma News Tribune* has reported that companies in eight of the ten regions under EPA jurisdiction have considered bankruptcy in order to elude responsibility. A 2007 study identified six companies connected to approximately 120 Superfund sites in 28 states filing for bankruptcy, with four of these companies successfully avoiding over half a billion dollars in cleanup costs. In 2009, eleven states involved in the ASARCO bankruptcy and the Justice Department reaffirmed the warning that more companies will follow suit.

Twice Cantwell has introduced bills to curtail companies' use of bankruptcies and other "legal" techniques to avoid responsibility; twice the bills have failed.

Texas State Senator Shapleigh has witnessed the city of El Paso's struggle with the high cost of environmental cleanup and jeopardized public health. Commenting on the bankruptcy and echoing Cantwell's concerns, he warns, "This is a strategy that will be used over and over again in the United States. The corporations will play out this environmental saga…this is the first one."

A Familiar Story

The story of ASARCO is a complicated one. It is a story of environmental degradation, of countless hidden occupational health hazards, of a corporation comfortably connected to federal and state administrations, and of a broken safety net that offers little compensation for communities impacted by a century of industrial operations.

Yet the story of ASARCO is not an unfamiliar one. The company's evasion of corporate responsibility in the face of weakened federal regulations demonstrates how companies can shift billions of dollars of environmental cleanup costs onto affected communities.

The special brew of corporate bankruptcies and an under-funded Superfund leaves us extremely vulnerable to industrial contamination. ASARCO's bankruptcy left thousands of exposed workers and family members, 21 states, two Indian tribal communities, and unions in limbo for years, and now with very limited reparation for life-altering health effects and degraded environments. Despite the company's responsibility for extensive environmental and health damage, the settlement holds them accountable for only a sliver of originally projected cleanup costs. A lack of political will from Congress to ensure corporate funding for Superfund and to pass legislation that tightens legal loopholes has left communities who believed they were protected by the 1980 CERCLA legislation strapped for cash and with few legal protections to enforce corporate responsibility.

Current and former ASARCO employees, affected communities, and allies are organizing to push for corporate accountability and government regulations. In El

Paso, as a result of the bankruptcy, the Superfund dysfunction, and the special burden of illegal hazardous waste incineration, community advocates are working to shape a strategy for activating workplace right-to-know for former employees at high risk for illness. They are further insisting on transparency in the cleanup and corporate accountability for public health.

In February 2010, a group of over two dozen organizations and individuals, including current and former ASARCO employees and several Mexican government officials, wrote to the EPA with concerns that the cleanup plan for the El Paso site is "inadequate to protect the health of the [El Paso] community and does not address offsite-pollution in [New Mexico], Mexico and Texas." The current plan only addresses hazards in El Paso, but according to Mariana Chew of the Sierra Club, "Cuidad Juárez in Mexico and Sunland Park in [New Mexico] are the communities most affected by ASARCO's legal and illegal operations and yet are not taken in account." Chew and others are especially concerned about the health of children at an elementary school in Cuidad Juárez that sits just 400 feet downwind from the smelter.

The group demands larger payments from ASARCO, specifically for its illegal incineration of hazardous waste. In the interim, the group claims that federal monies from the Superfund should be used.

The 2010 National Latino Congress has also condemned ASARCO's contamination of the border region and the company's bankruptcy. The Congress, supported by hundreds of organizations and over 40 elected U.S. officials, demanded full disclosure of the illegal incineration of hazardous waste, and comprehensive testing and treatment for workers and community members who may have been exposed.

Meanwhile, in Hayden, Ariz., site of the company's only operating U.S. smelter, ASARCO officials have reassured residents that blowing dust from mine tailings is not a hazard. According to ASARCO vice president Thomas Aldrich, "Across the board these are very low in metals, about what you'd expect here, comparable to the background levels in soil."

Such statements offer little comfort for communities still struggling for information, protection, and accountability. ❑

This article is based on the project "No Borders: Communities Living and Working with Asarco" based at Evergreen State College and guided by Fischel and Nelson. The project examines the occupational and environmental health and social justice implications of ASARCO's operations with a focus on three communities: Ruston/Tacoma, Wash., Hayden, Ariz., and El Paso, Texas. A documentary film, "Borders of Resistance," to be released in the summer of 2010, documents the El Paso story of community and labor advocates pressing for accountability and health protections. Other films and writing are forthcoming.

Sources: Office of Texas Senator Eliot Shapleigh, "Asarco in El Paso," September 2008; Les Blumenthal, "Asarco Mess Reveals Superfund Failings," *Tacoma News Tribune*, March 21, 2006; Les Blumenthal, "Lawyers Dissect Asarco's cleanup obligation in the US," *Tacoma News Tribune*, May 20, 2006; Les Blumenthal, "Grupo México wins Asarco back in court ruling," *Tacoma News Tribune*, September 3, 2009; Joel Millman, "Asarco Bankruptcy Leaves Many Towns with Cleanup Mess," *Wall Street Journal*, May 24, 2006; Office of U.S. Senator Maria Cantwell,

"Cantwell Introduces Legislation to Prevent Corporate Polluters from Evading Toxic Cleanup Responsibilities," June 15, 2006; Center for Health, Environment and Justice, "Superfund: In the Eye of the Storm," March 2009; Center for Health, Environment and Justice, "America's Safety Net in Crisis: 25th Anniversary of Superfund," 2005; The Smelterworker rank-and-file union newsletter, circa 1970-75, Tacoma Wash.; Marianne Sullivan, "Contested Science and Exposed Workers: ASARCO and the Occupational Standard for Inorganic Arsenic," Public Health Chronicles, July 2007; Ralph Blumenthal, "Copper Plant Illegally Burned Hazardous Waste, EPA Says," *New York Times*, October 11, 2006; Government Accountability Office, "Environmental Liabilities: EPA Should Do More to Ensure That Liable Parties Meet Their Cleanup Obligations," August 2005; Government Accountability Office, "Hazardous Waste: Information about How DOD and Federal and State Regulators Oversee the Off-site Disposal of Waste from DOD Installations," November 2007; Department of Justice, "Largest Environmental Bankruptcy in US History Will Result in Payment of $1.79 Billion Towards Environmental Cleanup and Restoration," December 10, 2009; Seattle and King County Department of Public Health, Arsenic Facts, 2010; The Center for Health, Environment & Justice, "Letter to the Environmental Protection Agency," February 16 2010; The Center for Health, Environment & Justice, "News Release," February 16 2010; The 2010 National Latino Congress, "Draft Amended ASARCO Resolution," 2010; Interview, Dr. Philip Landrigan, Mt Sinai Medical School, August 27 2009; Interview, Daniel Solis, El Paso, Tex, August 2007.

Article 2.5

BETWEEN THE DEVIL AND THE DEEP BLUE SEA
Workers in the Global Environment

BY ALAN DURNING
June 1991, updated May 2009

> "Our enormously productive economy ... demands that we make consumption our way of life, that we convert the buying and use of goods into rituals, that we seek our spiritual satisfaction, our ego satisfaction, in consumption... We need things consumed, burned up, worn out, replaced, and discarded at an ever increasing rate."
>
> —*Victor Lebow, U.S. retailing analyst, 1955*

In 1988, I was recalled to work at General Electric Appliance Park in Louisville, Kentucky, after a four-year layoff. This was not the first long layoff and, as always, getting called back unleashed a complex emotional response. I felt a great rush of relief to be delivered from a series of miserable, low-paying jobs and mounting piles of overdue bills. But I was humiliated that, once again, I hadn't found that perfect job, once again I jumped when GE snapped its fingers.

I was assigned to Building 4, "Refrigeration Components." As jobs went at Appliance Park, this was a good place to work. Building 4 was in the middle of a long and messy restructuring process—moving some work to a nonunion plant and automating production lines while still recovering from a major design screw-up. Workers were transferring to other buildings right and left. As an incentive for workers to stick out the transition, GE raised pay in Building 4. The new systems replaced a lot of people with robots, but it was easier work than the traditional assembly line. And, we got all the overtime we could handle. Despite mixed emotions, I settled in to recover from years of personal fiscal austerity.

But there was a new complication in the emotional mix—environmental disaster on a global scale. Building 4 works on the parts that enable refrigerators to refrigerate, components that circulate the chemicals that withdraw heat from inside the unit and disperse it outside. The refrigerant used at the time was Freon, one of the most prominent chlorofluorocarbons (CFCs)—the class of chemicals responsible for depleting the ozone layer that shields the earth from harmful ultraviolet radiation. When I went to work in Building 4, the Montreal Protocol on Ozone Depletionwas in the final stages of negotiation. No thanks to GE, I was aware of the Montreal Protocol and its implications both for the environment and the appliance industry. From the company I saw only brief mention in the building newsletter of the "challenges" of meeting conflicting government regulations to reduce energy usage and end CFC use. (Substitutes for Freon under consideration were, according to the industry, less efficient and would need more electricity to work effectively.) Later, in an interview with the plant-wide newspaper, a GE executive claimed he had sleepless nights over ozone depletion.

The company was not so passive in its outward stance. The appliance industry lobbied fiercely against the Montreal Protocol. GE's internal indifference and external opposition to the resolution of a major environmental crisis was typical for a company that tops the list of Superfund sites. Ozone depletion was a nonissue among plant workers. Among the workforce, jobs were the only concern. Appliance Park has lost thousands of jobs since I first worked there in 1974 and continues to do so. Building 4 itself has been half empty since GE moved compressor production to a nonunion plant in 1984. I cannot recall any comments from the union about ozone depletion. Once the agreement was passed and the Clean Air Act amendments of 1990 scheduled the phase out of CFCs, GE redesigned its evaporators to comply with new requirements. The company played on the workers' anxiety for all it was worth. Management put the cost of getting evaporators from another source on the table and demanded that the union meet or beat that price in order to keep evaporator production at Appliance Park.

The union won that round, but now, 10 years later, all refrigerator production at Appliance Park is at risk. New energy requirements will become effective in the next few years and GE will have to redesign and retool for a more energy-efficient refrigerator. The union proposed a plan that would cut $30 million from production costs. They are still waiting for a response from the company.

After my experience at Appliance Park (I got laid off in 1991 and never returned), I was not surprised when Pacific Northwest loggers fought against measures to protect old-growth forests or when the AFL-CIO opposed the Kyoto Treaty on global warming. These positions are disappointing, but the issue of jobs versus the environment is not simple to sort out. Recent studies indicate small net job gains from environmental regulation and regulations can open opportunities for jobs in new, environmentally friendly industries. For workers, however, the critical question is not what is the net economic effect of "regulation," but rather, what will happen to my job? This question speaks to a profound anxiety about the loss of livelihood and loss of control—an anxiety that is well grounded in the realities of today's global economy.

The dangers of corporate environmental recklessness are also grounded in reality. More and more labor groups recognize this reality and are attempting to define an agenda that both protects the environment and ensures that workers do not pay a disproportionate part of the costs of transition to an environmentally sound economy. The Work and Environment Initiative (WEI) at Cornell University investigated union efforts on environmental issues. Their report, "Labor and Climate Change and the Environment," published shortly before the December 1997 Kyoto conference on climate change, found that while the labor movement is concerned with protecting its members' jobs, many unions are also deeply concerned about the environment and struggle to reconcile both issues. Workers are, after all, human beings who have to survive on this planet.

Among those most aware of environmental issues are unions involved in environmentally "dirty" industries such as the United Auto Workers. In a particularly forward-thinking resolution, adopted in 1991, the United Steelworkers of America (USWA) called the destruction of the environment potentially the greatest threat to our children and the destruction of the Earth's resource base a serious threat to the economy. Putting this philosophy into practice, in April the Steelworkers filed suit against the California Department of Forestry and Fire Protection challenging the sustained yield plan of the Headwaters Forest agreement with Pacific Lumber. In the press release, USWA spokesperson Jon Youngdahl stated that the plan "authorizes unsustainably high harvests of old growth timber and fails to consider the long-range economic impacts of these unsustainably high harvests."

According to Youngdahl, steelworkers began reaching out to environmentalists in Humboldt County, California, when they realized that the same corporation (Maxxam Corporation) owned both Pacific Lumber and Kaiser Aluminum. Steelworkers have been engaged in a protracted struggle against Kaiser, while environmentalists have long challenged Pacific Lumber's destructive forestry practices. Youngdahl also pointed out that, while the desire to build mutual support against a common enemy forged the initial connection between USWA members and environmentalists, the Headwaters lawsuit goes beyond specific labor disputes to put into action the Steelworkers' long term commitment to sustainability.

Testifying before a hearing on the Sustained Yield Plan, steelworker Don Kegley of Local 338 in Spokane, Washington made a link between the deterioration of Kaiser's record of environmental responsibility since it became part of Maxxam and thedanger that another Maxxam company would squander the resources of the Headwaters Forest. Kegley also articulated the link between preserving forest resources for the long term and preserving jobs: "Without the forest, our culture will crumble and worse, our planet will die. And there are no jobs on a dead planet." In May, the USWA and environmental allies took their fight to the Maxxam board meeting. The Oil, Chemical and Atomic Workers (OCAW), now merged into the Paperworkers, Allied Industrial, Chemical and Energy Workers Union (PACE), has been one of the most environmentally active unions. OCAW was the union involved in the Karen Silkwood case (made famous in the movie Silkwood), and has long fought for health and safety on the job. Because they deal with dangerous and environmentally hazardous substances in their workplaces, this union's leaders and members have a heightened consciousness of the ecological impact of their jobs. They have also suffered heavily from deindustrialization in the last few decades and are well aware that workers often bear the brunt of change. Several years ago OCAW proposed a Superfund for workers that would be used to ease workers' transition to more environmentally friendly industries. The Superfund idea has evolved into a campaign for a "Just Transition," and under that banner has begun to reverberate throughout the labor and environmental movements.

Les Leopold of the Labor Institute in New York City, a consultant to OCAW—and now PACE—on environmental issues and himself a PACE member, views "Just Transitions" as a far-reaching program along the lines of the G.I. Bill following World War II. To his mind, it can provide a model for managing workplace change resulting from environmental mandates or the next generation of technology. The key is to provide security and options for workers to move to a new stage of life and work. Older workers may choose to retire early and should be able to do so without loss of income. Other workers may accept subsidized pay to move to lower paying jobs. Still others will return to school to gain up-to-date skills and embark on new careers. The concept of a "Just Transition" is not confined to the workplace—it embraces communities which suffer both from environmental hazards and economic loss when plants close. One of PACE's most promising programs, from

Leopold's point of view, is building connections between the union and environmental justice movement. Minority communities are particularly harmed by being close to polluting factories yet are generally denied the benefits of the high-wage jobs in these industries. PACE is bringing its members together with representatives of the Ponco tribe in Oklahoma, neighbors of oil refineries in southern California, and residents of other endangered communities to develop appreciation of each other's fears and frustrations.

The recent merger that formed PACE is a pivotal event, and is being closely watched by those who care about the emerging Blue Collar-Green Alliance. Themerger directly confronts the Paperworkers'—which are traditionally defensive about environmental protection—with the proactive, "do the right thing," stance of OCAW. According the Leopold and also PACE Communication Director, Lynn Baker, the merged union will continue the "Just Transition" programs initiated by OCAW. The AFL-CIO itself has taken up the struggle for a "Just Transition" and is actively seeking relationships with environmentalists. Soon after taking office, AFL-CIO President John Sweeney appointed Jane Perkins as Environmental Liaison. Perkins has one foot in both labor and environmental worlds. She has been an officer in Service Employees International Union (SEIU) locals, an activist around the Three Mile Island nuclear power plant disaster, and was executive director of the environmental organization Friends of the Earth.

Climate Change now tops Perkins' agenda. The United Mine Workers (UMW), a stronghold of the new AFL-CIO leadership, put climate change on the AFL-CIO's table with resolutions, statements and rallies protesting the Kyoto agreement. UMW members feel especially threatened by initiatives to reduce coal in power generation. Rather than lock horns with environmentalists over specifics of the Kyoto agreement, Perkins set out to find topics both labor and green groups could discuss productively. Three topics emerged: exploring green technologies on a sector by sector basis; "Just Transitions"; and developing countries. In April of this year, at a two day meeting at the AFL-CIO conference center, Carl Pope, head of the Sierra Club, and Bob Wages, now a PACE official who was a long-time proponent within OCAW of environmental initiatives, were chosen to take the lead in developing a joint strategy on climate change.

The AFL-CIO fears, not without reason, that less stringent caps on carbon emissions in developing countries (at least until the next round of talks), will give them cheaper production costs and, therefore, an advantage in global markets. Although many corporations indeed shift production to low-wage countries in search of lower costs, Ed Cohen-Rosenthal of Cornell's WEI believes that energy costs in the United States will remain comparatively low even when complying with Kyoto requirements. Developing countries have legitimate grievances with the developed countries which emit the overwhelming majority of greenhouse gases. The standard of living in wealthy countries reflects generations of industrialization, relatively free of environmental restrictions. In the report issued by WEI, Boyd Young of the (then) United Paperworkers International Union argues that it is wrong to regulate only one part of the world. He notes that applying climate change controls to developing countries will provide incentives for them to develop clean energy technologies and reduce the need to retool at a later date. However, the same report summarizes findings of the European Union (EU) Environmental Council which point out that the costs of implementing clean technology are prohibitive for developing countries. The EU Council calls for the developed world to conduct the necessary research and development and to fund vehicles for financing technology transfer to poorer countries. The AFL-CIO's Perkins hopes to involve labor and environmental activists from many countries in putting together a strategy for reducing carbon emissions while protecting workers at the same time.

The International Confederation of Free Trade Unions (ICFTU) and the Trade Union Advisory Committee to the OECD (TUAC) issued a joint statement to the November 1998 Buenos Aires conference on climate change. The ICFTU and TUAC are sympathetic to the dilemmas faced by both developed and developing country workers. Their statement calls for immediate participation on the part of developing countries in reducing carbon emissions, but also states that: "Industrial countries should provide substantial financial and technical assistance as a means of enabling developing countries to adopt binding targets within the context of differentiated goals and long-term implementation strategy." The ICFTU and TUAC claim that the failure to confront employment issues is a major weakness of the Kyoto climate change treaty. But dislocation of workers in energy-intensive sectors of the industrialized world is not the only problem they cite. Workers will also suffer from the failure to check global warming since 70% of the world's population lives and works within 60 kilometers of seacoasts. With global warming on the rise, and ocean levels with it, the potential exists for 60 million environmental refuges by 2030.

Labor organizations point out that workers' knowledge can help create environmental solutions; they know production technology and are in a good position to suggest changes that reduce energy waste and introduce cleaner production options.

Many unions, particularly in Europe where there is a tradition of worker participation in decisions affecting workplace conditions, have conducted eco-audits. In these programs, workers evaluate the environmental impact of the materials and techniques they use and recommend ways to reduce waste and institute cleaner processes. The Swedish Confederation of Professional Employees developed a program called The Way to 6E—A Practical Model for Sustainable Workplaces, a blueprint for involving all workers in developing workplace improvements in ergonomics, economy, ecology, emissions, efficiency, and energy.

WEI research confirms the value of workers participation in workplace decisions. In a recent study of toxics, they found that businesses with employee participation programs release fewer toxic substances into the environment than businesses without such programs.

Other programs try to involve communities to reduce pollution that harms both workers and neighborhood residents near industrial sites. The Silicon Valley Toxics Coalition, based in the high tech industry's stronghold, has been a major force in focusing public attention on environmentally unsound practices of the electronics industry.

A recent story in Sierra, the 500,000 circulation magazine of the Sierra Club, described the emerging connections between labor and environmentalists as the "coalition that gives corporate polluters fits." The article points out that OCAW, a strong advocate of environmental safety on and off the job, always connected threats to the environment and to workers to the same culprit: corporations. Its "Just Transitions" project is exactly the kind of program that can cut the Gordian knot entangling the issues of jobs and the environment. It demands that the economic burdens of greening industry be shared fairly among all economic actors and has the potential to build a powerful new Blue-Green Alliance to fight for the agenda. ❑

Article 2.6

WE NEED A (GREEN) JOBS PROGRAM

Clean-energy investment would promote job growth for a wide swath of the U.S. workforce.

BY JEANNETTE WICKS-LIM
September/October 2010

Fourteen months of an unemployment rate at or near 10% clearly calls for the federal government to take a lead role in job creation. The White House should push its clean-energy agenda as a jobs program but steer clear of all the hype about "green-collar" jobs. Green-collar jobs are widely perceived as job opportunities accessible only to an elite segment of the U.S. workforce—those with advanced degrees, such as environmental engineers, lab technicians, and research scientists. Such jobs are inaccessible to the 52% of unemployed workers with no college experience. The truth is, however, that clean-energy investments could serve as a powerful engine for job growth for a wide swath of the U.S. workforce.

My colleagues at the Political Economy Research Institute and I examined a clean-energy program that includes making buildings more energy efficient, expanding and improving mass transit, updating the national electric grid, and developing each of three types of renewable energy sources: wind, solar, and biomass fuels. Here's what we found.

First, clean-energy activities produce more jobs, dollar for dollar, than fossil fuel-related activities. This is because clean-energy activities tend to be more labor intensive (i.e., more investment dollars go to hiring workers than buying machines), have a higher domestic content (i.e., more dollars are spent on goods and services produced within the United States) and have lower average wages than fossil fuel-related activities. The figures in the table below show how a $1 million investment in clean-energy activities would create more than three times the number of jobs that would be created by investing the same amount in fossil fuels.

Second, many clean energy sector jobs would be accessible to workers with no college experience. The table also shows how the jobs created by a $1 million investment in clean energy would be spread across three levels of education: high school degree or less, some college, and B.A. or more. Nearly half of the clean energy jobs would be held by workers with a high school degree or less. These

JOB CREATION: CLEAN ENERGY VS. FOSSIL FUELS

Number of jobs created by investing $1 million dollars in clean energy versus fossil-fuels activities, by education credentials

Education Credentials	Clean Energy	Fossil Fuels
Total	16.7 jobs (100%)	5.3 jobs (100%)
High school diploma or less	8.0 jobs (47.9%)	2.2 jobs (41.5%)
Some college, no B.A.	4.8 jobs (28.7%)	1.6 jobs (30.2%)
B.A. or more	3.9 jobs (23.3%)	1.5 jobs (28.3%)

include jobs for construction laborers, carpenters, and bus drivers. Fewer than one-quarter of clean-energy jobs would require a B.A. or more. The figures for the fossil fuels sector (second column) show that they are more heavily weighted toward jobs requiring college degrees.

Does this mean green investments will just create lots of low-paying jobs? No. The figures in the table below show that investing $1 million in green activities rather than fossil fuel-related activities would generate many more jobs for workers at *all three levels* of formal education credentials. Compared to the fossil fuels sector, the clean energy sector would produce nearly four times the number of jobs that require a high school degree or less, three times the number of jobs that require some college experience, and 2.5 times the number of jobs that require a B.A. or more. Green investments would produce more jobs at all education and wage levels, even while generating proportionately *more* jobs that are accessible to workers with a high school degree or less.

Workers are right to worry about whether these high school degree jobs would offer family-supporting wages. Construction laborers, for example, average at $29,000 annually—awfully close to the $22,000 official poverty line. In addition, women and workers of color have historically faced discrimination in the construction industry, which would be the source of a lot of the lower-credentialed jobs in the clean energy sector. Workers will need to do some serious organizing to put in place labor protections such as living-wage laws, strong collective bargaining rights, and affirmative action policies to insure that these jobs pay decent wages and are equally accessible to all qualified workers. ❑

Sources: Robert Pollin, Jeannette Wicks-Lim, and Heidi Garrett-Peltier, *Green Prosperity: How Clean-Energy Policies Can Fight Poverty and Raise Living Standards in the United States*, Political Economy Research Institute, 2009, www.peri.umass.edu/green_prosperity.

Article 2.7

SAVING ENERGY CREATES JOBS

BY HEIDI GARRETT-PELTIER
May/June 2009

Improving energy efficiency—using less energy to do the same amount of work—saves money and cuts pollution. But today, the other benefit of investing in energy efficiency may be the best draw: saving energy creates jobs.

Let's look at energy use in residential and commercial buildings. In the United States, buildings account for 40% of all energy use and are responsible for 38% of U.S. carbon emissions. Homes and other buildings lose energy through wasted heat, air-conditioning, and electricity. Following Jimmy Carter's suddenly fashionable example, we can turn down the thermostat in the winter and put on a sweater. We can unplug appliances that aren't used and save "phantom" power.

Beyond these personal changes, though, lie massive opportunities for systematic energy efficiency gains. These include insulating buildings, replacing old windows, and updating appliances and lighting. All of these generate new economic opportunities—read, jobs—in construction, manufacturing, and other sectors.

For instance, retrofitting existing homes, offices, and schools to reduce heating- and cooling-related energy waste (also known as weatherization) creates jobs of many kinds. Recent media attention has spotlighted "green jobs" programs that are hiring construction workers to add insulation, replace windows, and install more efficient heating systems. Perhaps less visible, retrofitting buildings also creates jobs for the engineers who design the new windows and furnaces, the factory workers who build them, and the office workers who make the appointments and handle the bookkeeping.

In fact, retrofitting creates more than twice as many jobs per dollar spent than oil or coal production, according to a detailed study that my colleagues and I at the Political Economy Research Institute conducted in 2008. For each $1 million spent, retrofitting creates about 19 jobs while spending on coal creates nine jobs and oil only six. Retrofitting also creates more jobs per dollar spent than personal consumption on typical items such as food, clothing, and electronics. Personal consumption does better than fossil fuels, but not as well as retrofitting, generating about 15 jobs per $1 million spent.

Why does retrofitting create more jobs? First, retrofitting is more labor-intensive than fossil-fuel production, meaning that more of each dollar spent goes to labor and less to machinery and equipment. Retrofitting also has higher domestic content than either fossil fuels or consumer goods; in other words, more of the supplies used to retrofit buildings are produced in the United States. In fact, about 95% of spending on retrofits stays in the domestic economy, versus only 80% of spending on oil (including refining and other related activities). Since more of its inputs are produced in the United States, retrofitting employs more U.S. workers. And this raises its multiplier effect: when those workers spend their earnings, each retrofitting dollar leads to yet more demand for goods and services.

To be fair, not all energy efficiency improvements will create jobs. When a more energy-efficient appliance or window design is widely adopted, the manufacturing worker who produced a less efficient good yesterday is simply producing a more efficient good today, with no net increase in employment. On the other hand, many retrofitting activities are pure job creators. Insulating attics and caulking leaky windows are activities that necessitate new workers—not just a shift from producing one good to another. With the collapse of the housing bubble and the huge rise in construction industry unemployment, retrofitting is an activity that could put tens of thousands of people back to work.

The Obama administration's stimulus package contains a wide variety of energy efficiency incentives, from 30% rebates for home insulation and for installing efficient windows, to rebates for builders of energy-efficient new homes and commercial buildings. These provisions will drive energy-saving improvements, accelerating the transition to a low-carbon economy while also creating jobs. ❑

Sources: U.S. Department of Energy, EERE Building Technologies Program; Robert Pollin, Heidi Garrett-Peltier, James Heintz, and Helen Scharber, "Green Recovery," Political Economy Research Institute, September 2008.

Article 2.8

THE PHANTOM MENACE

Environmental regulations are not "job-killers" after all.

BY HEIDI GARRETT-PELTIER

July/August 2011

Polluting industries, along with the legislators who are in their pockets, consistently claim that environmental regulation will be a "job killer." They counter efforts to control pollution and to protect the environment by claiming that any such measures would increase costs and destroy jobs. But these are empty threats. In fact, the bulk of the evidence shows that environmental regulations do not hinder economic growth or employment and may actually stimulate both.

One recent example of this, the Northeast Regional Greenhouse Gas Initiative (RGGI), is an emissions-allowance program that caps and reduces emissions in ten northeast and mid-Atlantic states. Under RGGI, allowances are auctioned to power companies and the majority of the revenues are used to offset increases in consumer energy bills and to invest in energy efficiency and renewable energy. A report released in February of this year shows that RGGI has created an economic return of $3 to $4 for every $1 invested, and has created jobs throughout the region. Yet this successful program has come under attack by right-wing ideologues, including the Koch brothers-funded "Americans for Prosperity"; as a result, the state of New Hampshire recently pulled out of the program.

The allegation that environmental regulation is a job-killer is based on a mischaracterization of costs, both by firms and by economists. Firms often frame spending on environmental controls or energy-efficient machinery as a pure cost—wasted spending that reduces profitability. But such expenses should instead be seen as investments that enhance productivity and in turn promote economic development. Not only can these investments lead to lower costs for energy use and waste disposal, they may also direct innovations in the production process itself that could increase the firm's long-run profits. This is the Porter Hypothesis, named after Harvard Business School professor Michael Porter. According to studies conducted by Porter, properly and flexibly designed environmental regulation can trigger innovation that partly or completely offsets the costs of complying with the regulation.

The positive aspects of environmental regulation are overlooked not only by firms, but also by economists who model the costs of compliance without including its widespread benefits. These include reduced mortality, fewer sick days for workers and school children, reduced health-care costs, increased biodiversity, and mitigation of climate change. But most mainstream models leave these benefits out of their calculations. The Environmental Protection Agency, which recently released a study of the impacts of the Clean Air Act from 1990 to 2020, compared the effects of a "cost-only" model with those of a more complete model. In the version which only incorporated the costs of compliance, both GDP and overall economic welfare were expected to decline by 2020 due to Clean Air Act regulations. However, once the costs of compliance were coupled with the benefits, the model showed that both GDP and economic welfare would increase over time, and that by 2020 the economic benefits would outweigh the costs. Likewise, the Office of Management and Budget found that to date the benefits of the law have far exceeded the cost, with an economic return of between $4 and $8 for every $1 invested in compliance.

Environmental regulations do affect jobs. But contrary to claims by polluting industries and congressional Republicans, efforts to protect our environment can actually create jobs. In order to reduce harmful pollution from power plants, for example, an electric company would have to equip plants with scrubbers and other technologies. These technologies would need to be manufactured and installed, creating jobs for people in the manufacturing and construction industries.

The official unemployment rate in the United States is still quite high, hovering around 9%. In this economic climate, politicians are more sensitive than ever to claims that environmental regulation could be a job-killer. By framing investments as wasted costs and relying on incomplete economic models, polluting industries have consistently tried to fight environmental standards. It's time to change the terms of the debate. We need to move beyond fear-mongering about the costs and start capturing the benefits. ❑

PART 3

HOW CAN WE DO BETTER?

Article 3.1

CLIMATE REALITY ELUDES THE BUSINESS PRESS

BY JOHN MILLER
July/August 2008

> Cap and Spend. As the Senate opens debate on its mammoth carbon regulation program this week, the phrase of the hour is "cap and trade." This sounds innocuous enough. But anyone who looks at the legislative details will quickly see that a better description is cap and spend. This is easily the largest income redistribution scheme since the income tax.
> —*Wall Street Journal editorial, June 2, 2008*

> Climate Reality Bites. Cap and trade is a tax imposed on business, disguising the true costs and thus making it more politically palatable. In reality, firms will merely pass on these costs to customers.

> ... politicians like cap and trade ... because it gives them a cut of the action and the ability to pick winners and losers. Some of the allowances would be given away, at least at the start, while the rest would be auctioned off, with the share of auctions increasing over time. This is a giant revenue grab.

> The Environmental Protection Agency estimates that this meddling would cause a cumulative reduction in the growth of GDP by between 0.9% and 3.8% by 2030.
> — *Wall Street Journal editorial, May 27, 2008*

The *Wall Street Journal*'s editors are celebrating having dodged a big-government bullet when the cap-and-trade global warming bill sponsored by Joe Lieberman and John Warner, as amended by Barbara Boxer, went down to defeat this June in the Senate.

But the Lieberman-Warner Climate Security Act of 2008 was a fairly low caliber munition in the fight against global warming. While undoubtedly the most comprehensive global warming bill ever to reach the Senate floor, its emission reductions fell well short of those called for by environmental groups or by the Clinton and Obama campaigns.

Inside Cap-and-Trade

"Cap-and-trade," introduced in the 1990 Clean Air Act to regulate sulfur dioxide (SO_2) emissions or acid rain, is now the favorite form of environmental regulation for politicians and big business. They find it far preferable to either command-and-control regulation, such as federal directives ordering electrical power plants to install smokestack scrubbers, or emissions taxes, such as a broad-based carbon tax.

Cap-and-trade, referred to variously as incentive-based regulation or market-based regulation, works this way. The federal government sets a mandatory, nationwide cap on carbon dioxide (CO_2) emissions that it gradually reduces. At the same time the government requires companies, or any emitter, to hold allowances for their emissions. Typically each allowance entitles a company to emit one ton of CO_2.

After the government either auctions off allowances or issues them to companies based on their energy output or usage, holders are free to buy and sell them. Companies that can reduce emissions cheaply, usually those with newer plants, will likely cut their emissions below the standard for their industry and sell their unused allowances (or, if allowances are auctioned rather than issued for free, buy fewer of them), reducing their abatement costs. Companies with relatively high abatement costs, usually those with older plants, can be expected to buy additional permits (either from other companies or the government) at a price well below their cost of abatement so that they can reduce emissions by less than the industry standard. The flexibility, or "non-uniform abatement," afforded by permit trading allows the least costly abatements to be carried out first, lowering the overall cost of meeting any given environmental target.

The Climate Security Act would have required the Environmental Protection Agency (EPA) to establish a cap-and-trade program to cover U.S. electrical power, transportation, manufacturing, and natural gas sources that together account for 87% of U.S greenhouse-gas emissions. Beginning in 2012, the EPA would steadily reduce the cap on total emissions, down to 71% below their 2005 level by 2050.

Over the life of the program the EPA would auction off the majority of allowances, but initially about 40% would be given away, ostensibly to help industries make the transition to lower emissions. Revenue from the auctions, estimated at $5.6 trillion over the life of the bill, would be used to finance some relief for the poor to offset increases in utility bills, training and assistance for workers, deficit reduction, research on clean-energy technologies, and an array of subsidies for electric and gas utilities, the coal industry, auto manufacturers, oil refiners, and the nuclear industry.

Big but Not Big Enough

That is the giant revenue grab the *Journal*'s editors protest. Still, it's over the top to compare $5.6 trillion over four decades—that's $147 billion a year, or less than 6% of current federal government revenue—to the income tax, which increased government revenue nearly eightfold when it became a broad-based tax during World War II. And today, the $869.6 billion collected in payroll taxes in 2007 and redistributed through the Social Security system dwarfs the revenues that would be collected by this cap-and-trade proposal.

Alas, as big as the editors say it is, the Lieberman-Warner plan would not have brought about the 80% emissions reduction (below 1990 levels) the Nobel Prize-winning Intergovernmental Panel on Climate Change (IPCC) says is necessary by 2050 to avoid the worst effects of climate change.

Next year's new president will be more favorably disposed to regulating greenhouse gases than the Bush administration, which threatened to veto the

Lieberman-Warner bill. Barack Obama favors a cap-and-trade system that would reduce carbon emissions to "80% below 1990 levels by 2050" and would "require all pollution credits to be auctioned."

John McCain supports what could best be described as "cap-and-trade lite." His plan would set limits on greenhouse gases at 66% below 2005 levels, not so different from the Lieberman-Warner proposal, but well short of the level recommended by the IPCC. It would issue permits to polluters for free, at least initially, then convene a commission to determine what share of future allowances would be provided for free versus auctioned.

McCain opposed the Climate Security Act because in his view it did not offer enough aid to the nuclear industry. While the support for nukes in the Lieberman-Warner bill was not explicit, it was quite generous. Karl Grossman, host of the nationally syndicated TV program "Enviro Close-Up," estimates that $544 billion in subsidies for the development of new nuclear power plants were buried in the bill. The bill would have effectively doubled government subsidies for the nuclear industry, already the single most subsidized industry in the energy sector—but that was not enough for McCain.

Auction or Issue?

Besides this alleged revenue grab, what has got the *Wall Street Journal* editors in a lather is that the Senate bill would have auctioned off the majority of its permits instead of giving them away free.

For environmental groups such as Friends of the Earth, the "polluter pays" principle demands that 100% of pollution permits be auctioned. The amended Lieberman-Warner plan fell well short of that standard. The 40% of permits it would have given away in the initial phase went well beyond the 15% level the Congressional Budget Office estimates affected companies would need to compensate their shareholders for any decline in the value of their stock caused by a drop in demand for energy and energy-intensive products following regulation. In fact, the CBO worries that the bill's permit giveaways could end up as "windfall profits" for oil, gas, coal, and other polluting industries.

Even mainstream, conservative economists disagree with the editors. Greg Mankiw, former chair of Bush's Council of Economic Advisers, headed the list of hundreds of economists who signed the Southern Alliance for Clean Energy (SACE) Economist Statement urging that permits be auctioned off, not given away.

As the SACE statement made clear, whether permits are issued or auctioned will not affect energy prices or deter corporations from passing on the cost of abatement to consumers through higher prices. In either case, market forces of supply and demand will determine those price changes for any particular product. Giving away permits to polluters will not protect families and businesses from higher energy prices.

Indeed, higher energy prices carry a benefit: they prompt energy conservation. That is already evident this summer in the United States, where rising gas prices have driven spending on energy as a share of wage income above 6%—higher than during the 1974-75 and 1990-91 oil price shocks. Cars now outsell SUVs by the largest margin since 1996, GM is preparing to sell off its Hummer brand, mass transit ridership has increased, and bicycle sales are up.

For an economist, auctions are superior to allocations not because they prevent higher prices but because they ensure the government has the resources necessary to offset those higher costs. How the government spends the auction revenue determines who bears the burden of the cost of cutting CO_2 emissions.

Energy price increases are regressive, hitting low-income consumers hardest. The CBO estimates that a 15% reduction in greenhouse gas emissions, the goal of the Lieberman-Warner bill for 2020, would cost the poorest fifth of families 3.3% of their after-tax income, but only about half that (1.7%) for the richest fifth of families.

But using only about 14% of the total value of the permits, lawmakers could fund a rebate program that would erase the bill's impact on the poorest 20% of households and provide significant relief to those in the next poorest fifth, according to a recent study by the Center on Budget and Policy Priorities (CBPP). Unfortunately, the Lieberman-Warner bill would have allotted low-income consumers only about half of what the CBPP recommends, and it would have delivered those benefits via a hodgepodge of mechanisms as opposed to the straightforward climate tax credit the center proposed.

Other proposals would devote most or all of the revenue from allowance auctions to compensating consumers for the higher energy costs they would face following new CO_2 regulations. For instance, the "sky trust" plan is modeled after the Alaska Permanent Fund, which pays out an annual share of oil earnings to each resident of the state. A sky trust would use the revenue from auctioning off CO_2 permits to issue an annual dividend check to every U.S. resident.

How much compensation would such a plan provide? The MIT Emissions Prediction and Policy Analysis model estimates that a cap-and-trade program that cuts carbon emissions to 50% below 1990s levels by 2050, somewhat less stringent than the amended Lieberman-Warner bill, would generate $392 billion in auction revenues in 2020. That sum would finance dividend checks of $963 per person— enough to compensate all but the most well-to-do households for the higher energy costs they would face if the Lieberman-Warner emissions goal for 2020 were met, according to the CBO.

But these results are predicated on auctioning off 100% of initial allowances and on a political willingness to devote the revenues generated by cap-and-trade regulation to promoting economic justice.

Strangely enough, both of these policies should be popular with the *Wall Street Journal* set. Auctioning all permits would eliminate corporations' incentive to lobby for favorable treatment (i.e., the free permits). In addition, distributing every dollar of auction revenue to the public in the form of dividends would drain Washington's coffers of the money that the federal government might otherwise use to finance the kind of industrial policy adventure that so concerns the *Journal* editors.

How Fast Will We Grow?

Lawmakers could also devote allowance revenues from a cap-and-trade program to reducing the cost to corporations of meeting the new emissions targets, in an effort to sustain economic growth.

Would the Lieberman-Warner plan, or even a more aggressive cap-and-trade policy, slow economic growth? How much? The answer is not altogether clear and depends heavily on the responsiveness of innovation to higher carbon or energy prices.

The EPA estimates suggesting that cap-and-trade will cause a cumulative reduction in GDP growth of between 0.9% and 3.8% by 2030 reported by the editors are quite alarming. But those estimates need to be examined critically and put into context. First, the Congressional Research Service (CRS) described the upper range of the EPA's estimates as an outlier, quite different from the estimates produced by the seven other models the CRS examined. Among the other models, 2.7% was the largest projected decline in GDP, and five of the seven models projected a loss of 1% of GDP or less.

On top of that, the models' predictions of U.S. GDP in the year 2030 under business as usual (i.e., without cap-and-trade) vary far more than their projections of the economic impact of a carbon cap. When Nathaniel Keohane and Peter Goldmark of the Environmental Defense Fund examined these same studies, they found that each of them projects average U.S. economic growth of 2.5% to 3% a year over this period, and each predicts the U.S. economy will be more than twice as large in 2030 as it was in 2005 even after taking into account whatever dampening effect cap-and-trade has on economic growth.

As they put it, these economic models predict that U.S. GDP will reach $26 trillion around January of 2030 under business as usual. With a carbon cap, it will get there by April.

While not cost free, cap-and-trade regulation is "surprisingly affordable" according to Keohane and Goldmark. Plus, the size of U.S. GDP two or four decades from now will depend more on other macroeconomic conditions than on the cost of curbing carbon emissions.

A Green Industrial Policy

Along with a partial cap-and-dividend program or a rebate for low-income consumers, there is a case to be made for spending much of the revenue from auctioning permits on an environmental industrial policy to dramatically reduce our dependence on fossil fuels. Pioneering environmental scientist and activist Barry Commoner insists that public policy needs "to confront the corporate domain at its most powerful and guarded point—the exclusive right to govern the systems of production" if it is to transform the environment and the economy.

"If managed properly, ending dependence on fossil fuels and building a clean energy economy could generate millions of good jobs," argues economist Robert Pollin, co-director of the Political Economy Research Institute. Pollin estimates that investments in conservation and renewable energy to match a 25% cut in spending on fossil fuels over a 20-year period would produce a net increase of about 2.5 million jobs.

Sadly, that is not what the Climate Security Act of 2008 was about. It devoted more monies to fossil fuel and coal than to promoting renewable energy, clean technology, and mass transit.

But fixing the climate, as Commoner has always said, will not happen with half-measures that reward corporate America. ❏

Sources: "McCain's Climate Market," *Wall Street Journal*, 5/13/08; Robert Pollin, "Green Investments and the Path to Prosperity," New Labor Forum, Fall 2008; N. Keohane and P. Goldmark, "What Will It Cost To Protect Ourselves from Global Warming?" Environmental Defense Fund, 2008; "Diverse Coalition Calls on Senate to 'Fix or Ditch' Lieberman-Warner Bill," Friends of the Earth Action, 6/2/08; Peter Barnes, "Carbon Capping: A Citizen's Guide," Tamales Bay Institute, 2007; "Containing the Cost of a Cap-and-Trade Program for CO_2 Emissions," Congressional Budget Office, 5/20/08; Peter Barnes, "Lieberman-Warner amended but still flawed," Cap and Dividend; "Assessment of U.S. Cap-and-Trade Proposals," MIT Joint Program on the Science and Policy of Global Change Report No. 146, April 2007; Larry Parker and Brent Yacbucci, "Climate Change: Costs and Benefits of S. 2191," Congressional Research Service, 5/15/08; "How Low-Income Consumers Fare in the Senate Climate-Change Bill," Center on Budget and Policy Priorities, 6/3/2008; David Roberts, "McCain's Climate Plan," Gristmill, 5/11/08; Southern Alliance for Clean Energy, "Economists for Auctions Statement"; Karl Grossman, "Half-Trillion Dollars for Nukes!" Common Dreams.org, 5/29/08; Jeffery Ball and Stephen Power, "Firms Weigh Climate Bill's Cost," WSJ, 5/5/08; Sudeep Reddy, "Gasoline Hits Average of $4 a Gallon," WSJ, 6/9/08; "S.3036—the Lieberman-Warner Climate Security Act of 2008," Pew Center on Global Climate Change; Ken Bensinger, "Pickup truck, SUV sales run out of gas," Los Angeles Times, 6/4/08; "Promoting Energy Independence and Fighting Global Warming," HillaryClinton.com; "Plan For a Clean Energy Future," barackobama.com; "Protecting Our Environment And Addressing Climate Change: A Sound Energy Strategy Must Include A Solid Environmental Foundation," johnmccain.com.

Article 3.2

BUSINESS AND CLIMATE CHANGE
Privatizing Environmental Regulation?

BY DAVID L. LEVY
January/February 2001

Human-caused emissions of greenhouse gases have "contributed substantially to the observed warming over the past 50 years" and, if left unchecked, could cause the earth's average surface temperature to rise between 2.7 and 11 degrees Fahrenheit. So concluded an October 2000 report of the Intergovernmental Panel on Climate Change (IPCC), the international group of scientists charged with assessing the causes, extent, and impact of climate change. The IPCC's language is much stronger than in its previous report, issued five years ago, and the range of warming is nearly twice the previous estimate. Industries dependent on fossil fuels, however, did not react to the 2000 report with the stonewalling that once typified their public declarations on climate change.

Before the November 1997 Kyoto Protocol, an international agreement which established mandatory limits on the emission of greenhouse gases, large sectors of U.S. industry waged an intense and well-funded campaign against international regulation. Companies organized a strong industry association, the Global Climate Coalition (GCC), challenging the scientific basis for action and highlighting the economic costs of curtailing emissions. In the months leading up to the meeting of more than 150 country delegates in Kyoto, U.S. industry put $13 million into the Global Climate Information Project, a public relations campaign against any international agreement.

Even before Kyoto, however, the first signs of a major shift were visible in Europe. In May 1997, John Browne, the Group Chief Executive of oil giant British Petroleum (BP), declared publicly, "The time to consider the policy dimensions of climate change is not when the link between greenhouse gases and climate change is conclusively proven, but when the possibility cannot be discounted and is taken seriously by the society of which we are part." By 1998, U.S. industry was also showing a change in stance. The GCC was weakened by a series of defections: BP left in late 1997, Shell in April 1998, and Ford in December 1999. In 1998, General Motors (GM) joined an initiative of the World Resources Institute called "Safe Climate, Sound Business," agreeing that precautionary action should be taken on climate change. That same year, 13 companies, including BP, Toyota, Boeing, Lockheed, and Enron, joined the newly formed Pew Center on Global Climate Change. The companies endorsed a series of newspaper advertisements stating that they "accept the views of most scientists that enough is known about the science and environmental impacts of climate change for us to take actions to address its consequences."

Smoke and Mirrors

Many environmentalists doubt the sincerity of big business's sudden conversion. Given the history of industry hostility to emission controls, changed public statements can easily be dismissed as cynical posturing or "greenwashing." In May 1999, for example, William Clay Ford, Jr., the new chairman of Ford Motor Company, proclaimed that "more and more, the marketplace will demand vehicles that are truly clean." At the same time, Ford continued to produce ever larger trucks and sports utilities vehicles (SUVs), like the 12-mile-per-gallon Expedition, contributing to the continuing decline in U.S. fuel economy. Even Shell and BP, the apostles of the new movement, have not curtailed their oil exploration or refining activities at all. The $100 million a year Shell has pledged to invest in renewables is only about 7% of the company's total annual expenditure on petroleum exploration and production. Incomplete though the conversion may be, investments of hundreds of millions of dollars cannot be discounted as mere public relations. Since its acquisition of Amoco, BP has become the world's largest producer of solar photovoltaic panels, with plans to reach $1 billion in sales by 2010. Shell has also announced that it will invest $500 million in photovoltaics over five years as part of a new International Renewable Energy Division. In 1998, European automakers (including European subsidiaries of U.S.- based companies) accepted a "voluntary" agreement to reduce carbon emissions by about 25% over the following decade. European car companies have introduced very small, light-weight cars, like Daimler-Chrysler's SMART car, and invested substantial amounts in a range of technologies from diesel to fuel cells. Even the most ardent opponents of mandatory emission controls have begun to invest in low-emission technologies.

In December 1997, Ford invested about $400 million in a fuel-cell joint venture with Daimler-Chrysler and the Canadian company Ballard. Texaco was the first major U.S. oil company to break ranks and proclaim the need for precautionary action on climate, and in May 2000 it invested $67 million in Electronic Conversion Devices, a company which develops advanced batteries and solar technology. This shift suggests something more than mere PR "greenwashing," though less than a conversion to sustainable practice. It is not surprising that large sectors of industry viewed action on climate change as a major stategic threat. Controls on the emission of carbon dioxide, the main greenhouse gas, would raise the price of fuels and hurt the revenues and profits of oil, coal, and car companies, as well as other energy-intensive industries. The companies seem to have concluded, however, that open defiance of the climate-change consensus could jeopardize their long-run interests even more—causing them to lose political legitimacy and therefore the power to shape the eventual regulatory outcome. This change of attitude illustrates the resilience of capitalism and the strategies by which business attempts to sustain hegemony —dominance based on consent, the projection of moral leadership, and an ability to present one's goals as the general interest. In the face of strong challenges from state institutions and civil society, companies are moving away from confrontation, and instead towards a strategy of accommodation, compromise, and cooptation.

Explaining the Turnaround

The change in Europe can be understood mostly as a response to political and social pressures. From a European perspective, the ratification of the Kyoto Protocol and the imposition of mandatory emission controls appear inevitable. European firms were concerned that, if they aggressively opposed emission controls, they might be jeopardizing their privileged access and influence with policymakers. In international negotiations, the European Union has called for bigger emission cuts than the United States, and European politicians were sensitive to charges that they talked tough but lacked the will to act. Therefore, they looked to industry for substantial, early emission reductions. The auto industry was already on the defensive for environmental reasons, even facing a total ban on cars in some cities.

This complex of factors resulted in the European car industry's agreement to the "voluntary" emission reductions. U.S. companies, meanwhile, have experienced growing pressure to respond to their competitors' moves in other countries. In the auto industry, Ford and GM saw Toyota launch the Prius, a hybrid electric-gasoline engine car, in Japan in 1998 and the United States in 2000. Honda leapfrogged Toyota, launching its own hybrid, Insight, in the U.S. market in December 1999. While U.S. companies publicly expressed skepticism about the market potential for small, expensive, fuel-efficient cars, they stepped up their own plans for low-emission technologies. Companies often prefer to make mistakes together rather than risk ceding a major advantage to competitors. After Daimler-Chrysler announced a target date of 2004 for introducing a commercial fuel cell vehicle, Ford, GM, BMW, and Honda followed with similar announcements. Ford's and GM's European subsidiaries had already agreed to substantial emission cuts, so these companies needed to develop the appropriate technologies anyway. When Ford announced in the spring of 2000 that it would improve the fuel economy of its SUVs by 25%, GM quickly followed suit.

Within the GCC, more companies were questioning the value of aggressively denying te climate problem. The public effort to challenge the legitimacy of the IPCC ad little impact, and even threatened to backfire on industry. Environmental groups n Europe and the United States seized upon the lobbying and public relations efforts f the fossil fuel industry, issued a number of reports that documented industry support for climate skeptics, and attempted to frame the issue as big business using its money and power to distort the scientific debate. In the run-up to the Kyoto conference n December 1997, the GCC decided to shift strategy. Instead of challenging he science, industry's message shifted to the high cost and limited environmental ffectiveness of an agreement that excludes developing countries from emission controls. After Kyoto, companies increasingly worried that they were losing political access. The Pew Center's Eileen Claussen was blunt in stating that "joining Pew gives companies credibility, and credibility means political access and influence."

In the years since Kyoto, companies have begun to reevaluate the threat posed o their economic interests by emission controls. In the oil industry, companies have ome to realize that their primary markets for oil and gas will enjoy significant growth for at least 20 years. Rapid growth of car ownership in developing countries and the continued growth of vehicle-miles traveled in industrialized countries will offset the gradual introduction of low-emission car technologies. With global air travel growing at about 5% annually, aviation remains a strong market for the oil industry. Demand for natural gas, a relatively low-carbon fuel, is also booming worldwide, as small, efficient gas turbines replace large coal-fired electric power plants. In the auto industry, companies are realizing that they can stay in the business of making and selling cars, even if the engine undergoes radical change. Change is likely to be slow, in any event, because new technologies are expensive and could require massive investments in alternative fuel infrastructure.

The likelihood of stringent emission controls in the short term has also receded. Parties to the Kyoto Protocol only reached agreement in 1997 by deferring difficult decisions about implementation. It has therefore become easier for companies to win public sympathy and political credibility by expressing support for a weak and ineffective international treaty. As details have emerged, companies have realized that there will be plenty of room for fudging. The United States is planning to comply with its commitments on emissions by buying emissions credits from other countries. Russia and other East European countries, whose economies collapsed along with the Soviet Union, now emit far less carbon dioxide than in the 1990 baseline year, allowing them to sell billions of tons of carbon credits, labeled "hot air" by critics. The United States has resisted European efforts to restrict the percentage of a country's commitments that can be met by emissions trading. It has also pushed for credits rewarding hard-to-measure increases in "carbon uptake" (due to such factors as expanded forest lands).

There is still some danger that the whole process could collapse. It is becoming clear that even the modest emission-reduction targets established in Kyoto are unlikely to be met. The United States agreed to reduce emissions to 7% below 1990 levels by the "budget period" 2008-2012, but by 1999 its emissions were already 13.1% above 1990 levels. Although an agreement was reached in Kyoto, industry efforts have succeeded in blocking its ratification by the U.S. Senate. The Senate is unlikely to ratify the treaty without major revisions, which will be opposed by most other countries. Without the participation of the United States, which accounts for nearly one-quarter of global emissions, the Kyoto Protocol is meaningless. According to one anonymous industry source, the GCC did not collapse; it was more a case of "mission accomplished; now we can avoid the political cost of membership."

The Privatization of International Environmental Governance

Even as some environmentalists have welcomed industry's changed stance on climate change, some observers have expressed concern that increasing industry participation in shaping regulation amounts to the privatization of environmental governance. In fact, industry has been closely involved in international climate policy from the outset. The Business Council for Sustainable Development, a group of industrialists representing 48 of the world's largest multinational corporations, was particularly active at the UN Rio conference in 1992, and helped to ensure that the original Framework Convention on Climate Change contained no binding commitments.

Governments have encouraged industry involvement. In a 1996 speech announcing that the United States would no longer oppose binding international emission controls, U.S. State Department negotiator Tim Wirth proclaimed that "meeting this challenge requires that the genius of the private sector be brought to bear on the challenge of developing the technologies that are necessary to ensure our long term environmental and economic prosperity." The U.S. Environmental

Protection Agency and Department of Energy have adopted the same stance. The Climate Wise program, jointly administered by the two agencies, bills itself as "a unique partnership that can help you turn energy efficiency and environmental performance into a corporate asset." At the international level, IPPC head Bob Watson attempted to head off criticism of its 2000 report by recruiting corporate experts as chapter authors and reviewers.

In the absence of an international mechanism to limit emissions, private bodies have been taking the initiative. The World Bank Prototype Carbon Fund (PCF) was established in 2000 as "public-private partnership" between a few national governments, including the Netherlands, Sweden, Japan, and Canada, and 26 companies, including Hydro Quebec, Daimler-Chrysler, Shell-Canada, BP-Amoco, and numerous Japanese firms. The Fund's purpose is to raise $140 million for investments in renewables and efficiency in developing countries, projects that will earn carbon credits for the investing companies. The Environmental Defense Fund (EDF) brought together seven large companies, including Dupont, Alcan, Shell and BP, in the summer of 2000 to form the "Partnership for Climate Action," whose purpose is to enable emission trading among its members.

The Price of Accommodation

Compared to the history of corporate denial and hostility, these moves appear to be constructive and proactive. The cost of this accommodation and compromise with industry, however, is a loss of democratic process and accountability. Dan Becker of the Sierra Club has sharply criticized the EDF's emissions trading initiative, saying it offered only modest reductions in greenhouse gases while undercutting efforts to write strong regulations on emission controls as part of the 1997 Kyoto treaty. Peter Utting, in a UN report called "Business Responsibility for Sustainable Development," concluded that "the most significant concern with some forms of voluntary initiatives and partnerships is that they may serve to weaken key drivers of corporate responsibility, namely governmental and inter-governmental regulation, the role of trade unions and collective bargaining, as well as more critical forms of nongovernmental organization (NGO) activism and civil society protest."

The new business strategy on climate issues includes a strong dose of public relations, but it is not all hot air. Companies also have to demonstrate some tangible progress toward reducing emissions in order to blunt demands for more stringent regulation, and to protect their market positions in the event that mandatory emissions controls become a reality. While this strategy may sustain the political access and legitimacy of business, however, it is unlikely to result in the sustainable development that business now claims to champion. The IPCC report notes that greenhouse gases need to be slashed by more than 50% to stabilize the climate; the Kyoto Protocol called for a 5% cut in industrialized countries, and that target is fast becoming unreachable. There is still a long struggle ahead. ❑

Article 3.3

WHOSE RIGHT TO WATER?

Corporate water giants seek to privatize this most basic of all natural resources.
Consumers and communities are fighting back.

BY KEVIN MURRAY

November/December 2003

> *"[Water is] one of the world's great business opportunities. It promises to be to the*
> *21st century what oil was to the 20th."*
> — *Fortune,* May 2000

Arriving in Haiti by air provides a dramatic visual introduction to a country facing a long-term problem with water. From the sky, a few lush patches of green stand out against dry hillsides totally devoid of vegetation. The Haiti-Dominican Republic border appears as a sharp line where forest cover ends abruptly—on the Dominican side of the frontier.

Haiti receives enough rain that floods are common. But climate change is slowly changing rainfall patterns, and poor resource management policies mean that most of the rain that does fall rushes quickly back to the sea, taking with it large amounts of precious topsoil.

Topsoil erosion and deforestation have combined to put tremendous pressure on small-scale agriculture, still the only source of livelihood for millions of Haitians. Manielus Exil and his fellow members at the Kopa Koton agricultural cooperative face this pressure every day. But through learning and experimentation, they have slowly improved their management of local water and soil resources. For example, they have invested in a system that allows them to store water from a source located in the hills above their farmland. They use gravity to irrigate their crops in the dry season and have terraced their land to protect it from erosion during the rainy season. Now they are investigating the potential benefits of installing a drip irrigation system. They have established a tree nursery where they cultivate and then plant hundreds of saplings a year to reverse deforestation.

Still, the cooperative's members continue to live at the very margin of economic viability. By mid-2003, lack of rain threatened to push them over that edge. "We haven't seen hardly any rain for two years," explains Manielus. "Now the spring has almost dried up. No one remembers that ever happening before. Our water problem is getting worse." The cooperative faced catastrophic crop losses that would mean economic ruin and hunger bordering on starvation for co-op members and their families. What little food they had been able to store had long since been eaten. Early-season rains did come to Papaye this year in amounts that allowed Kopa Koton and most of its neighbors to salvage some of their production. While they will be happy to have a harvest, cooperative members are under no illusion that their water problem has been solved.

Manielus Exil and his neihbors are not alone. One could tell a parallel story about the water woes of township dwellers in South Africa who face a cholera epidemic because they can no longer afford to pay for clean water. Local water authorities, under pressure from the World Bank to recover their costs, began metering water and hiked the price. In both rural and urban areas, chronic water shortage is a way of life for an increasing percentage of the world's population. Why is this the case? We are using this resource much faster than it can be renewed, pumping aquifers dry in the process. The United Nations forecasts that, at current rates of population growth and water use, the per capita supply of usable fresh water will drop by one-third over the next 20 years. Even conservative projections suggest that one-third of the world's population will face serious water shortages by 2025.

The overall supply of water is not the only issue. Like most resources, water is unequally distributed within and among countries, making water equity an important issue. Part of this distribution problem is the "natural" result of population levels, climate, and ecological factors, but much of it reflects power relations and policy choices at national and international levels. Around the world, one in five people (1.1 billion) lack access to safe drinking water and over half (2.9 billion) lack adequate sanitation facilities—many in countries where national water supply is not a serious problem. Without safe water, people drink to their own death and disease.

Each year there are 250 million new cases of water-related disease—mostly cholera and dysentery—and 10 million people die from those diseases. Beyond drinking water, the world's water crisis is undermining millions of smallscale farmers across the globe. Agriculture accounts for 70% of world water use, but large-scale, corporate agriculture swallows up most of that water. As aquifers are pumped dry and water is diverted for commercial purposes, water tables fall and small farmers in many regions are finding it increasingly diffi cult to sustain their harvests.

The Global Challenge, the Market Response

No one disputes the fact that our unsustainable use of water has created a global water crisis of overuse, pollution, waste, and lack of access. A widely shared sense of crisis opens up the possibility of real change, and the international community has taken some important steps. However, privatization of water resources threatens to exacerbate the problem and throw millions more people into the ranks of the "water-poor." At major international summits in 2000 and 2002, nations committed themselves to cutting the number of people without access to safe water or sanitation in half by 2015. Meeting these goals will require providing new water hookups for 300,000 people every year and new sanitation facilities for 400,000 per year. But most public water authorities are hard pressed to maintain existing services, let alone expand. Enter Suez, Vivendi, Thames Water, and a small number of other corporations that have burst onto the global water scene over the past decade. These water giants offer to build large-scale water infrastructure in return for increased corporate involvement in the provision of water services via "public-private partnerships," a.k.a. water privatization. The private for-profit water industry has grown explosively over the past decade. Vivendi alone already supplies water to 110 million people. In 1990, private water companies operated in 12 countries; today they are in nearly 100. And industry analysts expect the private drinking water market to grow from its current level of about $500 billion to about $3 trillion in just the next five years.

The corporotions typically sign long-term (25 to 30 year) contracts with a municipal or regional water authority that cedes to the corporation complete control over the water supply in question. The company sets rates and makes all investment decisions. Many contracts guarantee the private provider a minimum rate of return on investment, regardless of the quality of service. These contracts transfer control over a local or regional water supply to a single private company that is much more accountable to its shareholders than it is to any public entity or to water consumers. The collapse of a public authority may drive the privatization process, but con- ditions placed on water loans by lenders like the World Bank have also played a key role. The Bank used to help countries build public water utilities, but, in a recent three-year period, 60% of Bank loans for water infrastructure carried conditions related to privatization. To date, most privatizations have occurred in Africa, Asia, and Latin America, but all of the water giants are now targeting Europe and the United States as priority areas for expansion.

The International Center for Investigative Journalism conducted an in-depth study of the track record of the water corporations and found that while privatization has improved service in some cases, "they [the companies] can be ruthless players who constantly push for higher rate increases, frequently fail to meet their commitments and abandon waterworks if they are not making enough money." For example, some residents of metro Manila greeted privatization as a miracle when two water companies were handed control over the city's water supply in 1997. Five years later, corruption charges, poor service, and the near collapse of one of the companies left the miracle more than a little tarnished. Suez pulled out of a celebrated agreement with the city of Buenos Aires, Argentina, when general economic collapse meant the company's profits did not meet expectations. And the city of Atlanta, Georgia, recently voted to cancel its $500 million contract with Suez's U.S. subsidiary, United Water, after widespread public complaints about poor service, declining water quality, and high user fees.

Privatization boosters point to a modest list of examples where water privatization has shown positive results. But they typically falter when asked to explain how privatization is going to bring water to the hundreds of millions of people who currently do not have access to it. Speaking to the Canadian Broadcasting Company, Gerard Payen, the architect of Suez's international expansion program, explained, "Water as a business is very effective when you look at the needs. We purify water and bring this water to your home. We provide a service, it has a cost, and somebody has to pay for it." Then how will the market bring water to people who can never afford to pay for it? Privatization turns water, an essential common good, into a commodity like any other, to be owned, shifted across borders, and sold in search of the highest profit. For the corporate "water elites," water fits neatly into a vision of corporate-led global economic integration—along with sneakers, corn flakes, intellectual property rights, and the genetic material on which life is based. Water elites are often criticized for failing to recognize access to safe water as a right. But they clearly do have a rightsbased perspective. Water corporations and their allies place a high priority on the establishment and protection of the unfettered right of corporations to own and trade the world's water as they see fit.

The Real Rights Solution

A growing network of social movements, community groups, and nongovernmental organizations supports a different notion of the right to water. National and cross-border networks like the Water for All Campaign, the Blue Planet Project, and the People's World Water Forum share with the water establishment a sense of urgency about water, but reject the notion that water is just another commodity or service. Instead, they consider it a fundamental human right. They share the water establishment's interest in conservation and limiting water waste, but question its reliance on large infrastructure projects, especially dams, and on water privatization.

The new water activists recognize the limitations of many public water authorities. Clearly, some water authorities are inefficient bureaucracies that politicians use to reward relatives and supporters. Even where water authorities are committed to providing water to all, public disinvestment and the "hollowing out" of the state over the past two decades have made their job very difficult. A massive public investment program is part of the solution to the water crisis; redirecting the subsidies and investment capital now flowing to private corporations would provide a good start.

Money alone, however, will not solve the water crisis. Public water authorities are going to have to become much more creative and democratic, finding new ways to turn water "customers" into active participants in the development of water policy. There are already plenty of examples of public water authorities—Porto Alegre, Brazil, and Bogota, Colombia, for example—that have built successful programs encouraging public involvement in campaigns against water waste and in the implementation of new technologies.

In many rural areas, water activists favor decentralized, community-based resource management, supported but not dominated by public authorities. Farmers all over the world are joining those of Haiti's Central Plateau in taking steps to become more effective stewards of water resources. Too often, those farmers end up facing the opposition of public water or power authorities interested in developing a dam or other large infrastructure project, or in giving a private corporation control over local resources. In a new vision of "public-public partnership," activists advocate public support for community-based watershed management rather than the handoff of public water resources to private, for-profit corporations.

Adherents to radically different views of how to solve the water crisis are working to put their visions into practice in urban and rural communities all around the world. In some cases, the result has been creative solutions to local water challenges. In many others, local groups have challenged and blocked plans to increase private control over the water supply. For example:

- In Mecosta County, Michigan, a determined citizen coalition has opposed the efforts of a bottled water subsidiary of the Nestle corporation to gain private control of important groundwater supplies. In 2001, the county licensed the company (then a Perrier subsidiary) to open a bottling plant in Stanwood, Michigan, for a fee of less than $100 a year. Almost before anyone knew about it, the company was pumping a half million gallons of water a day from an aquifer beneath a hunting reserve. After learning about the plan, Michigan Citizens for Water Conservation launched a direct action campaign against Nestle and sought a temporary injunction to stop the pumps while the court decided on the legality of Nestle's use of the water. The injunction has yet to be granted.

- In Cochabamba, Bolivia, violent conflict broke out in 1999, when a Bechtel subsidiary signed a 40-year contract to operate municipal water services there. The private operator dramatically raised water fees during the first year. Well-organized public resistance led the municipality to rescind the contract with Bechtel, but the corporation sued Cochabamba for damages before a secret World Bank panel. The water is back in public hands, but the public authority still faces the same daunting challenges it faced before its flirtation with privatization. Plans exist to upgrade water services and extend them to more residents, but it is unclear where the authority will get the necessary $200 million.

- In many locations, governments, power companies, and irrigation interests have promoted the construction of large-scale dams in response to water and electricity problems. Dams often flood out thousands of local residents and completely destroy regional watershed systems, but they continue to get political support because they supply electricity to power-hungry urban areas and facilitate large-scale irrigation projects supporting corporate agriculture. In August 2003, activists from the Brazilian Movement of Dam-Affected People (MAB) occupied dams throughout Brazil. Among other things, MAB was demanding reparations for Brazilians whose lives have been destroyed by dam projects.

Kyoto Blues

In March 2003, 24,000 government and U.N. officials, civil society activists, corporate executives, journalists, and water specialists gathered in Kyoto, Japan, for the third World Water Forum. Organized by the Marseilles-based World Water Council (WWC), the forum quickly became a stage for debate over the water crisis and potential solutions.

It was "asymmetrical warfare," given the enormous resources at the disposal of corporate representatives and their control over the forum agenda. Those promoting the notion of a universal right to water did, however, get their voices heard. Freely referring to corporate water giants by name, activists charged that the forum had become a public relations event promoting a corporate view of the water crisis. The anti-dam International Rivers Network insisted that the forum was controlled by a "mafia" of irrigation- and power-agency representatives in tandem with the water multinationals. The forum may pose as a search for solutions to benefit the world's poor, but, according to an IRN representative, "in reality, their pseudo-solutions are driven by personal, institutional, corporate, and political interests."

A look at the composition of the WWC lends credence to the charge of elite control. The organization is led by Egypt's Minister of Water Resources and Irrigation. Its vice presidents include a Suez executive and a former vice president of the World Bank, and its Board of Governors is an elite club of power players in the world of dams, irrigation, hydropower, and water privatization.

To no one's surprise, the forum's final Ministerial Declaration failed to commit governments to review individual dam projects. It also quite consciously declined to recognize a universal human right to water. Activists did claim a victory in the forum's decision to declare that the results of water privatization have been mixed and that "the debate concerning public-private partnerships has not been resolved."

This last issue is extremely important to the corporations. They seem willing to invest some of their own money in water privatization projects in the developed countries, where users can pay fees that guarantee sufficient profits. In the global South, however, higher risk and lower rates of return mean that the water giants require massive public financing to make privatization work. Whether the World Bank and other international financial institutions continue to promote the current "public-private partnership" model will thus play a critical role in the outcome of the new water wars.

Toward a New Social Contract on Water

While the World Water Forum met in Japan, water activists held alternative gatherings in Florence, New Delhi, New York, and São Paulo to protest the approach being taken in Kyoto and to promote the notion that water is a human right and a common resource.

Activists are committed to creating a vision that moves beyond opposing dam construction and blocking water privatization to develop principles for a sustainable global water system and concrete proposals to bring that system into existence. They continue down the challenging path of integrating the vision of Haitian farmers struggling for community control of water with that of Michigan environmental activists fighting to keep public water out of the hands of bottled water companies. In September 2003, many members of this network were in Cancún, working to keep water out of the World Trade Organization's agreement on services. The end of this debate is not in sight.

In 1998, an international group of politicians, academics, and NGO leaders formed the Committee for a World Water Contract. Their World Water Manifesto opens with a challenge:

> 1.4 billion of the planet's 5.8 billion inhabitants do not have access to drinking water, the fundamental source of life. This fact is intolerable. Now, the risk is great that in the year 2020 when the world population reaches around 8 billion human beings, the number of people without access to drinking water will increase to more than 3 billion. This is unacceptable. We can and must prevent the unacceptable becoming possible. How?

The committee points to the recognition of a universal right to water, the need for a massive global educational campaign on the water crisis, and the creation of citizen "water parliaments" to address water issues. For their part, the new corporate water giants plan to continue turning water into a profitable commodity—"blue gold." The water wars have just begun. ❑

Resources: Maude Barlow and Tony Clarke, *Blue Gold* (New Press, 2002); International Center for Investigative Journalism, "The Water Barons: A Handful of Corporations Seek to Privatize the World's Water" (Feb. 2003) <www.icij.org/water>; Leah C. Wells, "In Iraq, Water and Oil Do Mix," Counterpunch 5/16/03; Vandana Shiva, "Bechtel and Blood for Water," Z-Net 5/12/03.

Article 3.4

WHAT AN ENVIRONMENTALLY SUSTAINABLE ECONOMY LOOKS LIKE

BY THAD WILLIAMSON
July/August 1999

Greens and economic progressives are seen as uncertain, uneasy allies—and perhaps not allies at all. Think of those spotted-owl-loving, middle-class activists clashing with blue collar loggers in the Pacific Northwest. Or the clash between liberal economists who still count progress in terms of jobs created, growth generated, and increases in consumption, and environmental activists who challenge those very ways of measuring progress. "Growth" to these activists is part of the problem, not the solution.

But do green politics necessarily conflict with progressive economic goals? Or can environmental protection live and thrive in a world dedicated to eradicating poverty, nurturing equality and economic security, and the continued advancement of productivity and technology?

In a word, yes. An environmentally "sustainable" economy is one that neither depletes natural resources nor pollutes at levels that overwhelm the ability of ecosystems to absorb waste. Such an economy would almost certainly need to overlap with many of the traditional goals of economic progressives, allowing us to envision an ideal world that is both socially and ecologically sustainable. What would that world look like?

First, it would provide economic security for individuals and communities. So long as most citizens are less than six months' paychecks away from insolvency, and so long as they worry that their income may be taken away, economic expansion (i.e., growth) and job creation will, most of the time and for most people, always be a higher political priority than environmental protection.

The link between economic security and sustainability runs at a deeper level as well. In a highly inegalitarian society such as ours, where the quality of public goods like neighborhood safety and public schools varies widely, individuals and families are pressured not just to subsist, but to earn enough to live an ecology-straining middleclass lifestyle.

At the community level, if localities remain dependent on the investment decisions of private businesses for their economic health, protection of the environment will tend to take a back seat. Just look at the way poor, deindustrialized cities such as Chester, Pennsylvania, court particle-spewing trash incinerators for the modest revenue they provide.

If we want to move to a society in which acquiring more and more goods is not the highest priority for individuals, and "growth" is not the highest priority for most communities, then we need a baseline of economic security.

Second, we must create a sense of self based on something besides consumerism. Of course, economic insecurity is not the only reason Americans are driven to consume at extraordinarily high levels. As Thorstein Veblen first argued in 1899, and as Juliet Schor documented in the 1990s, consumption is often used to mark social status, particularly with regard to goods that can be made visible to one's peers, such as cars, clothes, and lipstick. As workers, most Americans are provided with little scope for individual expressiveness, but as consumers, they feel free to follow their wishes in making decisions—decisions which then form a critical part of American identities. The result is a nation of individuals shaped by a compulsion to consume goods and services, and to increase that consumption over time. By contrast, in an ecologically sustainable society, people's core satisfactions could not come from buying decisions, and they would need to have a sense of when enough is enough.

Third, producers who damage the environment must also bear the costs of their damage. As it stands, private enterprises force the public to pay the costs of their polluting and depletion of natural resources. Since the true costs of production are not reflected in the prices of goods on the market, firms benefit by shifting costs such as pollution cleanup to the public. This system gives businesses an incentive to "externalize" environmental costs off their own balance sheets if they can get away with it—and to resist attempts by governments to minimize the costs through regulation. Advocates of ecological sustainability thus argue that firms should bear the full cost of their activities. A major question, of course, is how to best accomplish this goal.

Fourth, we must also use as much environmentally friendly technology as we can in our new world. Unfortunately, over the course of this century, the U.S. government intervened in the economy to promote ecologically inefficient and destructive economic practices. While giving a pittance to the development of solar and wind power, the government sank about $100 billion of subsidies into nuclear power between 1950 and 1990. Similarly, the government lavished funds upon the Highway Trust Fund and created the interstate highway system while allowing public transit of all types to decay. To this day, over 80% of federal transportation spending supports automobile-related infrastructure, leaving less than 20% for mass transit. Such spending patterns, along with additional subsidies like tax write-offs for home mortgages, help generate suburban sprawl (and thereby exacerbate the ecological damage caused by cars). At the same time, regulators often tackle problems at the "end of the pipe" instead of seeking to change the productive processes themselves.

In any sustainable society, these sorts of choices will need to be reversed and priority given to implementing the most environmentally friendly technology possible. Environmental technology, in fact, could be the source of millions of new jobs in the next century—and jobs building high-speed rail cars would likely pay just as well as jobs making automobiles. Similarly, labor-intensive public work projects could be undertaken in support of ecological goals—to beautify cities, build bike paths, install solar panels, remove lead paint, and insulate buildings. Governments could also aggressively use their purchasing policies to help promote the development of cutting-edge environmentally sound products.

Within the current structure of power, however, the private interests that stand to lose public funds—such as the oil and car companies—thwart any shift in public spending toward more ecologically and socially rational goals and resist any laws that would mandate certain kinds of production processes. They have the money to intervene in elections and (even more importantly) shape legislation—and they are aided by the fact that few politicians are eager to support measures that may damage companies in their districts. Just look at the way the energy lobby thoroughly discredited and defeated Vice President Al Gore's modest proposal for an energy tax in 1993. In contrast, an ecologically sustainable society would require that politics not be dominated by corporate or private interests—a very tough structural requirement rarely mentioned in the conventional policy debate about the environment.

Finally, a world where ecological and progressive economic goals are unified would be one where growth is no longer the top priority. In our corporate capitalist economy, banks and investors consider whether profits and the economy as a whole will grow before sending their capital the way of any business. In contrast, an environmentally sustainable economy would not need high rates of growth to function in a healthy manner. Growth would not be the goal of a sustainable economy, nor would the fair distribution of economic goods depend on continual growth. Instead, with every individual and community guaranteed a stake in the economy, it would not be necessary to focus so much on expanding production. Also, the gains from more efficient production would be distributed to people as reduced work-hours or more stringent environmental protection.

Still, even in a sustainable economy, economic growth per se need not be eliminated entirely. While one way to cut the use of resources and pollution is to cut production and shrink the economy, another is to make productive systems more efficient. We also might choose to produce those goods that cause less ecological damage. There is no inherent reason why a society that commits itself to ecologically efficient production, both in the actual production process and in the kinds of goods created, might not generate what we today call economic growth. For instance, if we decided to hire more elementary school teachers—and at the same time to consume fewer lawn care products—ecological damage would drop even as the size of the economy stayed roughly the same. The difference is that economic growth as a good in itself would not be the central aim of such an economy.

The Institutions of a Sustainable Economy

Ecological problems might be very easy to solve if we imagine an all-powerful state that enforces strict ecological standards on both individuals and businesses. Not only is such a vision unattractive on its own terms, it probably provides only a temporary solution to the ecological problem. Sooner or later, an ecofascist regime that tried to impose sound ecological practices without the support of its citizens would probably be overthrown, leading us back to square one: how to make the goals of democracy, economic justice, and ecological sustainability fit together.

How would that be possible? Is it possible?

At the community level, perhaps the fundamental questions to consider are: Who owns capital?, and, Who gets to make basic decisions over how production is carried out? The usual answers—small businesses, corporations, the government, or workers—would all have the incentive to pollute or use ecologically wasteful production strategies. A fifth possible solution is local community ownership. To see why, it's worth reviewing the shortcomings of the other possible answers.

Styles of regulation that allow private businesses to organize production as they see fit will always face an uphill struggle in trying to get businesses to pay for the ecological costs they generate, a hill that is especially steep in the case of nations like the United States where social democratic politics are weak. Moreover, even the success stories associated with social democratic-style environmental regulation have limitations. For example, no industrialized country has yet succeeded in constraining the growth of the automobile/highway complex, as we must to reduce greenhouse gases. Worker-owned firms are an attractive solution, it seems, since workers may be less likely to pollute their own communities (or risk their own health in the workplace), and more subtly, because worker-owned firms (as Douglas Booth argues) will have less incentive to grow than capitalist firms. Perhaps, but workers within a given enterprise still may have interests different from the public's. Given the reins of management, workers may come to see ecological responsibility as a threat to the bottom line, as Gar Alperovitz and Herbert Gintis have each suggested—especially if they can send the pollution from their plant downstream or to the next town. State ownership of firms also poses problems. When government officials are not held accountable and when ecological values are subordinated to other aims, both state-owned enterprises and general government operations are capable of doing disastrous damage to the environment. Even in the most favorable circumstances, public companies may find it rational to compromise the needs of local ecosystems in the name of some larger public interest. At worst, we've seen the Energy Department contaminate desert stretches of Nevada from nuclear weapons tests carried out in the "public interest."

This brings us to a fifth possible answer to the "who should control capital?" question: local-level community ownership. "Community-owned" firms might include municipally owned enterprises, firms owned by nonprofit organizations that represent community interests (such as community development corporations), or companies whose stock can be owned only by local residents (as in Michael Shuman's concept of "community corporation.") In theory, community-owned enterprises are more likely to take full responsibility for the ecological costs of their activity to the degree that they are made accountable to the community. If the managers of a community- owned firm chose to sacrifice ecological goals for the sake of higher production, citizens would have the opportunity, via the political process, to remove them. Moreover, profits from a community-owned firm could be distributed to citizens as a second income, thus helping to meet the economic security requirement previously noted. And perhaps best of all, there is no threat that a community firm would move away—removing the sword hanging over towns that want tough ecological standards but not at the cost of jobs.

The most widespread form of community ownership in the United States in the 20th century are the roughly 2,000 local-level, nonprofit, public electric utilities, which offer lower rates, more public accountability, and a better (although far from perfect) environmental record than their private counterparts. But many other forms of community ownership have sprouted up in the past two decades as well. These include businesses owned and operated by community development corporations, community land trusts, community-supported agriculture operations, community credit unions, and municipal enterprises.

Community-owned firms, then, would appear to be the best answer to the question of "who should control capital," at least within medium-size and large firms, and the recent growth of various forms of community ownership indicates this is a plausible solution. This does not mean that other forms of ownership need to be obliterated; on the contrary, community-owned firms could coexist along with small businesses, worker-owned firms, joint public-private enterprises, and some larger scale public enterprises. The key is that the local community must have substantial control over the practices of enough enterprises to anchor the local economy and set a tone for overall production practices.

Community control of land—especially downtown land and undeveloped land—would also be important to optimizing local communities' ecological health. Patterns of land development driven by private developers have resulted in autodominated, sprawled out forms of urban development. Community ownership of land would make shifting to ecologically friendly, resource-saving urban designs far more plausible—and rents collected from leases to downtown businesses could also be directly distributed to residents or given to them as services to help solve the economic security problem.

A picture thus emerges of a local economy characterized by a critical mass of community ownership, along with substantial community ownership of land, allowing local level democratic politics to steer firms toward ecological goals and allowing any community dividend to be distributed to citizens (enhancing their economic security). Even if this vision could be achieved with every locality in America, would such an achievement be enough to create a sustainable society?

Hardly. We'd still need mechanisms at the state or perhaps regional level to ensure that one community does not dump on another and meets ecological standards. There would also need to be a planning mechanism to allocate enough capital to each community to guarantee local-level full employment and to help communities adjust when some industries decline due to market shifts.

Governments would also provide important public goods relevant to sustainability, including rail and public transit, development of alternative energy sources, oversight of needed ecological clean-ups, and coordination of the overall macroeconomy. But by essentially removing the private corporation with its disproportionate sway over the political process, and replacing it with firms directly tied to community interests, it ought to be easier to decide how to spend the public works budget, how long the standard work week should be, and so on in an ecologically rational manner.

Continental or global forms of ecological governance may be appropriate on specific ecological issues such as greenhouse gas emissions.

This kind of system would have a far better chance of meeting the needs of a sustainable society than any industrial society that exists now (be it capitalist, social democratic or state socialist.)

But can it be said that this proposed system is inherently sustainable? No—or, at least, not exactly. In fact, it is probably impossible to design a modern economy that could guarantee ecological sustainability while also preserving other crucial norms such as liberty, equality, and democracy. The best we can hope for is an economy that meets the logical prerequisites for a sustainable society and permits citizens to make democratic social choices about what sort of world they wish to live in. Some citizens may chafe at any state-mandated shifts in their lifestyle and consumption habits (such as one bag of garbage per household per week) while others will believe that the trade off is worth it. The outcome of such political struggles is uncertain, and from time to time the public no doubt would make the wrong choices from a rigorous ecological point of view. But at least such bad choices would be made in the name of the public interest, not in response to private interests or as steps needed to grease the wheels of a growth-oriented economy.

To be sure, in the long interval before a truly sustainable society is built, there will continue to be episodes in which zero-sum tradeoffs between the economy and the environment must be made. But those episodes should not blind either greens or economic progressives to the common ground both groups share and will no doubt need to share if either group is to achieve its political aims in the 21st century ❑

Reources: Ted Howard, "Ownership Matters," (National Center for Economic and Security Alternatives, 1999), www.ncesa.org; Mark Hertsgaard, *Earth Odyssey* (Broadway Books, 1999); Gar Alperovitz, "Sustainability and the System Problem," *PEGS Journal*, 1996.

Article 3.5

ACHIEVING THE GOOD LIFE

Adapted from Graceful Simplicity: Toward a Philosophy and Politics of Simple Living

BY JEROME M. SEGAL
July/August 1999

The recent enthusiasm for "simple living" in the United States is largely apolitical, with acolytes maintaining that ours is an affluent society, whose central problem is an unenlightened consciousness. An entire self-help literature has blossomed in the last decade, showing people how they can live well with vastly lower income. Certainly, there is some truth to the idea that we need to be liberated from our ever expanding sense of what constitutes a necessity. However, our biggest problem is not warped perceptions at the individual level, but extreme inefficiency at the structural level: fundamental human needs can be met only with high levels of income. Simple living, espoused by individuals and groups as diverse as Gandhi, Thoreau and the Quakers, can be most easily defined by what it is not. At its core, the simple living philosophy is that "the good life" is not achieved through ever increasing getting- and-spending. Those rejecting the dominant American dream on an individual level may focus on friends, lovers, and family, or religion, or art and literature, or political struggle, or service to others, or the pursuit of knowledge.

A politics of simplicity—focused at the societal level—is similarly broad-based. Rather than promoting one particular way of life, it promotes a society in which people with even modest incomes can have the freedom to engage in fundamental projects beyond merely making a living. Rather than evaluating economic progress in terms of an ever-expanding cornucopia of goods and services, a politics of simplicity measures economic progress by how well core economic needs are being met and whether leisure time is expanding.

Over the last hundred years, satisfying certain basic needs has become much cheaper, while others have sky-rocketed in cost. The number of work hours the average person in the United States must devote to meeting their needs for food and clothing has fallen dramatically. In 1900, food and clothing constituted 56% of the household budget; today it is 20%. Meanwhile, costs for housing, transportation, health care, education and child care have increased. "Need required income" (income required to meet our needs) has gone up markedly.

In many critical ways, this shift is not the result of rising standards. In fact, we have lowered our expectations. Take the example of housing—the largest component of the average household budget. Certainly, the typical middle class house has changed dramatically, from having an outhouse to indoor plumbing to multiple bathrooms. Still, for most American families, the key to choosing housing is not the physical house, but the neighborhood: not too far from work and services, with access to good public schools, and safe enough for children to play outside. This standard is increasingly out of reach of moderate income families. In the Washington, DC area where I live, houses in such a neighborhood cost upward of $250,000. The solution is not higher incomes; more effective demand would only push prices higher. The real issue is supply, but not in the physical sense. We need to make existing urban neighborhoods viable places to live.

Consider transportation. One hundred years ago transportation represented 3% of the household budget. Today the figure is 19%. We have built a suburbanized society with extremely limited public transportation. A car is a necessity in most areas—families with two wage earners generally need two of them. Reducing household expenditures on transportation requires greater investment in public transport and the design of a simple living automobile: one that is safe, inexpensive, long lasting and can be repaired by anyone handy with tools.

Education is another key example. In the nineteenth century the battle for free public education was waged and won. Free public schooling through high school became the norm nationwide. Relatively few people went to college. The vast majority of jobs required only high school education. Today, access to most interesting work requires a college education, and often an advanced degree. Costs reach $30,000 per year. One hundred years ago, free education provided you with a viable point of entry into the economy. Today, it provides access to very little: only a small number of jobs available with a high school education provide a living wage. We could take major steps in this area with surprisingly limited funds. For $25 billion annually we could eliminate virtually all tuition at state universities for both undergraduate and graduate education. In an $8 trillion economy, this is only a fraction of our annual expenditures.

To make simple living an option for all, a politics of simplicity must go beyond reducing cost of meeting core needs and address a living wage for all, education for simple living, and increased leisure time.

From the mid-1800s until the Great Depression, reduction in work time was a central criterion of economic progress. Work time decreased from 70 hours to 40 hours per week. In 1933 legislation mandating a 30 hour work week passed the U.S. Senate, but died in the House. In recent years, fuller participation by married women in the formal workforce has led to an explosion in total family work time. We need to take the benefits of productivity growth and divide them between higher incomes and increased leisure time, like earlier generations did. Here is one possibility: add 16 three-day weekends to the ten enjoyed by most workers in this country, giving us a three-day weekend every other week. Introduced at the rate of two new holidays a year for the next eight years, this would reduce work time about 1% a year. With productivity growth around 2%, this would still allow for marginally higher incomes.

None of the policies I propose here are truly radical. They could be accomplished through ordinary politics and the creative use of referenda. What is radical is what lies behind them: a recognition of the limited place of money in the good life and a commitment to making simple living feasible for all ❏

Article 3.6

NOT THE OWNERS OF THE EARTH:
CAPITALISM AND ENVIRONMENTAL DESTRUCTION

An Interview with John Bellamy Foster

March/April 2003

The success of the environmental movement in raising public consciousness can be seen and felt almost on a daily basis. From local recycling efforts to tighter automobile inspection standards, we are constantly reminded of environmental issues. Daily newspapers and nightly newscasts shower us with issues as varied as global warming, the plight of lobsters, and Arianna Huffington's recent attacks on SUVs. For many of us, this may all get a bit overwhelming. Fortunately, John Bellamy Foster takes a step back and uncovers the connecting threads that tie together these diverse questions. Touching on history, economics, ecology, and philosophy, Foster delves seriously into the complexity and vast scale of today's environmental problems. He also reminds us that many of today's reforms treat the symptoms rather than curing the disease—which is capitalism itself. Foster is coeditor of Monthly Review: An Independent Socialist Magazine *and a professor at the University of Oregon at Eugene. His books on society and ecology (including* The Vulnerable Planet: A Short Economic History of the Environment, Marx's Ecology: Materialism and Nature, *and* Ecology Against Capitalism*), as well as numerous articles on these issues, have provided those concerned about the environment with a critical analytical foundation for thinking about and acting on today's environmental crisis. Here, he takes on the largest and most pressing environmental and economic issues in a conversation with* Dollars & Sense's *Skip Barry.*

-- Eds.

D&S: Since Earth Day in 1970, the environmental movement has been successful in raising public awareness of the plight of the environment. To what extent has it been successful in winning environmental protections and more ecological forms of economic development?

JBF: Environmentalists have scored a lot of important victories over the last three decades. However, this has not prevented the environmental crisis as a whole from getting much worse. One difficulty is that those environmental problems that are easiest to fix within the present system (such as the elimination of lead in gasoline) get addressed, while others that go against the grain of the system, like reducing carbon dioxide emissions, continue on without amelioration. Another difficulty is that the scale and complexity of environmental problems keep on increasing along with the scale and complexity of the world economy—and indeed new problems not previously imagined keep on arising. If you look back three decades to the period following the first Earth Day and compare it to today you will notice two things: First, most of the issues raised at that time, such as the role of toxins in our environment, are still with us, and more often than not on a much larger scale. Second, new problems have arisen that were scarcely on the radar screen thirty years ago—or problems that we recognized then have been qualitatively transformed and present themselves to us now in new forms.

We are still faced with the issue of pesticides raised by Rachel Carson in Silent Spring. Although a few of the worst pesticides, such as DDT, were banned for use in the rich countries, we now produce in the United States several times the quantity of pesticides that we did when Rachel Carson raised the alarm and most such chemicals are effectively untested and unregulated for their effects on humans.

But if the old environmental problems continue to haunt us, new ones have arisen that are equally or more threatening. Global warming and depletion of the ozone layer were not threats that one heard about commonly within the environmental movement in the early 1970s. Species extinction was often raised but the idea that we were entering a period of the "sixth extinction," in which the extinction rate would rise to a minimum of 1000 times the background (or normal) rate—comparable to the five great mass extinctions in the history of the planet (the most recent being the destruction of the dinosaurs 65 million years ago)—that was not something that was or could have been foreseen on the first Earth Day.

The Worldwatch Institute talks about the "acceleration of history" where the environment is concerned. This acceleration is the product of the exponential growth of an unsustainable economic system, which now operates on a scale that rivals the basic biogeochemical processes of the planet. For example, carbon dioxide is not a pollutant. It is part of our own respiratory system. But when hundreds of millions of cars are driven trillions of miles per year, all pumping carbon dioxide into the atmosphere, the scale of human economic activity becomes of planetary significance, changing the balance within the biosphere. When one considers that a 3% annual rate of growth in world output means a doubling in the size of the economy every twenty five years, so that the size of the world economy would increase by sixteen times in a century, 250 times in two centuries, and 4,000 times in three centuries—it becomes clear that the main reason for what environmentalists call the "acceleration of history" is the exponential growth of the economy itself. China has the highest rate of economic growth in the world at present and this is fueling expectations about its future energy demands. The U.S. Department of Energy has estimated that China's demand for petroleum will increase by almost 1000% between 1997 and 2020.

D&S: **The Bush Administration rejected an already watered down version of the Kyoto Protocol on global warming. Is the United States government the main barrier to adequately addressing environmental reform?**

JBF: There is no doubt that the United States is the single most important political entity blocking environmental reform. The U.S. refusal to ratify the Kyoto Protocol was a major blow to the struggle against global warming. But this response was virtually inevitable given that the giant corporations were strongly opposed to the climate treaty. The Kyoto Protocol required the United States to reduce its greenhouse gas emissions to 7% below the 1990 level. But U.S. carbon dioxide emissions have actually risen by as much as 18% since 1990. The Clinton administration declared in 2000 that the United States would have to cut its carbon dioxide emissions by up to 30% if it were to meet its meet its targeted reductions under the Kyoto Protocol by 2010. This was viewed as potentially catastrophic by the vested interests (for example, the corporate lobbying group the Global Climate Coalition), since U.S. wealth and power is built around the auto-petroleum complex. The Clinton administration therefore made no attempt to ratify the Kyoto Protocol and did everything it could do to water down and escape the agreement. The Bush administration has simply been more honest in rejecting the climate treaty outright.

D&S: **How has mainstream economics traditionally dealt with the environment? Does the mainstream perspective lend support to U.S. policies on issues like global warming?**

JBF: Traditionally, mainstream economics has scarcely dealt with the environment at all. Neoclassical economists construct abstract models which treat the economy as a total system that does not exist within a larger biosphere. When environmental problems, such as pollution, have come up economists have traditionally viewed these as "externalities"—essentially outside the private market, falling on society as a whole. Nowadays, however, there are a lot of attempts by neoclassical economists to bring environmental problems within their models. This usually starts with the view that there are "market imperfections" that prevent the system from adequately valuing nature.

For example, society has created "market imperfections" in the area of fresh water by treating water as a free good, leading to an imbalance of demand and supply and hence growing water shortages. From a mainstream standpoint this points to the need to have the entire environment brought within the price system. A book was published a number of years ago by leading environmental economists entitled, significantly, *Pricing the Planet.* The environment is conceived as if it is a set of commodities with prices or values (awaiting to be discovered) that allow for its incorporation into the logic of the self-regulating market system. Of course, most of this is bogus since the natural environment cannot be reduced to commodities to be bought and sold on the market.

But various ways of artificially imposing prices on nature have been tried. Mainstream economists actually believe that in doing all of this they are seriously tackling environmental problems. If nature is incorporated into market relations, they contend, this will solve nearly all ecological problems. It is only economists, however, who believe this. One of the continual sources of frustration for orthodox economists applying this kind of analysis is that the population stubbornly refuses to view everything in nature as having a price tag or as constituting a salable commodity.

With respect to global warming, mainstream economists have taken the issue seriously up to a point. But they tend to underestimate the costs associated with it (since they perceive only the direct costs to the market) and are critical of measures that attempt to cut emissions, such as the Kyoto Protocol, which they see as too costly. William Nordhaus, the most famous establishment economist to address this problem extensively, argues that rather than supporting the Kyoto Protocol and attempting to control emissions the United States should opt for some kind of grand technological solution, like carbon sequestration, designed to increase carbon absorption by the oceans. The fact that such technologies don't exist doesn't seem to matter.

There is a tragic-comic aspect to this. A decade ago atmospheric scientists objected to an article that Nordhaus wrote for Science magazine in which he claimed that the losses to U.S. GDP over the next century as a result of global warming would be on the order of 1%. In response to these criticisms, Nordhaus admitted that he had not taken into account losses in nonmarket sectors, such as the costs associated with the loss of wetlands or a rise in species extinctions. He therefore went on to carry out a survey of a select group of economists and natural scientists on their estimates of the costs to the world economy associated with various global warming scenarios. When he raised the scenario of a 6°C (10.8°F) rise in the earth's average temperature by 2090 (within the range of what the UN Intergovernmental Panel on Climate Change currently believes possible) most conventional economists that he surveyed thought it would have an impact on the Gross World Product of only a few percent. In contrast, natural scientists who were asked about the effect of the same increase in global temperature generally thought it catastrophic, with losses to world economic output ranging from several percent all the way up to 100% (since one scientist assigned a 10% chance to the virtual destruction of all civilization). Nordhaus concluded that those who knew most about the economy were optimistic. Stephen Schneider, a leading atmospheric scientist, retorted that those who knew most about the planet were worried.

D&S: Does the environmental crisis call into question the sustainability of capitalist development?

JBF: The questioning of capitalism is omnipresent in the ecological critique. That is why I entitled my latest book *Ecology Against Capitalism*. Capitalism is all about the accumulation of capital. The commodification of nature in the service of accumulation involves the systematic disruption of spatial and temporal relations that are integral to a sustainable system. It frequently means not just the exploitation of nature but the robbing or pillage of the biosphere. I have tried over the years to find a way of conceptualizing the damaging effects that capitalism has on the environment.

In *The Vulnerable Planet* I looked at how capital accumulation conflicts with Barry Commoner's four informal "laws" of ecology: (1) everything is connected to everything else, (2) everything must go somewhere, (3) nature (i.e. evolution) knows best, and (4) nothing comes from nothing. Capitalism, I argued, has its own built-in anti-ecological tendencies: (1) the only lasting connection between things is the cash nexus, (2) it doesn't matter where something goes (how it is externalized) as long as it doesn't reenter the circuit of capital, (3) the self-regulating market knows best, and (4) nature's bounty is a free gift to the property owner.

Recently I concluded that the most powerful way of understanding capitalism's destructive relation to the environment is in terms of what Marx called the "metabolic rift"—or the material estrangement of human beings from the natural conditions and processes that form the bases of their existence. (Marx's concept of metabolic rift is discussed in detail in my book Marx's Ecology.) Such a rift occurs when the circulation of commodities and exchange under capitalism ruptures the basic processes governing the circulation of matter and energy—the biogeochemical interactions on which ecosystems and the biosphere depend. For example, prior to growth of modern agribusiness livestock was raised on farms where it provided fertilizer for crops. This is of course part of an ecological cycle stretching back over the ages. Now, however, cattle are forced into giant feedlots and their manure, which cannot under these circumstances be used to fertilize the soil, collects in huge amounts and gives off methane gas, which has become a major factor in global warming.

D&S: The "command" economies of the former USR and Eastern Europe were environmental disasters. Why were they such failures ecologically? What would sustainable non-capitalist economies have to look like?

JBF: I don't think that the environmental destruction in the Soviet Union and Soviettype economies was due mainly to their being "command" economies (although the fact that they were societies that were not socialist in the sense of being controlled by the direct producers was a major factor in their demise). The key here is that the Soviet Union was what is called, in economic terms, a "war economy." It not only operated with little or no excess capacity or unemployment, but it also overdrafted labor and resources. In the resource realm the Soviet Union attempted to extract energy and materials at maximum rates and to absorb them into production in order to promote the maximum short-term economic growth. It soon however came up against the limitations, many of them environmental, to such a strategy. It also got dragged into the massive use of toxic chemicals, nuclear power, giant dams and the like. Part of this tragedy was that in the Cold War context the Soviet Union was trying to compete militarily and economically with the United States, a much bigger economy, and was doing so in a state of constant crisis. According to the principles of mutual assured destruction (MAD) they needed thousands of missiles to point at the United States to counter the thousands of missiles pointed at them, along with all the other paraphernalia of destruction. Consequently, they were unable to use their resources rationally.

The result was a kind of "ecocide" in the Soviet Union, as many observers have noted. However, we tend to be less aware of our own ecocide. Global warming, the destruction of the ozone layer, the elimination of tropical forests, the mass extinction of species, etc.—the panoply of planetary ecological problems that now threaten all life on earth—were not problems produced by the Soviet Union but by the capitalist world economy, which has been far more destructive overall.

The question of how we can create a sustainable economy is obviously difficult to answer. We know a lot of the things that have to be done—the elimination of nuclear power, the shift to solar power, drastic cutbacks in carbon emissions, reductions in throughput of energy and materials, less reliance on toxic chemicals, preservation of natural habitat, etc. But to effect these changes we need to break away from an economic system dedicated to the accumulation of capital by means of the exploitation of labor and the natural environment. It is necessary to abandon those conditions hat guarantee unsustainability on a planetary scale.

Marx said that the labor process can be defined as the metabolic relation between human beings and nature. He argued that socialism/communism necessitated that the direct producers rationally regulate this metabolic relation, in harmony with both human needs and the eternal nature-imposed conditions of production. "Even an entire society, a nation, or all simultaneously existing societies taken together," he wrote, "are not owners of the earth, they are simply its possessors, its beneficiaries, and have to bequeath it in an improved state to succeeding generations, as boni patres familias [good heads of the household]." Marx argued that we need to focus on reciprocity, demanding in many cases "restoration." For example, in our relation to the soil those vital elements that are taken away (in this case essential soil chemicals) must be put back. Engels, in line with Marx, was already arguing in the nineteenth century that capitalism had led to the "squandering of our reserves of energy, our coal, ore, forests, etc." He raised the issue of climate change, including rising temperatures, as a result of the destruction of forests.

D&S: Since lower-income people worldwide are disproportionately affected by adverse environmental conditions, it seems that the environmental movement must incorporate issues such as class, race, and the third world. To what extent have environmental movements done this? How do you think this can be achieved?

JBF: Within the environmental movement itself, which is really a collection of movements, the most vital element since the late 1980s has been the "environmental justice" movement—or that part of the movement that sees environmental degradation as inseparably connected to issues of class, race, gender, and international oppression. Leadership in this realm has come from those fighting environmental racism. But ecofeminists have also made crucial contributions. The anti-toxic movement as a whole has had a working class base. And more and more there is a globalization of the environmental struggle that recognizes the reality of ecological imperialism. It was this growth of the environmental justice movement, and the way that it has altered environmental struggles, that allowed environmentalists and labor activists to come together in Seattle in 1999 and in subsequent anti-globalizations struggles. I think that this is the tendency of the future. Capitalism in its relentless commodification and accumulation is breaking down all the barriers. Exploitation, once understood to be centered in factory labor, is now universalized. The earth itself has been brought within the factory, so to speak. In this context all struggles become one. ❑

PART 4

CAN WE RESOLVE GLOBAL ISSUES?

Article 4.1

TOWARD A GLOBAL ENERGY TRANSITION

What would it take to reverse climate change?

BY ROSS GELBSPAN
March/April 2004

In 1998, Hurricane Mitch killed 10,000 people in Central America. Last May [2003], the worst flooding in memory in Sri Lanka killed about 300 people, left another 500 missing, and left 350,000 homeless. The president of Tuvalu, an island nation in the Pacific threatened by rising sea levels, calls climate change "a form of slow death." These are just a few recent natural disasters that scientists fear may be linked to global warming.

To avert climate catastrophe, humanity needs to cut its use of fossil fuels by at least 70% in a very short time. That is the consensus of more than 2,000 scientists from 100 countries reporting to the U.N.-sponsored Intergovernmental Panel on Climate Change in the largest and most rigorously peer-reviewed scientific collaboration in history.

The urgency of the threat is spelled out in two other recent peer-reviewed studies corroborating the U.N. panel's findings. The first, written in 2001 by researchers at the Hadley Center, Britain's principle climate research institute, estimated that the climate will change 50% more quickly than scientists had previously believed. Earlier computer models had assumed a relatively static biosphere. But when researchers factored in the warming that has already taken place, they found that the rate of change is compounding. They project that most of the world's forests will begin to die off and emit, rather than absorb, CO_2 by around 2040.

The other study is equally troubling. Several years ago, a team of 11 researchers published a study in Nature suggesting that unless the world gets half its energy from non-carbon (that is, non-fossil fuel) sources by 2018, a doubling—and possible tripling—of pre-industrial carbon dioxide (CO_2) levels later in this century will be inevitable. A follow-up study, published in Science in November 2002, calls for a crash program to develop a carbon-free energy economy. Using conservative projections of future energy use, the researchers concluded that within 50 years, the world will need to generate at least three times more energy from alternative sources than it currently produces from fossil fuels in order to avoid a catastrophic build-up of atmospheric CO_2.

The science is taken very seriously outside the United States. In other countries, hardly anyone debates whether human activities are affecting the climate. Policymakers in Europe are in agreement about the urgency of the climate threat. Holland has completed a plan to cut emissions by 80% in the next 40 years. The United Kingdom has committed itself to 60% reductions in 50 years. Germany is planning for 50% cuts in 50 years.

By contrast, the White House has become the East Coast branch office of Exxon-Mobil and Peabody Coal, and climate and energy policy has become the pre-eminent case study in the contamination of the U.S. political system by money.

Two years ago, U.S. President George W. Bush reneged on a campaign promise to cap carbon emissions from coal-burning power plants. He then unveiled his administration's energy plan, which is basically a shortcut to climate hell. In a truly Orwellian stroke, the White House excised all references to the dangers of climate change on the Environmental Protection Agency's website in mid-2003. Finally, Bush withdrew the United States from the Kyoto climate negotiations, and the administration's chief climate negotiator declared that the United States would not engage in the Kyoto process for at least 10 years.

A Strategy to Reverse CO$_2$ Emissions

A plan that could actually stabilize the climate does exist. Provisionally called the World Energy Modernization Plan, it was developed by an ad hoc group of about 15 economists, energy policy experts, and others who met at the Center for Health and the Global Environment at Harvard Medical School three years ago.

The plan addresses a stark reality: The deep oceans are warming, the tundra is thawing, the glaciers are melting, infectious diseases are migrating, and the timing of the seasons has changed. All this has resulted from only one degree of warming. The U.N.-sponsored Intergovernmental Panel on Climate Change (IPCC) expects the earth to warm another three to 10 degrees later in this century.

To date, no other policy proposals have adequately addressed either the scope or the urgency of the problem. While some of its particulars may require revamping, the World Energy Modernization Plan reflects an appropriate scale of action, given the magnitude of the crisis.

The plan calls for three interacting strategies. One is a subsidy switch: industrial countries would eliminate government subsidies for fossil fuels and establish equivalent subsidies for renewable, non-carbon energy technologies. Another is a clean-energy transfer fund—a pool of money on the order of $300 billion a year to provide renewable energy technologies to developing countries. The last element is a progressively more stringent fossil-fuel efficiency standard that would rise by 5% per year.

While each of these strategies can be viewed as a stand-alone reform, they are better understood as a set of interactive policies that could speed the energy transition far more rapidly together than if they were implemented piecemeal.

Subsidy Switch

The United States now spends more than $20 billion a year to subsidize fossil fuels through corporate tax write-offs and direct payments to oil, gas, and coal companies (for research and development, and oil purchases for the Strategic Petroleum Reserve, for example). Subsidies for fossil fuels in industrial countries total an estimated $200 billion a year.

Under this proposal, industrial countries would withdraw those subsidies from fossil fuels and establish equivalent subsidies for renewable energy sources. A small portion of U.S. subsidies must be used to retrain or buy out the nation's approximately 50,000 coal miners. But the lion's share of the subsidies would go to aggressive development of fuel cells, wind farms, and solar systems. The major oil companies would be forced to re-tool and retrain their workers to stay afloat in the renewable energy economy.

Fund to Help Poor Countries Go Green

The second element of the plan involves the creation of a new $300-billion-a-year fund to help transfer renewable energy technologies to the global South. Developing countries such as China, Mexico, Thailand, and Chile contain some of the world's smoggiest cities. Many would love to go solar, but virtually none can afford to. One attractive source of revenue to fund the transfer lies in a so-called "Tobin tax," named after its developer, Nobel prize-winning economist James Tobin. This tax would be levied on banks and other agents that conduct international currency transactions.

Tobin conceived his tax as a way of damping volatility in capital markets by discouraging short-term trading and encouraging longer-term capital investments. But it would also generate enormous revenues. Today currency swaps by banks and speculators total $1.5 trillion per day. A tax of a quarter-penny on a dollar would net $300 billion a year, which could go for wind farms in India, fuel-cell factories in South Africa, solar equipment assemblies in El Salvador, and vast, solar-powered hydrogen-producing farms in the Middle East.

If a Tobin tax proves unacceptable, a fund of the same magnitude could be raised from a tax on airline travel or a carbon tax in industrial countries, although both these sources are more regressive.

Regardless of its revenue source, the fund would be allocated according to a United Nations formula. Climate, energy use, population, economic growth rates, and other factors would determine each developing country's allocation. Recipient countries would negotiate contracts with renewable energy vendors to ensure domestic ownership of new energy facilities and substantial employment of local labor in

---

CAP AND TRADE: ENVIRONMENTAL COLONIALISM?

The global South has long contended that the Kyoto cap and trade system is unjust. Under Kyoto, each country's emissions cap is based on its 1990 emission levels—but developing countries argue that only a per-capita allocation of emission rights is fair. What's more, they argue, provisions in the Kyoto Protocol allow industrial nations to buy limitless amounts of cheap emission reductions in developing countries and to bank them indefinitely into the future.

As the late Anil Agarwal, founder of the Centre for Science and Environment in new Delhi, has pointed out, when developing nations eventually become obligated to cut their own emissions (under a subsequent round of the Kyoto Protocol), they will be left with only the most expensive options. Agarwal considered this a form of environmental colonialism.

their construction and operation. Although not explicitly mentioned in the initial version of the plan, it would be important for governments to be required to include representatives of ethnic and indigenous minorities, universities, nongovernmental organizations (NGOs), and labor unions in making decisions about the procurement and deployment of new energy resources.

An international auditing agency would monitor transactions to ensure equal access for all energy vendors and to review contracting procedures between banks, vendors, and recipient governments.

Individual countries would decide how to use their share. For example, if India received $5 billion in the first year, it could pick its own mix of wind farms, smalls-cale solar installations, fuel cell generators, and biogas facilities.

In this hypothetical example, the Indian government would entertain bids for these clean energy projects. Vendors might include large or small private compa-nies, state-owned entities, and even nonprofit organizations. As these contractors met specified development and construction goals, they would be paid directly by the banks. And the banks would receive fees for administering the fund. As developing countries acquired technology, the fund could simply be phased out, or the money in it could be diverted to other global needs.

If funded by a Tobin tax, it would transfer resources from speculative, nonpro-ductive finance-sector transactions to the industrial sectors of developing nations for productive, job-creating, wealth-generating projects. A clean-energy transfer fund of this sort could have a massive impact on developing and transitional economies, similar to the Marshall Plan's effect on Europe after World War II.

Strict International Efficiency Standards

Third, the plan calls on the parties to the Kyoto talks to adopt a simple and equi-table fossil-fuel efficiency standard that becomes 5% more stringent each year. This mechanism, if incorporated into the Kyoto Protocol, would harmonize and guide the global energy transition in a way that the current ineffectual and inequitable sys-tem of international emissions trading cannot.

The system of international emissions trading at the heart of the Kyoto Protocol is based on the concept that a country that exceeds its allowed quantity of carbon emissions can buy emission credits from a country that emits less than its allowed quantity. The United States, for instance, can pay Costa Rica to plant more trees to absorb carbon dioxide, and subtract the resulting reduction from its own allowance. This system of international "cap and trade," as it is called in the jargon of the Kyoto negotiators, has significant failings: It's not enforceable and is plagued by irreconcil-able equity disputes between the countries of the North and South.

International carbon trading cannot be the primary vehicle to propel a world-wide energy transition. Alone, it simply will not succeed in reversing—or even slowing—global CO_2 emissions at anywhere near an adequate rate. Even if all the problems with monitoring, enforcement, and equity could be resolved, emissions trading would at best be a fine-tuning instrument to help countries meet the final 10 to 15% of their obligation to reduce CO_2 emissions. We simply can't finesse nature with accounting tricks.

Instead, the parties to the Kyoto talks should increase their fossil-fuel energy efficiency by 5% every year until the global 70% reduction is attained. That means a country would either produce the same amount of goods as in the previous year with 5% less carbon fuel, or produce 5% more goods with the same amount of carbon fuel use as the previous year. During the first few years under the proposed efficiency standard, most countries would likely meet their goals by implementing low-cost improvements to their existing energy systems. After a few years, however, more expensive technology would be required to meet the progressively higher standard, making renewable energy sources more cost effective in comparison to fossil-fuel efficiency measures. The growing demand would create mass markets and economies of scale for renewables.

Given both fossil-fuel efficiency improvements and the growing use of alternatives, emissions reductions would outpace long-term economic growth, benefiting the environment.

Every country would begin at its current baseline for emission levels, which would reduce the inequities inherent in the cap-and-trade system. This approach would be far simpler to negotiate than the current protocol, with its morass of emissions trading details, reviews of the adequacy of commitments, and differentiated emission targets for each country. It would also be easier to monitor and enforce. A nation's compliance would be measured simply by calculating the annual change in the ratio of its carbon fuel use to its gross domestic product. That ratio would have to change by 5% a year. Although this plan does not include an enforcement mechanism, one would be devised.

The approach has a precedent in the Montreal Protocol, under which companies phased out ozone-destroying chemicals. That protocol was successful because the companies that made the destructive chemicals were able to produce their substitutes with no loss of competitive standing within the industry. The energy industry must be restructured in the same way. Several oil executives have said in private conversations that they could, in an orderly fashion, decarbonize their energy supplies—but only if the governments of the world regulate the process to require all companies to make the transition in lockstep. A progressive fossil-fuel efficiency standard would provide that type of regulation.

A Regulated Transition

Even from the perspective of capitalist financial institutions, this plan should make perfect sense. Recently, Swiss Re-Insurance said it anticipates losses from climate impacts to reach $150 billion a year within this decade. Munich Re, the world's largest reinsurer, estimates that within several decades, losses from climate impacts will reach $300 billion a year. Climate change will destroy property; raise health care costs; ruin crops; and damage energy, communications and transportation infrastructures. It will likely wound the insurance and banking sectors in the process. Last year, the largest re-insurer in Britain said that unchecked climate change could bankrupt the global economy by 2065. And its effects hit poor countries hardest—not because nature discriminates against the poor, but because poor countries can't afford the kinds of infrastructure needed to buffer its impacts.

By contrast, a worldwide energy transition would create a dramatic expansion of the overall wealth in the global economy. It would raise living standards in the South without compromising those in the North. Rewiring the planet with clean energy in time to meet nature's deadline will generate a staggering number of new jobs for the global labor force. By blocking a transition to clean energy, the coal and oil industries are hindering a huge surge in new jobs all over the world.

This transition cannot be accomplished by unregulated free markets. A global energy conversion will require the world's governments to put in place a strong regime of mandatory regulation to control the economic activity of some of the world's largest and most powerful corporations. Without a binding structure of regulation to level the corporate playing field, competing energy companies will undercut today's voluntary initiatives by selling artificially cheaper oil and coal products. This would turn any investment in solar, wind, and hydrogen into money losers. On the other hand, energy firms that submit to the strong new regulations would gain a new $300-billion-a-year market.

A meaningful solution to the climate crisis could potentially be the beginning of a much larger transformation of our social and economic dynamics. This proposal is ambitious. But the alternative—given the escalating instability of the climate system and the increasing desperation caused by global economic inequities—is truly too horrible to contemplate. ❏

Adapted with permission from Foreign Policy In Focus (FPIF) <www. fpif.org>, a joint project of the Interhemispheric Resource Center and the Institute for Policy Studies. A longer version of this article was prepared for the PetroPolitics conference co-sponsored by FPIP and the Sustainable Energy and Economy Network (SEEN), a project of the Institute for Policy Studies. For more information, and to read the web version of the article online, see <www.PetroPolitics.org>.

Article 4.2

SUSTAINABLE SANITATION
A Global Health Challenge

BY LAURA ORLANDO
May/June 2001

In late October 1995, in the small town of Greenland, New Hampshire, Wheelabrator Water Technologies, Inc. dumped 650 tons of sewage sludge on Rosamond Hughes' field. The sludge contained not only the dregs left over from sewage treatment but also 700 pounds of a nitrogen-based polymer (used to remove water from sludge) and 24,000 pounds of lime. After sitting for several days, the sludge was chain-dragged across the field's surface with a tractor, and then spread repeatedly for the next three weeks. As it dried, it was blown by steady winds toward the home of 26-year-old Shayne Conner, just 300 feet away.

Almost immediately, Conner, his family, and their neighbors began to get sick. Overcome by the stench, they started vomiting. They felt burning sensations in their eyes, throats, and lungs. They experienced nosebleeds, headaches, congestion, fever, and nausea, and they had difficulty breathing. And then, on a quiet day in November—less than one month after the sludge was dumped on the Hughes' property— Shayne Conner died.

When sanitation is practiced successfully, it can promote health and prevent disease. But its effectiveness depends on many factors—education, behavioral changes, access to clean water, solid and industrial waste management, and the safe disposition of human excreta. What happened to Shayne Conner is just one tragic example of how, in rich as well as poor countries, improper sanitation can cause environmental degradation, illness, and death.

Rich Nation, Poor Sanitation

In rich countries, sewers and sewage treatment systems are considered signs of progress, but they are the reason we have toxic sludge. First comes the sewage, a mixture of undifferentiated industrial and household wastes. Then there's the treatment process, which attempts to clean the wastewater that the sewage contains. What's left over— after the dead cats and cardboard are screened out and hauled away to the dump—is a concoction of whatever was flushed down the drain: motor oil, dioxin, asbestos, polychlorinated biphenyls (PCBs), heavy metals, bacteria, viruses, industrial solvents, any combination of the 70,000 chemicals used in U.S. industries, and so on. And the better the water at the end of the treatment cycle, the nastier the sludge will be.

At one time, sludge's pungent smell was considered offensive only on aesthetic grounds. But new research in the Journal of Agromedicine confirms that sludge's olfactory assault can have serious physical health consequences as well. So, while it might seem safe and convenient to have our waste whisked out of sight, we're paying the piper at the end of the pipe.

In spite of sludge's poisonous properties, the federal government keeps calling it a fertilizer and putting it on land. The Environmental Protection Agency (EPA) is in charge of regulating the disposal of sewage sludge. Since 1992, when Congress banned the practice of dumping sludge in the ocean, the EPA has geared its regulations and public relations efforts toward one goal: To dump sludge wherever possible, primarily on U.S. farmland. That's the cheapest way to dispose of sludge and launder the toxic waste that goes into sewers. The EPA now goes to great lengths to convince people that sludge makes good fertilizer. For instance, the agency refers to sludge as "biosolids"—the winning entry in a 1990 contest sponsored by the sewage industry to make its main product more marketable.

Despite the preponderance of pro-sludge propaganda, however, not everyone is fooled. When Shayne Conner's mother, Joanne Marshall, filed a wrongful death suit against Wheelabrator, Dr. David Lewis—an EPA microbiologist and whistleblower— testified in the case. According to Lewis, the symptoms reported by Greenland, New Hampshire, residents were "consistent with a growing number of cases where people have been exposed to airborne contaminants from land-applied sewage sludge." It was well-established in the scientific and medical literature, Lewis noted, that "inhaling of irritant gases and pathogen-contaminated, limed sludge dust" could "lead to infections of respiratory and gastrointestinal systems and serious, life-threatening complications."

Why, then, is the United States so invested in the sewers and sewage treatment plants that produce toxic sludge? Since passage of the Clean Water Act in 1972, many communities have had no choice but to put in sewers and build expensive sewage treatment plants. The resulting multi-billion dollar sewering effort created a powerful wastewater industry. The EPA, while ostensibly charged with protecting the environment, caters to that industry and other corporate interests.

What we do with sludge now is a public health and environmental disaster. Instead, sludge should be treated as hazardous waste. We need to promote public policies that aim to reduce its production, by not extending existing sewers or building new ones. In addition, source separation should be the mantra of the EPA (and you and me): Keeping waste products separate at the point of production will greatly facilitate safe recycling and reuse.

Sanitation Crisis in the Global South

In the wealthiest country in the world, people are dying from the industrial end product of state-of-the-art sewage treatment systems. In the Global South, where 65% of the population have no sanitation facilities at all, people are dying from exposure to excreta that carry disease.

The state of global sanitation, according to Akhtar Hameed Khan, is "unconscionable." Khan is the director of the Orangi Pilot Project, a low-cost sanitation project that has reached thousands of people in Karachi, Pakistan. "On the brink of the 21st century," he wrote in Progress of Nations, a 1997 UNICEF study, "half the world's people are enduring a medieval level of sanitation. Almost 3 billion individuals do not have access to a decent toilet, and many of them are forced to defecate on the bare ground or queue up to pay for the use of a filthy latrine."

The "medieval level of sanitation," Khan points out, results in a "medieval level of disease." The improper management of human excreta wreaks havoc on people's health in both rich and poor countries. But its consequences are most brutal for poor people in developing nations, where it results in the deaths of 2.2 million children each year. In densely settled areas where there is no containment of human waste, disease-causing organisms—primarily found in feces—easily move from one person to the next. (Water is the ideal but by no means the only conduit.) These organisms cause many illnesses, including diarrhoeal diseases, which are responsible for killing the majority of children who die before reaching the age of five. In addition to promulgating disease and degrading water and soil quality, the lack of ecological excreta management is a dignity issue in people's everyday lives.

When it comes to investing in environment sanitation, however, bringing health and dignity to poor people is not high on the list. The lion's share of such investment goes to sewerage in urban areas, subsidizing services for industrial development, the middle class, and the rich. According to the United Nations, in 2000, only 34% of rural residents in developing countries had access to sanitation, compared with 80% of urban residents. During the UN-declared International Water and Sanitation Decade (1980-1990), funding for sanitation skyrocketed. But according to Frank Hartvelt, deputy director of the Science and Technology Private Sector Division of the UN Development Programme, 80% of all investment went to "well-off urban areas, for expensive installations." As in wealthy countries, it is those with the most economic clout who decide what kinds of public services will be provided, and who will benefit from the expenditure of public funds.

These same priorities determine what types of solutions the world's sanitation "experts" devise. In 1998, the UN set up the World Water Commission to examine water issues. In its Vision Report, published last year, the Commission identified what it called "a vital need for high tech innovation." As an example of this, the Report suggested "the use of computer chips to control the digestion process in smart-composting toilets." Good for Intel—bad for the three billion people without any toilet. The digestion process in composting toilets needs carbon—chopped leaves, wood chips—not silicon. But then again, they wouldn't be able to add and subtract. People in the Global South live in a world rich enough to afford a universal level of sanitation that would help to protect their health. But regardless of how much money is available, we will trade one set of problems for another unless we radically rethink how that money is spent.

A Model for Sustainable Sanitation

The truth is, neither sewers nor computer chips in composting toilets are functionally or environmentally sustainable. Instead, what is needed are sanitation systems that keep toxic and human wastes separate, prevent pollution, and return the nutrients in urine and feces to the soil as fertilizers. (See sidebar.) Small projects have demonstrated systems that accomplish these goals while also being culturally appropriate, locally responsible, affordable, functional, and even beautiful.

One example can be found on the Caribbean coast of Mexico, a fragile ecosystem that is home to 554,000 people and four million tourists. Since 1993, the ReSource

Institute for Low Entropy Systems (RILES), a nonprofit concerned with sanitation, has built about 300 composting toilets in the Yucatan Peninsula. Most are paid for by their owners: maids, gardeners, masons, carpenters, schoolteachers, doctors, editors, tourism operators, hotels, municipalities, and retired Americans, to name a few. All of them are functioning well. Word has spread that they have no smell, do not fill up, can be in the house or outside, and can be hooked to a water toilet or not; that there is somebody around who knows how to maintain them; and that there are people who will gladly take away and use the fertilizer that these systems produce. The fact that these composting toilets are also beautiful is no small part of their success. The first few were built in houses with dirt floors, but soon people with beachfront homes wanted them. Because of their aesthetic appeal, the toilets have won acceptance across class boundaries. In an effort to build a local infrastructure to keep up with demand and maintain quality control, RILES has helped establish three Mexican corporations: a company to prefabricate the composting toilets; a workers' cooperative to maintain them and build the bathrooms that go on top; and a nonprofit organization to carry out education and policy-related work. (The author is director of RILES.)

Another project is in Cuernavaca, in central Mexico, where an architect named César Añorvé has been promoting two chamber (double-vault) dry toilets. (One chamber is used until full, then left to dehydrate while the other is used.) Añorvé has added an entrepreneurial element to his efforts by designing and selling attractive toilet fixtures. He collaborates with a nonprofit organization, Espacio de Salud, and together they have made the double-vault toilet widely available, with the construction supervision and maintenance necessary to build them correctly and keep them functioning properly.

HOW DOES A COMPOSTING TOILET WORK?

Human excreta—urine and feces—can be treated one of two ways, either aerobically (with oxygen) or anaerobically (without oxygen). The objectives of treatment are to contain this material, eliminate disease-causing organisms (pathogens), and—in ecological systems like composting toilets—return the nutrients to the soil.

There are different styles of composting toilets—some are built on site and others are commercially manufactured—but all have these objectives in common. For instance, a single chamber composting toilet contains excreta, toilet paper, and even kitchen food waste, in a tank below the bathroom floor. There, biological activity, much like that found in a backyard compost pile, aerobically digests this material. During the treatment process, up to 90% of the volume is driven out of the ventilation stack as carbon dioxide and water. What remains is called *humus*, a fertilizer that looks and smells like the kind of soil you would find in a greenhouse or on a Lancaster farm.

Time, not heat, kills pathogens in the tank. Pathogens generally need their human host to survive. But it's the highly competitive environment in the tank, where they cannot compete with the composting organisms, that does them in. This takes time, which the composting toilet has because of proper sizing and volume reduction. Compost is not removed for years. The urine, on the other hand, is available in days, after passing through a nitrification process inside the treatment tank. It becomes an odorless, stable, nitrogen-rich fertilizer capable, for instance, of doubling corn yields.

The maintenance involved is simple but necessary for proper functioning. It includes maintaining airflow in the tank, periodically adding a bulking agent like coarse sawdust, and removing and using the compost and liquid fertilizer.

Why not just hand out blueprints and leave it at that? It doesn't work. It has been demonstrated over and over again that there is an infinite number of ways to build a composting toilet so that it does not function well. Training and supervision take care of this. Regular maintenance keeps the toilets working. Homeowners need support for these things. Add to this the fact that there is a social change element to the project, and you can see why a blueprint won't do the trick.

Though do-it-yourself construction can be an effective way to get some on-site systems built for low-income households, many other components are needed to bring these efforts to scale. Providing sustainable sanitation technologies for billions of people will require replacing the existing engineering and financial infrastructure that currently supports sewerage with one that supports ecological innovations in waste treatment. That, in turn, will require massive government and organizational— for-profit sometimes, nonprofit other times, a combination of both most of the time—intervention. And whatever the technology, people will have to want it. What is needed is a new approach consisting of:

- Principles that put source separation first in the decision-making hierarchy;
- People who approach sanitation from both a health and ecological perspective;
- Financing—both private and public—to develop production and marketing capabilities;
- Easy access by those who want sustainable sanitation technologies to those who can deliver, install, and maintain them;
- Financial packages to help people pay for toilets; and
- Government policies that punish polluters, reward ecological innovators, and promote and help pay for universal sustainable sanitation coverage.

The fact that half of the people in the world do not have a toilet reflects government priorities that are politically and morally bankrupt. The fact that the other half has little or no access to sustainable sanitation reflects misconceptions about conventional sanitation systems and what they can and cannot do. Under the current system, everyone suffers. But it doesn't have to be that way. ❏

Article 4.3

FILIPINO DUMP ACTIVISTS TURN WASTE INTO WEALTH

BY EUGENIO GONZALES AND LIZ STANTON

November/December 2004

To visitors from outside, the Payatas dumpsite outside Manila is at best an eyesore and at worst a vision of hell on Earth. For the thousands of families who earn their livelihoods by recycling materials in Payatas, though, garbage is a form of wealth. "In good times, we can earn more than twice the minimum wage of factory workers just by picking through the garbage," says Zaldy Arevan, an officer of the Payatas Scavengers Association.

Metro Manila is the Philippines' largest urban center, with a growing population of over 10 million. In recent years, four dumpsites—Smokey Mountain, Carmona, Payatas, and San Mateo—have served the metropolis. One by one these sites have been closed, mainly because they were filled beyond their capacity. In early 2001, the last one, the San Mateo landfill, was closed following protests from nearby residents. They had had enough of the stench of the garbage and the daily rumbling of heavy garbage trucks that polluted the air and damaged their roads.

Mountains of garbage piled up on city streets as the 16 Metro Manila municipalities were left to fend for themselves. Illegal dumpsites sprang up in rural areas, endangering the water supply and the health of both rural and urban communities. The re-opening of the Payatas dumpsite and the opening of a new landfill in Rodriguez Town outside of Metro Manila have eased the situation, at least temporarily. The Ecological Solid Waste Management Act, signed into law in early 2001 at the urging of activists, NGOs, and sympathetic government officials, has encouraged recycling as one response to the landfill crisis. Of the 5,350 metric tons of waste generated daily in Metro Manila in the late 1990s, only 6% was being recycled. Thanks to the new law, the recycling rate now may have reached 15%, according to estimates by the Washington, D.C.-based Earth Day Network.

The Payatas Dump

Payatas, the country's largest open dumpsite, occupies 50 acres in Quezon City, the largest city in Metro Manila. Despite its lack of required liners and piping systems, it receives around 1,200 tons of trash per day. Since the mid-1970s when Payatas started operating, hundreds and later thousands of waste-pickers migrated to work and to live in the dump. They stayed in shacks—usually made from recycled wood, roofing materials, and cardboard—with no access to roads, water, or electricity. In exchange for votes, politicians slowly gave the waste-pickers access to basic utilities, but even today very few have title to their homes.

Roughly 6,000 waste-pickers make or supplement their livings by combing through this mountain of garbage. Families living on the margins of the dump sort out plastics, bottles, metal, and other materials to sell to junk shops that consolidate the recyclables and deliver them to factories for reprocessing. "They work in unsanitary and dangerous conditions but they have no other alternative livelihood," says Celia Tuason of the Vincentian Missionaries Social Development Foundation, an NGO that has worked in Payatas for more than 10 years.

When garbage trucks arrive at the dumpsite entrance, young boys jump onto the back of each truck to pick quickly through the load. These boys, called "jumpers," are hired by junk shop owners to do this work. Inside the entrance, hundreds of waste-pickers wait. They are called "mangangalahig," after the pointed tool called a kalahig that they use to pick through the garbage. They assemble behind the truck and immediately sift through the garbage as it falls off. They have mastered the art of avoiding being buried by the garbage or run over by the truck, but accidents sometimes happen.

Women and elderly scavengers who lack the physical abilities of the jumpers and the mangangalahigs are forced to rely on more tedious but less competitive ways to pick through the waste. They go to areas of the dump that are being leveled by bulldozers, in hope that plastics or metals will be unearthed that may still be of value. There are fewer waste-pickers, and consequently less competition, in these locations, but these workers—called "suros," a local term for dredging—face the added risk of being run over by the bulldozers.

The final stage of waste picking is performed by the "sala," literally, "to sift through." They go to the areas of the dump that have already been burned or are still burning. Using tongs, the workers sift through the ash looking for metal and other items of value. Others extract clumps of burnt garbage and use nearby waterways to remove the ash, hoping to find useful items. This least rewarding job in the dumpsite is also the riskiest: their chances of recovering items of much value are slim, and the sala are constantly subjected to smoke and flames.

On July 10, 2000, more than 200 waste-pickers lost their lives when a huge section of the garbage mountain collapsed after strong rains. Most of those who died were salas buried under smoldering garbage. After the accident, the government promptly closed the site. A few months later, however, the dump was re-opened at the request of the waste-pickers themselves, although the collapsed section has been permanently closed. The tragedy attracted more NGOs and government agencies to provide health care and other kinds of assistance to the Payatas scavengers, but their lives remain difficult, and the future of the site is still in question.

The Promised Land

In 1993, the Vincentian Missionaries Social Development Foundation started a savings and credit program for the scavengers of the Payatas dumpsite. The foundation's program catered mainly to women, using a modified Grameen Bank microloan approach that emphasized savings rather than outside funding as a source of capital. Borrowers founded a people's organization, the Lupang Pangako (or "Promised Land") Urban Poor Association, Inc. (LUPAI).

From initial seed capital of $2,000 in government funds, LUPAI now manages around $300,000 in savings accounts for its 7,000 members. Today, many LUPAI members engage in micro-enterprises such as small stores, junk shops, and metal-working, which provide goods and services to the scavengers and other local residents.

In addition to the revolving credit program, LUPAI has piloted a community mort-gage program through which some of its members have acquired ownership of the land where their houses stand. The program has also provided funds for improving streets and water systems. "I have seen how much they have improved their lot in spite of the difficulties and the little help that we could give them. This inspires me to carry on with my work," says Celia Tuason of the Vincentians.

In addition, LUPAI works with other organizations, like the Payatas Scavengers' Association, to improve the living conditions around the dumpsite. As a result of their advocacy, roads leading up to and inside the dump have been improved, and utilities like water and electricity have been provided to the scavengers' homes.

As the Payatas case shows, waste recycling can contribute to poverty reduction. A 1996 survey of waste-picker households in Payatas found that families earned an average of $175 per month, or 20% more than the legislated minimum wage. In addition to cash income, the dump provides some free household goods, such as building materials, furniture, and clothes. The scavengers lack secure rights to access the waste stream, though: they could be "evicted" from the dumpsite at any time because they have no title to the land. In addition, the scavengers' income has fallen as upstream recycling has increased with government regulation and incentives.

Whereas in previous years a scavenger typically earned $8 per day, now he or she is lucky to earn $3 per day. Some scavengers, seeing an opportunity, have already banded together to collect garbage upstream, before it arrives at the dump. For a fee, they collect garbage from homes, offices, and malls. This provides additional income to their sorting and recycling activities.

Still, the financial cost of handling solid waste in Metro Manila is estimated to be around $56 per ton. The scavengers, therefore, provide a vital environmental and cost-saving service by removing an estimated 65 tons of recyclables per day from the waste stream. If they were paid by the government for the savings they provide, they could earn roughly $3,600 per day, or $1.3 million a year. This would be equivalent to 30% of the average yearly income of all the waste pickers in Payatas—a signifi-cant boost to families barely eking out a living at the site.

By treating trash as an asset, the scavengers of Payatas not only secure liveli-hoods, but also help the Philippines to solve its garbage crisis. If the control and eventual closure of municipal dumpsites like Payatas leads to the proliferation of illegal dumpsites across the country, both the environment and public welfare will suffer. If, instead, creative strategies are adopted by groups like LUPAI, and the gov-ernment, the crisis could be turned into an opportunity to advance the twin goals of environmental protection and poverty reduction.

The central aim of the Natural Assets Project is to promote creative thinking internationally about strategies to advance simultaneously the goals of poverty reduction, environmental protection, and environmental justice. See <www.naturalassets.org>.

Article 4.4

HOOKED ON HYDROCARBONS
A Drug User's Guide to the Emirate of the North

BY MAURICE DUFOUR
January/February 2009

America has an oil addiction. George W. Bush himself said so, and in this case he was actually telling the truth. To make matters worse, suppliers are less and less dependable. OPEC dealers are becoming increasingly fickle (and some want to be paid in euros), China has been pushing out the competition all over Africa, and Iraq is going through withdrawal (ostensibly). Afghanistan looks promising…but only if you're looking to feed your heroin habit, and the "Chávez effect" in Latin America is turning into a bad trip. All of these trends have been threatening to choke supply lines just about everywhere, even in America's backyard.

What's an American dope fiend to do? Why, visit the pusher in the front yard, of course! The neighbor to the north has a cornucopia of crude, enough to provide a junkie with a lifetime of mined, altering experiences. The U.S. Department of Energy formally acknowledged as much in 2003, when it vaulted Canada's oil reserves from 21st to 2nd in the world, just after Saudi Arabia. Canada's growing importance as a purveyor of petroleum has also been recognized by Houston-based Energy Maga-zine, which named Canada "Country of the Year" earlier this year. So here's some advice to add to your vice: Get your 8-billion-barrel-a-year fossil-fuel fix exclusively from this northern dealer from now on.

The benefits of replacing a Prince Al-Saud with a Province Al-Berta, say, are as enormous as the deposits buried in the tar sands. For one, terrorism is practically non-existent. The only bin Ladens on Alberta's soil are the bins laden with oil. And the province's WMDs (weapons of mass depletion) pose a threat to no one: the entire arsenal is pointed downwards.

There would be no need for messy, budget-busting, Iraqi-style regime change or awkward rewriting of local laws to ensure untrammeled access to Alberta's crude. The potentates from the petroleum-producing province are far more obsequious than those in the Middle East. Unlike the Saudis' unpredictable religious fundamentalists, who can test the patience of even their American patrons, Alberta's fundamentalists are of a neoconservative kind—the kind that have never seen an oil contract they didn't like. And they are loathe to under-mine their bedrock principles. To put it crudely, instead of big-wig mullahs calling the shots, Alberta's big rigs making moolah would be providing you with the contents of your shots.

What's more, there's a pipeline for every urge to mainline. Spending to expand the Canadian pipeline network is expected to reach $6 billion this year, three times the amount spent in 2007. In the United States, $53 billion has already been slated towards the expansion and modification of existing refineries to process oil from the tar sands.

Just as potent as Saudi oil, Alberta's bitumen will provide a powerful octane rush, once the impurities—mostly sand—are removed. As it courses through

America's industrial arteries, Canadian crude will guarantee a perpetual high. The quality of our black gold easily rivals that of the kingdoms of the Persian Gulf.

Speaking of royalties, those in the United Cana-dian Emirates are extremely modest, unlike the haughty heirs to the throne in Saudi Arabia. In fact, the royalty regime is so generous it gives new meaning to that well-known line of the country's national anthem, "True North Strong and Free." In a score that would make a Colombian drug dealer envious, for example, Canadian Oil Sands Trust paid only $19.6 million in 2005 for a hit of Alberta crude worth $2 billion in revenues and $831 million in profits.

While there has been a recent increase in royalty rates, it was shrugged off by the oil industry. The reason? Compared to most other jurisdictions, the oil sands are still a bargain hunter's dream come true. As the OECD puts it, "the new royalty regime still leaves significant un-captured rents."

Translated into plain English, this means a killing can be made from drilling. Corporate profits in Alberta more than quadrupled to $54 billion in 2006 from $12 billion in 1998. PetroCanada, one of the biggest players in the oil sandbox, made a staggering $1 billion in the first quarter of this year alone. Four other major oil companies saw their wallets fatten by a record-setting $5 billion in the second quarter. One analyst anticipates a 60% increase in earnings this year.

A veritable candy store of subsidies, tax credits and other government handouts ensures that oil money stays in the hands of the most deserving (or rather disserving). Federal government subsidies to the oil industry in 2002 alone amounted to almost $1.5 billion. According to tax lawyer Jack Mintz, the effective tax rate on capital investments in the oils sands in 2007 was a paltry 5%, compared to 47.3% in Texas. It is estimated that the oil industry overall has saved $1.8 billion as a result of tax breaks on capital costs since 1996.

And let's not forget CanaBus (the street pushers' term for "Canadian business"), which can be purchased legally and shamelessly in any province as a supplement to America's fossil fuel addiction. Sweetening the pot, so to speak, are some of the laxest foreign investment rules around. Unless you're in the business of selling ultra-sensitive satellite technology, the chances Investment Canada will block any takeover bid are virtually nil. (In 23 years, and after "reviewing" more than 16,000 takeover bids, the federal government has turned down only one.)

The welcome mat for foreign buyers of CanaBus is so inviting, in fact, that Canada has gained the reputation of being the best place to do business among the G7 countries, according to the Economist Intelligence Unit's most recent global business rankings forecast. Foreign direct investment (FDI) flows are revealing in this regard. Just in the four years preceding 2006, FDI into Canada tripled, from $22.1 billion to $66 billion, the bulk of it going towards acquisitions. Foreign ownership of the Canadian oil and gas sector now stands at 50.5%, up from 31% in 1999. Even state-owned companies from China and India are snapping up assets in the oil sector, drawn to "probably the only major oil-exporting country in the world which im-poses virtually no restrictions on foreign ownership or takeover of petroleum reserves and facilities."

And now that the value of Canada's petro-currency—the loonie—has dropped dramatically as a result of the current global meltdown, CanaBus has become even cheaper.

No wonder the line-up to make the pilgrimage to the northern Mecca has been bulging with new converts from the oil industry. With resource nationalism gaining momentum around the world, and countries everywhere driving harder bargains with foreign investors, one of the few hydrocarbon havens remaining is Canada.

Drug-addled Americans can be assured that the demand from other buyers will not deplete Canada's supply of black gold, though. The United States is pretty much guaranteed an inside track to northern crude because of NAFTA (the North American Federation of Tar-sands Addicts), which actually requires Canada to keep feeding the junkie's habit. In particular, NAFTA's "proportional sharing" clause stipulates that Canada's current share of energy exports to the United States must be maintained even if Canada suffers shortages or wants to cut back for conservation purposes. Canada could be freezing in the dark, in other words, and it would still have to deliver "the merchandise."

True, there are some politicians in the United States who are trying to bar the entrance to the rehab center by proposing to cut back on imports of crude from the Alberta oil sands. Junkies have no cause for alarm, though. They have a powerful friend in a Canadian organization that is adamantly averse to therapy: the Canadian Association of Petroleum Pushers, er, Producers (CAPP). A well-lubricated propaganda machine, CAPP, along with its acolytes in both federal and provincial governments, has been seeking an exemption from the American Energy Independence and Security Act of 2007, which bans federal agencies from purchasing fuel from non-conventional sources that generate more greenhouse gases than conventional oil. The anti-anti-oil-sands lobby has been beavering away (in true Canadian fashion) to bypass this legislative obstacle through a clever bit of semantic gerrymandering. With powerpoint presentations slick as the oil it is pushing, the pitchmen are trying to get their tarry goo classified as conventional oil.

Never mind that extracting oil from the dirtiest industrial project in the world produces three to four times more greenhouse gas emissions than conventional oil. "The money is too big, as a former environment minister, Stephane Dion, put it, when he bluntly asserted that "no environment minister on earth…can stop the oil from coming out of the sand."

Dion's words pretty much summarize the current Ottawa mindset, which guarantees the continued trumping of pumping and dumping over the environment. Recently, for example, when a federal court ruling imposed a costly delay on Imperial Oil's $8 billion Kearl oil sands mine because of an incomplete environmental assessment, company executives picked up the hotline to the Prime Minister, Stephen Harper. Harper promptly agreed to remove the legal impediment to the sediment, and the project, which will emit 3.7 million metric tons of carbon dioxide annually (the equivalent of 800,000 cars), was fast-tracked.

To no one's surprise, Canada is expected to miss its reduction targets under Kyoto by a country kilometer. And unfettered oil sands development is largely to blame. The rhetoric coming out of Ottawa may be increasingly green, but the oil rigs of Alberta are dredging up daily reminders of the hypocrisy behind the words. Not one of the major political parties supports mandatory regulations on oil companies that would force them to adhere to Canada's Kyoto commitments.

All of this, of course, is heartening news to the addict south of the border. If the American junkie is not too strung out, then, the course of action should be obvious by now. Stop invading other countries to get a fix. Leave the troops behind and just bring syringes, spoons and other drug paraphernalia north of the 49th. There are plenty of safe injection sites here. ❑

Sources: David Ebner, "$250 Billion," *Globe and Mail*, February 28, 2008; Barrie McKenna and David Parkinson, "U.S. Law Puts Chill on Oil Sands," *Globe and Mail*, June 24, 2008; William Marsden, *Stupid to the Last Drop* (Toronto: Alfred A. Knopf, 2007); OECD, "Economic Survey of Canada, 2008"; David Parkinson, "Global Corporate-Earnings Picture Has Canada Sitting Pretty," *Globe and Mail*, August 29, 2008; Jack Mintz, "Perfect Oil Storm," *Financial Post,* January 10, 2007; Heather Scoffield, "Canada's Declining Share of FDI is Deceiving," *Globe and Mail*, July 5, 2008; Brent Jang, "U.S. Control of Canadian Oil Surges," *Globe and Mail*, September 30, 2003; CAW/TCA, "Building a Diversified, Value-Added Productive Economy," Submission to the Competition Policy Review Panel, Government of Canada, January 2008; Jad Mouwad, "As Oil Giants Lose Influence, Supply Drops," *New York Times*, August 18, 2008.

Article 4.5

BLOOD ON THE PALMS
Afro-Colombians fight new plantations.

BY DAVID BACON
July/August 2007

On September 7, 2006, paramilitary gunmen invaded the home of Juan de Dios García, a community leader in the Colombian city of Buenaventura. García escaped, but the gunmen shot and killed seven members of his family.

The paramilitaries, linked to the government of President Alvaro Uribe and to the country's wealthy landholding elite, wanted to stop García and other activists from the *Proceso de Comunidades Negras* (Process of Black Communities, or PCN), who have been trying to recover land on which Afro-Colombians have lived for five centuries. The PCN is a network of over 140 organizations among Black Colombian communities.

García later told Radio Bemba, "when the *paras* [paramilitary soldiers] came looking for me, I could see they were using police and army vehicles. They operate with the direct and indirect participation of high government functionaries. So denouncing their crimes to the authorities actually puts you at an even greater risk."

South of Buenaventura along the Pacific, in the coastal lowlands of the department of Nariño, oil palm plantations are spreading through historically Afro-Colombian lands. The plantation owners' association, Fedepalma, plans to expand production to a million hectares (about 3,861 square miles), and the government has proposed that by 2020 seven million hectares will be used for export crops, including oil palms.

Helping planters reach their goal is the U.S. Agency for International Development (USAID). In what the agency describes as an effort to resettle right-wing paramilitary members who agree to be disarmed, USAID funds projects in which they are given land to cultivate. The land, however, is often located in historically Afro-Colombian areas.

On paper these resettlement projects may appear to be effective components of a national peace process. On the ground, however, what typically happens is that the paramilitaries take on the task of protecting the plantation owners' (and the government's) investment. And Afro-Colombian activists who get in the way pay a price in blood.

Growing Plantations

In the 1960s, only about 18,000 hectares were planted with the trees. By 2003 oil palm plantations occupied 188,000 hectares—and closer to 300,000 counting fields planted but not yet producing. Colombia has become the largest palm oil producer in the Americas, and 35% of its product is already exported as fuel. Palm oil used to be used just for cooking. But the global effort to shift away from petroleum has created a new market for biofuels, and one of the world's major sources is the kernel of the oil palm.

Oil palm planters take advantage of the growing depopulation of the Afro-Colombian countryside caused by poverty, internal migration, and the civil war. But they also drive people off the land directly using armed guards and paramilitaries, who often seem to be the same people. "When the companies are buying land, if a farmer sells only part of what he owns, but not his house, he'll be burned out the next day," said Jorge Ibañez, an activist involved in land recovery, whose name has been changed to protect him from retaliation.

Ibañez organizes urban committees in Tumaco, a coastal city where many of the displaced Afro-Colombians in Nariño now live. Displaced people have traveled to the department capital, Pasto, to protest and demand services for the communities of shacks they've built on the edge of Tumaco's mangrove swamps. "But the government says the problem of displacement has been solved," Ibañez says, "even while those same displaced people are camping out in the plaza in front of the offices of the authorities, because they have no place to go."

Other community activists charge that coca production follows the palms. Raul Alvarez explains that "we never consumed coca here, but now it's all over our schools and barrios." Residents accuse the newly arrived armed plantation guards of involvement in the traffic and suspect the planters themselves are its financial backers. The earliest and largest plantation owners have been the sugar barons of Cali, in the Valle de Cauca department, who for years have been suspected of involvement in the drug trade. Ibañez says the gunmen are "people who come here from other regions, go to work for these companies, and threaten people."

In Tumaco, among the shacks of the displaced, the network of armed guards runs loan sharking operations and pawnshops, keeping watch on community activity by monopolizing the tiny phone stores where residents go to make their calls.

"These people aren't a political force themselves," García says. "They're mercenaries. In an area like the Pacific coast, where the average income isn't even $500 a year, they offer $400 a month to join up. Even Black and indigenous people get bought, and then they use one group to commit massacres against the other— Blacks against indigenous, indigenous against Black."

Regaining Land Rights

In the face of the displacement and dispersal of their communities, Afro-Colombians have fought with the government for decades, trying to force recognition of their land rights. Those persistent efforts have produced important legal gains. As a result of Afro-Colombian and indigenous community pressure, the country's constitution, rewritten in 1991, finally validated their right to their historical territories. Law 70, passed in 1993, said these communities had to be consulted and had to give their approval prior to any new projects planned on their land. But having a law is one thing; enforcing it is another.

In Nariño's interior, displaced residents have joined forces with those still on the land. Together they've filed a series of legal challenges to regain title to land where their ancestors settled centuries ago. Francisco Hurtado, an Afro-Colombian leader who began the effort over a decade ago, was assassinated in 1998. Nevertheless, Afro-Colombians recovered their first collective territories in the department in 2005. Since the passage of Law 70, Afro-Colombians have gained title to 6.1 million hectares of land. Recovery is still far from complete, however.

Tiny communities in the jungle, like Bajo Pusbi, still live in fear of the various armed groups who walk their dirt streets with impunity. And Palmeira, the largest of the Nariño planters, has ceded land planted in palms, but not the roads that lead to or through that land. As a result, the territory's inhabitants still earn their living by collecting wood. Most people can't read or write. Deep in the *selva*, or jungle, Bajo Pusbi has neither a school nor a clinic .

President Uribe's response to this poverty is his plan to force Afro-Colombian communities to become the planters' junior partners, maintaining and harvesting the trees and turning over the product to the companies for refining. Further, he wants to take even more land for this monoculture. To support expanding palm oil production, conservative parties in the Colombian Congress—with encouragement from USAID—have promulgated new laws for forests, water and other resources that require their commercial exploitation. If a community doesn't exploit the resources, it can lose title to its land.

At Fedepalma's 2006 congress in Villavicencio, Uribe told the growers' organization that he would "lock up the businessmen of Tumaco with our Afro-Colombian compatriots, and not let them out of the office until they've reached an agreement on the use of these lands." Leaders from the Community Councils of the Black Communities of Kurrulao condemned the idea in a letter to the president, claiming "it would bring with it great environmental, social and cultural harm." They argue that more palm plantations would affect the ability to reproduce Afro-Colombian culture, and would replace one of the most biodiverse regions of the planet with monocrop cultivation.

"Afro-Colombian communities on the Pacific Coast," García told Radio Bemba, "use the land, and are the owners of what the land produces, but don't believe they own the land itself, which belongs to us all. We follow the concept of collective property. The fact that we've recovered some of our lands and now hold them in this way has infuriated powerful economic forces in our country, as well as transnational corporations."

The PCN was organized to push for land recovery and to address the extreme poverty Afro-Colombians suffer. Some of its leaders have traveled to Washington to denounce the project in meetings with U.S. Congress members, trying to convince them to vote no on the proposed U.S.-Colombia free trade agreement. That agreement would vastly expand palm oil production.

A History of Forced Labor

Development projects like the palm oil plantations threaten more than just a group of families or a single town. They endanger the territorial basis for maintaining the unique Afro-Colombian culture and society, developed over the course of nearly 500 years.

The first Spaniard landed at what would eventually become Colombia in 1500, finding a territory already inhabited by Carib and Chibchan people. Before the century was out, musket-bearing troops of the Spanish king had decimated these indigenous communities, forcing survivors away from the coast and deep into remote mountains. To replace their forced labor in plantations and mines, colonial administrators brought the first slaves from Africa. By 1521, a hundred years before slavery began in the Virginia colony, the first Africans had already started five centuries of labor in the Americas.

In Colombia, as in the U.S. South, Africans were not docile. They fled the plantations in huge numbers, traveling south and west to the Pacific coast and inland to the jungle-clad mountains of the interior. The runaways called their towns "*palenques.*" By the time Simón Bolívar and Francisco de Paula Santander raised the flag of liberation from Spain in 1810, African rage was so great that slaves and ex-slaves made up three of every five soldiers in the anti-colonial army.

Yet emancipation was delayed another 40 years until 1851, a decade before Lincoln's Emancipation Proclamation freed slaves in the United States. By then, the rural Afro-Colombian communities founded by escaped slaves were as old as the great cities of Bogotá and Cartagena.

Poverty Polarized by Race

Today Colombia, a country of 44 million people, is the third largest in Latin America and one of the most economically polarized. Its Department of National Planning estimates that 49.2% of the people live below the poverty line (the National University says 66%). In the countryside, 68% are officially impoverished. And within rural areas, poverty is not evenly distributed.

The *Asociacion de Afro-Colombiano Desplazados* (the Association of Displaced Afro-Colombians) documents more than 10 million Black Colombians living on the Pacific Coast, making up 90% of the coastal population. Even in interior departments like Valle de Cauca and northern Cauca, they are a majority. In Afro-Colombian communities 86% of basic needs go unsatisfied, including basic public services from sewers to running water, according to a report given to the 23rd International Congress of the Latin American Studies Association. Most white and *mestizo* communities, by contrast, have such services.

The country's health care system, damaged by budget cuts to fund the government's counterinsurgency war, covers 40% of white Colombians. Only 10% of Black Colombians get health services, and a mere 3% of Afro-Colombian workers receive social security benefits. Black illiteracy is 45%; white illiteracy is 14%. Approximately 120 of every 1000 Afro-Colombian infants die in their first year, compared to 20 white babies. And at the other end of life, Afro-Colombians live 54 years on average; whites, 70 years.

And while non-Black Colombians have an average annual income of $1,500, Afro-Colombian families make $500. Only 38% of Afro-Colombian young people go to high school, compared to 66% of non-Black Colombians. Just 2% go on to the university.

Institutionalized inequality has been reinforced by decades of internal displacement. From 1940 to 1990, the urban share of Colombia's population grew from 31% to 77%. Afro-Colombians joined this internal migration in hopes of gaining a better standard of living. But those hopes were dashed—instead, they joined the ranks of the urban poor, living in the marginal areas of cities like Tumaco, Cali, Medellín and Bogotá. Currently, most Afro-Colombians are living in urban areas, according to Luis Gilberto Murillo Urrutia, the former governor of Choco state. "Afro-Colombians make up 36-40% of Colombia's people," he says, "although the government says it's only 26% (or about 11 million people). Only 25%, approximately three million people, are still based on the land."

More Displacement Expected

The Colombian government's current development program will depress that number even further. Afro-Colombian communities are in greater danger of disappearance and displacement than at any previous time in their history, thanks to huge new government-backed development projects, pushed by the United States and international financial institutions.

Local communities do not control these large development projects. Palm oil refineries create dividends, but the only Colombians who benefit from them are a tiny handful of planters in Cali and Medellín. But the Colombian government, like many in the thrall of market-driven policies, sees foreign investment in these projects as the key to economic development, and thus revenue. It cuts the budget for public services needed by Afro-Colombian, indigenous and other poor communities, while increasing military spending.

Plan Colombia, the U.S. military aid program, underwrites much of that growing military budget. Both Plan Colombia and a new free trade treaty, expected to be ratified by Congress this year, will lead to further displacement of rural Afro-Colombian and indigenous communities. Leaders who stand in the way of foreign investment projects will disappear or die.

PCN activists estimate that the proposed free trade agreement will force approximately 80,000 families working in agriculture off the land. They say this will be just the beginning, and point to the 1.3 million farmers displaced in Mexico under the North American Free Trade Agreement.

And while most displaced Colombians become internal migrants in the country's growing urban slums, that migratory stream will eventually cross borders into those wealthy countries whose policies have set it into motion. Since 2002, over 200,000 Colombians have arrived in the United States.

Preserving Land and Culture

García points out that Afro-Colombian communities are the historic guardians of the country's biodiversity. "The whole Pacific coast is made up of rich mangrove forests, to which we owe our subsistence," he explains. "Afro-Colombian and indigenous culture sees that territory as a place to live, and not as a potential source of economic wealth. But this is the basis for planning these megaprojects, so they are now using their private armies, the paramilitaries, and have assassinated thousands of our movement's leaders and displaced millions of people. That includes one million Black Colombians who have had to leave the Pacific coast."

Afro-Colombian communities and their centuries-old culture have no place in the current megadevelopment plans. "They see Black people as objects that have no value," García emphasizes. "Therefore sacrificing us, even to the extent of a holocaust, doesn't matter. That's the kind of racism to which we're subjected. We believe all acts against a people's culture should be considered crimes against human rights, because there is no human life without culture."

García and others warn that continued funding of Plan Colombia will produce more conflict and more displacement. The government often accuses the guerrillas of the *Fuerzas Armadas Revolucionarias de Colombia* (FARC) of committing massacres, and in fact uses their activity as a pretext for maintaining an extremely heavy military presence in the countryside. On the other hand, it says it has forced the paramilitaries to demobilize. "But at the same time they make these commitments in the U.S. and Europe, the *paras* are massacring people here," García told Radio Bemba. "The government asks for money for the peace process, but what happens on the ground is the opposite of peace."

The U.S. Congress has appropriated $21 million to aid the resettlement of paramilitaries. Local people say the same *paras*, with the same guns, are doing the same killing. High officials of the Uribe administration have been forced to resign because their links to the paramilitaries were exposed.

"The displacement of our communities isn't a consequence of conflict," García points out. "The conflict itself is being used to displace us, to make us flee our territories. Then the land is expropriated, because the state says it's no longer being used productively. We have no arms to fight this, but we will resist politically, because to give up our land is to give up our life." ❑

Article 4.6

LETTERS: OIL-PALM PLANTATIONS ON AFRO-COLOMBIAN LANDS
November/December 2007

> *We received the following letter from the U.S. Embassy in Bogotá, Colombia, in response to our article on the devastating effects of the expanding palm oil industry on Afro-Colombian communities of the Pacific coast, "Blood on the Palms." The author of the article, David Bacon, thought activists from the region should have a chance to respond to the embassy's claim that the U.S. government and USAID are having a positive impact on their communities. A joint statement by several activist groups from the region follows. The statement was translated by Daniel Fireside and Wil Escobar. —Eds.*

Letter to the Editors

Mr. David Bacon's article is an unfortunate mischaracterization of the palm oil industry in Colombia and of the U.S. government's related efforts to promote sustainable, legal economic opportunities in Afro-Columbian communities. The article is correct on many fronts—that paramilitary and guerrilla activity has wreaked havoc on Afro-Colombian and indigenous communities, that the palm oil industry in Colombia has ambitious expansion plans, and that Afro-Colombian communities face development challenges that are unparalleled in the rest of the country.

However, Mr. Bacon's assertions that U.S. government resources through the U.S. Agency for International Development (USAID) are being used to displace Afro-Colombians, to destroy cultural ties to the land, and to further the economic interests of the palm industry just for the sake of doing so are simply inaccurate. During the past five years, as part of U.S. government assistance to Plan Colombia, USAID has worked with President Uribe's administration, municipal governments, elected Afro-Colombian councils and representatives, farmer associations, and the private sector to develop models that meet the needs of the communities. Indeed, only one USAID-supported palm-oil investment is in an Afro-Colombian community, and almost all other USAID palm-oil activities are designed as alliances. These alliances are structured whereby large processors are linked to small, privately-held or community-held palm farms, and the processors provide seed funding, common infrastructure (roads, bridges, irrigation), social investments, and technical assistance to small farmers and communities. Further, USAID assists the small farmers and communities to become more capable of negotiating competitive forward contracts for their product.

Unfortunately, most of Colombia's agricultural sector has had experience with the issues that Mr. Bacon cites as palm-specific, and of course there remains a lot of work to do relating to palm cultivation and Afro-Colombian communities. The Colombian and U.S. governments and the robust private sector in Colombia will continue to be change agents in the agriculture sector, and USAID will continue to assist Afro-Colombian communities to identify opportunities for economic development, to strengthen representative councils and decision-makers with their ability to represent their communities' interests, and to protect their ties to the land and their cultural values in the face of very difficult development challenges.

Mark Wentworth, Counselor for Public Affairs Embassy of the United States of America, Bogotá, Colombia

Response from Activists

Having read the article by David Bacon as well as the letter by Mark Wentworth from the U.S. Embassy in Colombia, we wanted to contribute to a debate that has deep implications for our lives and rights.

Mr. Bacon's article is an accurate description of the impact that the monocultural production of palm oil has had, not only here in Colombia but in other parts of the world. U.S. officials have potentially valuable contributions to make in relation to the palm oil industry and to Colombia's forestry law. However, they cannot be effective when they push us to follow the dictates of the government and of Colombia's business class. These policy efforts are contrary to the ethnic and cultural production practices of Colombians of African descent, as well as to the ecological and conservation practices stipulated in Colombian law governing collectively-owned land.

Contrary to Mr. Wentworth's claims, activities are being promoted that are both environmentally and financially unsustainable for Afro-Colombian communities. For example, the communities have been forced to make "strategic alliances" with the large palm oil companies with unfavorable terms of credit, a lack of social security for small palm-oil producers, and fixed prices for products and transport, all resulting in disadvantageous terms for the small producers due in part to their lack of decision-making power. As far as environmental sustainability is concerned, there are many studies that show monocultural production, like that used for palm oil, to be incompatible with the simultaneously complex and fragile ecosystem of the Pacific coast bioregion.

The ambitious plans for expansion of palm oil in Colombia ignore the very serious environmental, cultural, social, and economic impacts on these communities, in both the medium- and long-term. The unprecedented development challenges faced by Afro-Colombians, and Colombian society as a whole, require an enormous societal effort that includes effective remedies for the inherited consequences of slavery and for the impact of the internal armed conflict that our communities have disproportionately suffered.

Such measures must not only respect the ethnic and cultural diversity recognized in the Colombian legal system, but must also respect the right of Afro-Colombians to develop economically in a way that is consistent with our own cultural aspirations. The failure to accept that racism and racial discrimination are problems that need to be overcome, and the failure to respect and support the proposals from the communities themselves, can only lead to the reproduction of the conditions that keep in place the racial inequality that our communities suffer, including massacres, displacement, loss of land and culture, acculturation, racism, invasion, dispossession, murder, persecution of our leaders, etc. Is there any difference between that scenario and the dawn of trafficking and slavery that resulted in the dispersion of the African diaspora in the Pacific Coast?

The progress of the palm oil industry is currently one of the most serious, complex, and systematic violations of rights against the Black communities of Colombia. Despite this, and with the support of USAID in Tumaco, there has been a growth of "strategic alliances," depriving the local Community Councils of their right to prior consultation in the areas where palm cultivation has been expanding. These so-called "associated businesses," promoted to advance the palm oil industry, divide communities and are both legally and culturally ignorant of the mechanisms established for the administration and management of collective territories—mechanisms which should be respected by the state, business, and international actors. Since 2006, those "associated businesses" have begun repaying their loans. Today, many are facing serious difficulty doing so as a result of crop infestations, fumigation with glyphosate [Monsanto's Roundup], the difficulty of adapting to the technical demands of monocultivation, and on top of it all, a sharp drop in prices from 490,000 pesos per ton of palm fruit to only 80,000 pesos per ton today.

In areas where communities use collective land titles, we face other challenges. Banks do not recognize communally-held titles and will neither issue a mortgage nor allow them to be used as credit guarantees, unless those communities apply for the loans through the "strategic alliances" formed for plantations that are already in production. Communities are thereby forced into these partnerships. Since loans are tied to the normal lifespan of a oil-palm tree, which can live 30 to 40 years, and given the interest charged and the life of the loan, the debts can last even longer. There is no guarantee that the loans will be paid off, so with the support of USAID, there is a grave risk that these lands will once again be stolen from us.

Further north in the area of Guapi and Charco, one of the regions of expanding oil-palm cultivation, communities are being subjected to repeated processes of displacement. Local leaders who have voiced concerns have received threats. We are still waiting for a response to our open letter of protest to President Uribe after he publicly threatened to "lock up" Afro-Colombians and local businessmen until we reached an agreement on how to use our lands. The government's megaproject to "fill the tanks, empty the lands" (of biological and cultural diversity) is incompatible with the life experience that we have accumulated for nearly 500 years in the Pacific coast bioregion, recognized as the second most biologically diverse region in the world.

Born out of our own knowledge of this land where we have been reborn, our communities have different approaches to palm cultivation than simple monoculture, although the government has refused to listen or support them. These methods are consistent with our way of life, responsible towards the future, respectful of our desire to remain in these territories, and loyal to the ways of our elders. We remain firm in our affirmation of life, happiness, and freedom.

[Signed,]
Consejo Comunitario Bajo Mira y Frontera
Consejo Comunitario del Río Grande del Patía, sus Brazos y la Ensenada
  ACAPA
Palenque Regional Kurrulao, Corporación Ancestros–Costa Pacífica Caucana

Palenque Regional El Congal
Asociación Popular de Negros Unidos del Río Yurumanguí–APONURY
AFROLIBERTARIOS del Río Grande De La Magdalena
Asociación de Consejos Comunitario de Timbiquí–Cauca
Proceso de Comunidades Negras en Colombia PCN ❑

Article 4.7

KEEP IT IN THE GROUND

An alternative vision for petroleum emerges in Ecuador. But will Big Oil win the day?

BY ELISSA DENNIS
July/August 2010

In the far eastern reaches of Ecuador, in the Amazon basin rain forest, lies a land of incredible beauty and biological diversity. More than 2,200 varieties of trees reach for the sky, providing a habitat for more species of birds, bats, insects, frogs, and fish than can be found almost anywhere else in the world. Indigenous Waorani people have made the land their home for millennia, including the last two tribes living in voluntary isolation in the country. The land was established as Yasuní National Park in 1979, and recognized as a UNESCO World Biosphere Reserve in 1989.

Underneath this landscape lies a different type of natural resource: petroleum. Since 1972, oil has been Ecuador's primary export, representing 57% of the country's exports in 2008; oil revenues comprised on average 26% of the government's revenue between 2000 and 2007. More than 1.1 billion barrels of heavy crude oil have been extracted from Yasuní, about one quarter of the nation's production to date.

At this economic, environmental, and political intersection lie two distinct visions for Yasuní's, and Ecuador's, next 25 years. Petroecuador, the state-owned oil company, has concluded that 846 million barrels of oil could be extracted from proven reserves at the Ishpingo, Tambococha, and Tiputini (ITT) wells in an approximately 200,000 hectare area covering about 20% of the parkland. Extracting this petroleum, either alone or in partnership with interested oil companies in Brazil, Venezuela, or China, would generate approximately $7 billion, primarily in the first 13 years of extraction and continuing with declining productivity for another 12 years.

The alternative vision is the simple but profound choice to leave the oil in the ground.

Environmentalists and indigenous communities have been organizing for years to restrict drilling in Yasuní. But the vision became much more real when President Rafael Correa presented a challenge to the world community at a September 24, 2007 meeting of the United Nations General Assembly: if governments, companies, international organizations, and individuals pledge a total of $350 million per year for 10 years, equal to half of the forgone revenues from ITT, then Ecuador will chip in the other half and keep the oil underground indefinitely, as this nation's contribution to halting global climate change.

The Yasuní-ITT Initiative would preserve the fragile environment, leave the voluntarily isolated tribes in peace, and prevent the emission of an estimated 407 million metric tons of carbon dioxide into the atmosphere. This "big idea from a small country" has even broader implications, as Alberto Acosta, former Energy Minister and one of the architects of the proposal, notes in his new book, *La Maldición de la Abundancia* (*The Curse of Abundance*). The Initiative is a "*punto de ruptura*," he writes, a turning point in environmental history which "questions the logic of extractive (exporter of raw material) development," while introducing the possibility of global "*sumak kawsay*," the indigenous Kichwa concept of "good living" in harmony with nature.

Ecuador, like much of Latin America, has long been an exporter of raw materials: cacao in the 19th century, bananas in the 20th century, and now petroleum. The nation dove into the oil boom of the 1970s, investing in infrastructure and building up external debt. When oil prices plummeted in the 1980s while interest rates on that debt ballooned, Ecuador was trapped in the debt crisis that affected much of the region. Thus began what Correa calls "the long night of neoliberalism:" IMF-mandated privatizations of utilities and mining sectors, with a concomitant decline of revenues from the nation's natural resources to the Ecuadorian people. By 1986, all of the nation's petroleum revenues were going to pay external debt.

Close to 40 years of oil production has failed to improve the living standards of the majority of Ecuadorians. "Petroleum has not helped this country," notes Ana Cecilia Salazar, director of the Department of Social Sciences in the College of Economics of the University of Cuenca. "It has been corrupt. It has not diminished poverty. It has not industrialized this country. It has just made a few people rich."

Currently 38% of the population lives in poverty, with 13% in extreme poverty. The nation's per capita income growth between 1982 and 2007 was only .7% per year. And although the unemployment rate of 10% may seem moderate, an estimated 53% of the population is considered "underemployed."

Petroleum extraction has brought significant environmental damage. Each year 198,000 hectares of land in the Amazon are deforested for oil production. A verdict is expected this year in an Ecuadorian court in the 17-year-old class action suit brought by 30,000 victims of Texaco/Chevron's drilling operations in the area northwest of Yasuní between 1964 and 1990. The unprecedented $27 billion lawsuit alleges that thousands of cancers and other health problems were caused by Texaco's use of outdated and dangerous practices, including the dumping of 18 billion gallons of toxic wastewater into local water supplies.

Regardless of its economic or environmental impacts, the oil is running out. With 4.16 billion barrels in proven reserves nationwide, and another half billion "probable" barrels, best-case projections, including the discovery of new reserves, indicate the nation will stop exporting oil within 28 years, and stop producing oil within 35 years.

"At this moment we have an opportunity to rethink the extractive economy that for many years has constrained the economy and politics in the country," says Esperanza Martinez, a biologist, environmental activist, and author of the book *Yasuní: El tortuoso camino de Kioto a Quito.* "This proposal intends to change the terms of the North-South relationship in climate change negotiations."

As such, the Initiative fits into the emerging idea of "climate debt." The North's voracious energy consumption in the past has destroyed natural resources in the South; the South is currently bearing the brunt of global warming effects like floods and drought; and the South needs to adapt expensive new energy technology for the future instead of industrializing with the cheap fossil fuels that built the North. Bolivian president Evo Morales proposed at the Copenhagen climate talks last December that developed nations pay 1% of GDP, totaling $700 billion/year, into a compensation fund that poor nations could use to adapt their energy systems.

"Clearly in the future, it will not be possible to extract all the petroleum in the world because that would create a very serious world problem, so we need to create measures of compensation to pay the ecological debt to the countries," says Malki Sáenz, formerly Coordinator of the Yasuní-ITT Initiative within the Ministry of Foreign Relations. The Initiative "is a way to show the international community that real compensation mechanisms exist for not extracting petroleum."

Indigenous and environmental movements in Latin America and Africa are raising possibilities of leaving oil in the ground elsewhere. But the Yasuni-ITT proposal is the furthest along in detail, government sponsorship, and ongoing negotiations. The Initiative proposes that governments, international institutions, civil associations, companies, and individuals contribute to a fund administered through an international organization such as the United Nations Development Program (UNDP). Contributions could include swaps of Ecuador's external debt, as well as resources generated from emissions auctions in the European Union and carbon emission taxes such as those implemented in Sweden and Slovakia.

Contributors of at least $10,000 would receive a Yasuní Guarantee Certificate (CGY), redeemable only in the event that a future government decides to extract the oil. The total dollar value of the CGYs issued would equal the calculated value of the 407 million metric tons of non-emitted carbon dioxide.

The money would be invested in fixed income shares of renewable energy projects with a guaranteed yield, such as hydroelectric, geothermal, wind, and solar power, thus helping to reduce the country's dependence on fossil fuels. The interest payments generated by these investments would be designated for: 1) conservation projects, preventing deforestation of almost 10 million hectares in 40 protected areas covering 38% of Ecuador's territory; 2) reforestation and natural regeneration projects on another one million hectares of forest land; 3) national energy efficiency improvements; and 4) education, health, employment, and training programs in sustainable activities like ecotourism and agro forestry in the affected areas. The first three activities could prevent an additional 820 million metric tons of carbon dioxide emissions, tripling the Initiative's effectiveness.

These nationwide conservation efforts, as well as the proposal's mention of "monitoring" throughout Yasuní and possibly shutting down existing oil production, are particularly disconcerting to Ecuadorian and international oil and wood interests. Many speculate that political pressure from these economic powerhouses was behind a major blow to the Initiative this past January, when Correa, in one of his regular Saturday radio broadcasts, suddenly blasted the negotiations as "shameful," and a threat to the nation's "sovereignty" and "dignity." He threatened that if the full package of international commitments was not in place by this June, he would begin extracting oil from ITT.

Correa's comments spurred the resignations of four critical members of the negotiating commission, including Chancellor Fander Falconí, a longtime ally in Correa's PAIS party, and Roque Sevilla, an ecologist, businessman, and ex-Mayor of Quito whom Correa had picked to lead the commission. Ecuador's Ambassador to the UN Francisco Carrion also resigned from the commission, as did World Wildlife Fund president Yolanda Kakabadse.

Correa has been clear from the outset that the government has a Plan B, to extract the oil, and that the non-extraction "first option" is contingent on the mandated monetary commitments. But oddly his outburst came as the negotiating team's efforts were bearing fruit. Sevilla told the press in January of commitments in various stages of approval from Germany, Spain, Belgium, France, and Switzerland, totaling at least $1.5 billion. The team was poised to sign an agreement with UNDP last December in Copenhagen to administer the fund. Correa called off the signing at the last minute, questioning the breadth of the Initiative's conservation efforts and UNDP's proposed six-person administrative body, three appointed by Ecuador, two by contributing nations, and one by UNDP. This joint control structure apparently sparked Correa's tirade about shame and dignity.

Within a couple of weeks of the blowup, the government had backpedaled, withdrawing the June deadline, appointing a new negotiating team, and reasserting the position that the government's "first option" is to leave the oil in the ground. At the same time, Petroecuador began work on a new pipeline near Yasuní, part of the infrastructure needed for ITT production, pursuant to a 2007 Memorandum of Understanding with several foreign oil companies.

Amid the doubts and mixed messages, proponents are fighting to save the Initiative as a cornerstone in the creation of a post-petroleum Ecuador and ultimately a post-petroleum world. In media interviews after his resignation, Sevilla stressed that he would keep working to ensure that the Initiative would not fail. The Constitution provides for a public referendum prior to extracting oil from protected areas like Yasuní, he noted. "If the president doesn't want to assume his responsibility as leader…let's pass the responsibility to the public." In fact, 75% of respondents in a January poll in Quito and Guayaquil, the country's two largest cities, indicated that they would vote to not extract the ITT oil.

Martinez and Sáenz concur that just as the Initiative emerged from widespread organizing efforts, its success will come from the people. "This is the moment to define ourselves and develop an economic model not based on petroleum," Salazar says. "We have other knowledge, we have minerals, water. We need to change our consciousness and end the economic dependence on one resource." ❏

Resources: Live Yasuni, Finding Species, Inc., liveyasuni.org; "S.O.S. Yasuni" sosyasuni.org; "Yasuni-ITT: An Initiative to Change History," Government of Ecuador, yasuni-itt.gov.ec.

Article 4.8

FAMINE MYTHS
Five Misunderstandings Related to the 2011 Hunger Crisis in the Horn of Africa

BY WILLIAM G. MOSELEY
March/April 2012

The 2011 famine in the Horn of Africa was one of the worst inrecent decades in terms of loss of life and human suffering. While the UN has yet to release an official death toll, the British government estimates that between 50,000 and 100,000 people died, most of them children, between April and September of 2011. While Kenya, Ethiopia, and Djibouti were all badly affected, the famine hit hardest in certain (mainly southern) areas of Somalia. This was the worst humanitarian disaster to strike the country since 1991-1992, with roughly a third of the Somali population displaced for some period of time.

Despite the scholarly and policy community's tremendous advances in understanding famine over the past 40 years, and increasingly sophisticated famine early-warning systems, much of this knowledge and information was seemingly ignored or forgotten in 2011. While the famine had been forecasted nearly nine months in advance, the global community failed to prepare for, and react in a timely manner to, this event. The famine was officially declared in early July of 2011 by the United Nations and recently (February 3, 2012) stated to be officially over. Despite the official end of the famine, 31% of the population (or 2.3 million people) in southern Somalia remains in crisis. Across the region, 9.5 million people continue to need assistance. Millions of Somalis remain in refugee camps in Ethiopia and Kenya.

The famine reached its height in the period from July to September, 2011, with approximately 13 million people at risk of starvation. While this was a regional problem, it was was most acute in southern Somalia because aid to this region was much delayed. Figure 1 provides a picture of food insecurity in the region in the November-December 2011 period (a few months after the peak of the crisis).

The 2011 famine received relatively little attention in the U.S. media and much of the coverage that did occur was biased, ahistorical, or perpetuated long-held misunderstandings about the nature and causes of famine. This article addresses "famine myths"—five key misunderstandings related to the famine in the Horn of Africa.

Myth #1: Drought was the cause of the famine.

While drought certainly contributed to the crisis in the Horn of Africa, there were more fundamental causes at play. Drought is not a new environmental condition for much of Africa, but a recurring one. The Horn of Africa has long experienced erratic rainfall. While climate change may be exacerbating rainfall variability, traditional livelihoods in the region are adapted to deal with situations where rainfall is not dependable.

The dominant livelihood in the Horn of Africa has long been herding, which is well adapted to the semi-arid conditions of the region. Herders traditionally ranged widely across the landscape in search of better pasture, focusing on different areas depending on meteorological conditions.

The approach worked because, unlike fenced in pastures in America, it was incredibly flexible and well adapted to variable rainfall conditions. As farming expanded, including large-scale commercial farms in some instances, the routes of herders became more concentrated, more vulnerable to drought, and more detrimental to the landscape.

Agricultural livelihoods also evolved in problematic ways. In anticipation of poor rainfall years, farming households and communities historically stored surplus crop production in granaries. Sadly this traditional strategy for mitigating the risk of drought was undermined from the colonial period moving forward as households were encouraged (if not coerced by taxation) to grow cash crops for the market and store less excess grain for bad years. This increasing market orientation was also encouraged by development banks, such as the World Bank, International Monetary Fund, and African Development Bank.

FIGURE 1: FOOD INSECURITY IN THE HORN OF AFRICA REGION, NOVEMBER-DECEMBER 2011.

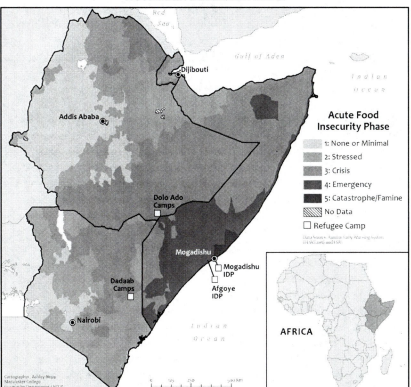

Based on data and assessment by FEWS-Net (a USAID-sponsored program).

Cartography by Ashley Nepp, Macalester College.

The moral of the story is that famine is not a natural consequence of drought (just as death from exposure is not the inherent result of a cold winter), but it is the structure of human society which often determines who is affected and to what degree.

Myth #2: Overpopulation was the cause of the famine.

With nearly 13 million people at risk of starvation last fall in a region whose population doubled in the previous 24 years, one might assume that these two factors were causally related in the Horn of Africa. Ever since the British political economist Thomas Malthus wrote "An Essay on the Principle of Population" in 1798, we have been concerned that human population growth will outstrip available food supply. While the crisis in Somalia, Ethiopia and Kenya appeared to be perfect proof of the Malthusian scenario, we must be careful not to make overly simplistic assumptions.

For starters, the semi-arid zones in the Horn of Africa are relatively lightly populated compared to other regions of the world. For example, the population density of Somalia is about 13 persons per sq. kilometer, whereas that of the U.S. state of Oklahoma is 21.1. The western half of Oklahoma is also semi-arid, suffered from a serious drought in 2011, and was the poster child for the 1930s Dust Bowl. Furthermore, if we take into account differing levels of consumption, with the average American consuming at least 28 times as much as the average Somali in a normal year, then Oklahoma's population density of 21.1 persons per sq. kilometer equates to that of 591 Somalis.

LAND GRABS IN AFRICA

Long term leases of African land for export-oriented food production, or "land grabs," have been on the rise in the past decade. Rather than simply buying food and commodity crops from African farmers, foreign entities increasingly take control of ownership and management of farms on African soil. This trend stems from at least two factors. First, increasingly high global food prices are a problem for many Asian and Middle Eastern countries that depend on food imports. As such, foreign governments and sovereign wealth funds may engage in long-term leases of African land in order to supply their own populations with affordable food. Secondly, high global food prices are also seen as an opportunity for some Western investors who lease African land to produce crops and commodities for profitable global markets.

In the Horn of Africa, Ethiopia (which has historically been one of the world's largest recipients of humanitarian food aid) has made a series of long-term land leases to foreign entities. The World Bank estimates that at least 35 million hectares of land have been leased to 36 different countries, including China, Pakistan, India and Saudi Arabia. Supporters of these leases argue that they provide employment to local people and disseminate modern agricultural approaches. Critics counter that these leases undermine food sovereignty, or people's ability to feed themselves via environmentally sustainable technologies that they control.

Despite the fact that Oklahoma's per capita impact on the landscape is over 45 times that of Somalia (when accounting for population density and consumption levels), we don't talk about overpopulation in Oklahoma. This is because, in spite of the drought and the collapse of agriculture, there was no famine in Oklahoma. In contrast, the presence of famine in the Horn of Africa led many to assume that too many people was a key part of the problem.

Why is it that many assume that population growth is the driver of famine? For starters, perhaps we assume that reducing the birthrate, and thereby reducing the number of mouths to feed, is one of the easiest ways to prevent hunger. This is actually a difficult calculation for most families in rural Africa. It's true that many families desire access to modern contraceptives, and filling this unmet need is important. However, for many others, children are crucial sources of farm labor or important wage earners who help sustain the family. Children also act as the old-age social security system for their parents. For these families, having fewer children is not an easy decision. Families in this region will have fewer children when it makes economic sense to do so. As we have seen over time and throughout the world, the average family size shrinks when economies develop and expectations for offspring change.

Second, many tend to focus on the additional resources required to nourish each new person, and often forget the productive capacity of these individuals. Throughout Africa, some of the most productive farmland is in those regions with the highest population densities. In Machakos, Kenya, for example, agricultural production and environmental conservation improved as population densities increased. Furthermore, we have seen agricultural production collapse in some areas where population declined (often due to outmigration) because there was insufficient labor to maintain intensive agricultural production.

Third, we must not forget that much of the region's agricultural production is not consumed locally. From the colonial era moving forward, farmers and herders have been encouraged to become more commercially oriented, producing crops and livestock for the market rather than home consumption. This might have been a reasonable strategy if the prices for exports from the Horn of Africa were high (which they rarely have been) and the cost of food imports low. Also, large land leases (or "land grabs") to foreign governments and corporations in Ethiopia (and to a lesser extent in Kenya and Somalia) have further exacerbated this problem. These farms, designed solely for export production, effectively subsidize the food security of other regions of the world (most notably the Middle East and Asia) at the expense of populations in the Horn of Africa.

Myth #3: Increasing food production through advanced techniques will resolve food insecurity over the long run.

As Sub-Saharan Africa has grappled with high food prices in some regions and famine in others, many experts argue that increasing food production through a program of hybrid seeds and chemical inputs (a so-called "New Green Revolution") is the way to go.

While outsiders benefit from this New Green Revolution strategy (by selling inputs or purchasing surplus crops), it is not clear if the same is true for small farmers and poor households in Sub-Saharan Africa. For most food insecure households on the continent, there are at least two problems with this strategy. First, such an approach to farming is energy intensive because most fertilizers and pesticides are petroleum based. Inducing poor farmers to adopt energy-intensive farming methods is short sighted, if not unethical, if experts know that global energy prices are likely to rise. Second, irrespective of energy prices, the New Green Revolution approach requires farmers to purchase seeds and inputs, which means that it will be inaccessible to the poorest of the poor, i.e., those who are the most likely to suffer from periods of hunger.

If not the New Green Revolution approach, then what? Many forms of bio-intensive agriculture are, in fact, highly productive and much more efficient than those of industrial agriculture. For example, crops grown in intelligent combinations allow one plant to fix nitrogen for another rather than relying solely on increasingly expensive, fossil fuel-based inorganic fertilizers for these plant nutrients. Mixed cropping strategies are also less vulnerable to insect damage and require little to no pesticide use for a reasonable harvest. These techniques have existed for centuries in the African context and could be greatly enhanced by supporting collaboration among local people, African research institutes, and foreign scientists.

Myth #4: U.S. foreign policy in the Horn of Africa was unrelated to the crisis.

Many Americans assume that U.S. foreign policy bears no blame for the food crisis in the Horn and, more specifically, Somalia. This is simply untrue. The weakness of the Somali state was and is related to U.S. policy, which interfered in Somali affairs based on Cold War politics (the case in the 1970s and 80s) or the War on Terror (the case in the 2000s).

During the Cold War, Somalia was a pawn in a U.S.-Soviet chess match in the geopolitically significant Horn of Africa region. In 1974, the U.S. ally Emperor Haile Selassie of Ethiopia was deposed in a revolution. He was eventually replaced by Mengistu Haile Mariam, a socialist. In response, the leader of Ethiopia's bitter rival Somalia, Siad Barre, switched from being pro-Soviet to pro-Western. Somalia was the only country in Africa to switch Cold War allegiances under the same government. The U.S. supported Siad Barre until 1989 (shortly before his demise in 1991). By doing this, the United States played a key role in supporting a long-running dictator and undermined democratic governance.

More recently, the Union of Islamic Courts (UIC) came to power in 2006. The UIC defeated the warlords, restored peace to Mogadishu for the first time in 15 years, and brought most of southern Somalia under its orbit. The United States and its Ethiopian ally claimed that these Islamists were terrorists and a threat to the region. In contrast, the vast majority of Somalis supported the UIC and pleaded with the international community to engage them peacefully. Unfortunately, this peace did not last. The U.S.-supported Ethiopian invasion of Somalia begun in December 2006 and displaced more than a million people and killed close to 15,000 civilians. Those displaced then became a part of last summer and fall's famine victims.

The power vacuum created by the displacement of the more moderate UIC also led to the rise of its more radical military wing, al-Shabaab. Al-Shabaab emerged to engage the Transitional Federal Government (TFG), which was put in place by the international community and composed of the most moderate elements of the UIC (which were more favorable to the United States). The TFG was weak, corrupt, and ineffective, controlling little more than the capital Mogadishu, if that. A low-grade civil war emerged between these two groups in southern Somalia. Indeed, as we repeatedly heard in the media last year, it was al-Shabaab that restricted access to southern Somalia for several months leading up to the crisis and greatly exacerbated the situation in this sub-region. Unfortunately, the history of factors which gave rise to al-Shabaab was never adequately explained to the U.S. public. Until July 2011, the U.S. government forbade American charities from operating in areas controlled by al-Shabaab—which delayed relief efforts in these areas.

Myth #5: An austere response may be best in the long run.

Efforts to raise funds to address the famine in the Horn of Africa were well below those for previous (and recent) humanitarian crises. Why was this? Part of it likely had to do with the economic malaise in the U.S. and Europe. Many Americans suggested that we could not afford to help in this crisis because we had to pay off our own debt. This stinginess may, in part, be related to a general misunderstanding about how much of the U.S. budget goes to foreign assistance. Many Americans assume we spend over 25% of our budget on such assistance when it is actually less than one percent.

Furthermore, contemporary public discourse in America has become more inward-looking and isolationist than in the past. As a result, many Americans have difficulty relating to people beyond their borders. Sadly, it is now much easier to separate ourselves from them, to discount our common humanity, and to essentially suppose that it's okay if they starve. This last point brings us back to Thomas Malthus, who was writing against the poor laws in England in the late 18th century. The poor laws were somewhat analogous to contemporary welfare programs and Malthus argued (rather problematically) that they encouraged the poor to have more children. His essential argument was that starvation is acceptable because it is a natural check to over-population. In other words, support for the poor will only exacerbate the situation. We see this in the way that some conservative commentators reacted to last year's famine.

The reality was that a delayed response to the famine only made the situation worse. Of course, the worst-case scenario is death, but short of death, many households were forced to sell off all of their assets (cattle, farming implements, etc.) in order to survive. This sets up a very difficult recovery scenario because livelihoods are so severely compromised. We know from best practices among famine researchers and relief agencies in that you not only to detect a potential famine early, but to intervene before livelihoods are devastated. This means that households will recover more quickly and be more resilient in the face of future perturbations.

Preventing Famines

While the official famine in the horn of Africa region is over, 9.5 million people continue to need assistance and millions of Somalis remain in refugee camps in

Ethiopia and Kenya. While this region of the world will always be drought prone, it needn't be famine prone. The solution lies in rebuilding the Somali state and fostering more robust rural livelihoods in Somalia, western Ethiopia and northern Kenya. The former will likely mean giving the Somali people the space they need to rebuild their own democratic institutions (and not making them needless pawns in the War on Terror). The latter will entail a new approach to agriculture that emphasizes food sovereignty, or locally appropriate food production technologies that are accessible to the poorest of the poor, as well as systems of grain storage at the local level that anticipate bad rainfall years. Finally, the international community should discourage wealthy, yet food-insufficient, countries from preying on poorer countries in Sub Saharan African countries through the practice of land grabs. ❏

Sources: Alex de Waal, *Famine That Kills: Darfur, Sudan*, Oxford University Press, 2005; William G. Moseley, "Why They're Starving: The man-made roots of famine in the Horn of Africa," *The Washington Post*. July 29, 2011; William G. Moseley and B. Ikubolajeh Logan, "Food Security," in B. Wisner, C. Toulmin and R. Chitiga (eds)., *Toward a New Map of Africa*, Earthscan Publications, 2005; Abdi I. Samatar, "Genocidal Politics and the Somali Famine," Aljazeera English, July 30, 2011; Amartya Sen, *Poverty and Famines*, Oxford/Clarendon, 1981; Michael Watts and Hans Bohle, "The space of vulnerability: the causal structure of hunger and famine," *Progress in Human Geography*, 1993.

Article 4.9

IS THE UNITED STATES A POLLUTION HAVEN?

BY FRANK ACKERMAN
March/April 2003

Free trade, according to its critics, runs the risk of creating pollution havens—countries where lax environmental standards allow dirty industries to expand. Poor countries are the usual suspects; perhaps poverty drives them to desperate strategies, such as specializing in the most polluting industries.

But could the United States be a pollution haven? A look at agriculture under NAFTA, particularly the trade in corn, suggests that at least one polluting industry is thriving in the United States as a result of free trade.

In narrow economic terms, the United States is winning the corn market. U.S. corn exports to Mexico have doubled since 1994, NAFTA's first year, to more than five million tons annually. Cheap U.S. corn is undermining traditional production in Mexico; prices there have dropped 27% in just a few years, and a quarter of the corn consumed in Mexico is now grown in the United States. But in environmental terms, the U.S. victory comes at a great cost.

While the United States may not have more lax environmental standards than Mexico, when it comes to corn U.S. agriculture certainly uses more polluting methods. As it is grown in the United States, corn requires significantly more chemicals per acre than wheat or soybeans, the other two leading field crops. Runoff of excess nitrogen fertilizer causes water pollution, and has created a huge "dead zone" in the Gulf of Mexico around the mouth of the Mississippi River. Intensive application of toxic herbicides and insecticides threatens the health of farm workers, farming communities, and consumers. Genetically modified corn, which now accounts for about one-fifth of U.S. production, poses unknown long-term risks to consumers and to ecosystems.

Growing corn in very dry areas, where irrigation is required, causes more environmental problems. The United States also has a higher percentage of irrigated acreage than Mexico. While the traditional Corn Belt enjoys ample rainfall and does not need irrigation, 15% of U.S. corn acreage—almost all of it in Nebraska, Kansas, the Texas panhandle, and eastern Colorado—is now irrigated. These areas draw water from the Ogallala aquifer, a gigantic underground reservoir, much faster than the aquifer naturally refills. If present rates of overuse continue, the Ogallala, which now contains as much fresh water as Lake Huron, will be drained down to unusable levels within a few decades, causing a crisis for the huge areas of the plains states that depend on it for water supplies. Government subsidies, in years past, helped farmers buy the equipment needed to pump water out of the Ogallala, contributing to the impending crisis.

Moreover, the corn borer, a leading insect pest that likes to eat corn plants, flourishes best in dry climates. Thus the "irrigation states," particularly Texas and Colorado, are the hardest hit by corn borers. Corn growers in dry states have the greatest need for insecticides; they also have the greatest motivation to use genetically modified corn, which is designed to repel corn borers.

Sales to Mexico are particularly important to the United States because many countries are refusing to accept genetically modified corn. Europe no longer imports U.S. corn for this reason, and Japan and several East Asian countries may follow suit. Mexico prohibits growing genetically modified corn, but still allows it to be imported; it is one of the largest remaining markets where U.S. exports are not challenged on this issue.

Despite Mexico's ban, genetically modified corn was recently found growing in a remote rural area in the southern state of Oaxaca. As the ancestral home of corn, Mexico possesses a unique and irreplaceable genetic diversity. Although the extent of the problem is still uncertain, the unplanned and uncontrolled spread of artificially engineered plants from the United States could potentially contaminate Mexico's numerous naturally occurring corn varieties.

An even greater threat is the economic impact of cheap U.S. imports on peasant farmers and rural communities. Traditional farming practices, evolved over thousands of years, use combinations of different natural varieties of corn carefully matched to local conditions. Lose these traditions, and we will lose a living reservoir of biodiversity in the country of origin of one of the world's most important food grains. The United States has won the North American corn market. But the cost looks increasingly unbearable when viewed through the lens of the U.S. environment, or of Mexico's biodiversity. ❑

Article 4.10

GENETIC ENGINEERING AND THE PRIVATIZATION OF SEEDS

BY ANURADHA MITTAL AND PETER ROSSET

March/April 2001

In 1998, angry farmers burned Monsanto-owned fields in Karnataka, India, starting a nationwide "Cremate Monsanto" campaign. The campaign demanded that biotech corporations like Monsanto, Novartis, and Pioneer leave the country. Farmers particularly targeted Monsanto because its field trials of the "terminator gene"—designed to prevent plants from producing seeds and so to make farmers buy new seed each year—created the danger of "genetic pollution" that would sterilize other crops in the area. That year, Indian citizens chose Quit India Day (August 9), the anniversary of Mahatma Gandhi's demand that British colonial rulers leave the country, to launch a "Monsanto Quit India" campaign. Ten thousand citizens from across the country sent the Quit India message to Monsanto's Indian headquarters, accusing the company of colonizing the food system.

In recent years, farmers across the world have echoed the Indian farmers' resistance to the biotech giants. In Brazil, the Landless Workers' Movement (MST) has set out to stop Monsanto soybeans. The MST has vowed to destroy any genetically engineered crops planted in the state of Rio Grande do Sul, where the state government has banned such crops. Meanwhile, in September 2000, more than 1,000 local farmers joined a "Long March for Biodiversity" across Thailand. "Rice, corn, and other staple crops, food crops, medicinal plants and all other life forms are significant genetic resources that shape our culture and lifestyle," the farmers declared. "We oppose any plan to transform these into genetically modified organisms."

Industrial Agriculture I: The Green Revolution

For thousands of years, small farmers everywhere have grown food for their local communities—planting diverse crops in healthy soil, recycling organic matter, and following nature's rainfall patterns. Good farming relied upon the farmer's accumulated knowledge of the local environment. Until the 1950s, most Third World agriculture was done this way.

The "Green Revolution" of the 1960s gradually replaced this kind of farming with monocultures (single-crop production) heavily dependent on chemical fertilizers, pesticides, and herbicides. The industrialization of agriculture made Third World countries increase exports to First World markets, in order to earn the foreign exchange they needed to pay for agrochemicals and farm machinery manufactured in the global North. Today, as much as 70% of basic grain production in the global South is the product of industrial farming.

The Green Revolution was an attempt by northern countries to export chemical- and machine-intensive U.S.-style agriculture to the Third World. After the

Cuban revolution, northern policymakers worried that rampant hunger created the basis for "communist" revolution. Since the First World had no intention of redistributing the world's wealth, its answer was for First World science to "help" the Third World by giving it the means to produce more food. The Green Revolution was to substitute for the "red."

During the peak Green Revolution years, from 1970 to 1990, world food production per capita rose by 11%. Yet the number of people living in hunger (averaging less than the minimum daily caloric intake) continued to rise. In the Third World—excluding China—the hungry population increased by more than 11%, from 536 to 597 million. While hunger declined somewhat relative to total Third World population, the Green Revolution was certainly not the solution for world hunger that its proponents made it out to be.

Not only did the Green Revolution fail to remedy unequal access to food and food-producing resources, it actually contributed to inequality. The costs of improved seeds and fertilizers hit cash-poor small farmers the hardest. Unable to afford the new technology, many farmers lost their land. Over time, the industrialization of agriculture contributed to the replacement of farms with corporations, farmers with machines, mixed crops with monocultures, and local food security with global commerce.

Industrial Agriculture II: The New Biorevolution

The same companies that promoted chemical-based agriculture are now bringing the world genetically engineered food and agriculture. Some of the leading pesticide companies of yesterday have become what today are euphemistically called "life sciences companies"—Aventis, Novartis, Syngenta, Monsanto, Dupont, and others. Through genetic engineering, these companies are now converting seeds into product-delivery systems. The crops produced by Monsanto's Roundup-Ready brand seeds, for example, tolerate only the company's Roundup brand herbicide.

The "life sciences" companies claim that they can solve the environmental problems of agriculture. For example, they promise to create a world free of pesticides by equipping each crop with its own "insecticidal genes." Many distinguished agriculture scientists, corporate bigwigs, and economists are jumping on the "biotechnology" bandwagon. They argue that, in a world where more than 830 million people go to bed hungry, biotechnology provides the only hope of feeding our burgeoning population, especially in the Third World.

In fact, since genetic engineering is based on the same old principles of industrial agriculture—monoculture, technology, and corporate control—it is likely to exacerbate the problems of ecological and social devastation:

- As long as chemical companies dominate the "life sciences" industry, the biotechnology they develop will only reinforce intensive chemical use. Corporations are currently developing plants whose genetic traits can be turned "on" or "off" by applying an external chemical, as well as crops that die if the correct chemical—made by the same company—is not applied.

- The biotechnology industry is releasing hundreds of thousands of genetically engineered organisms into the environment every year. These organisms can reproduce, cross-pollinate, mutate, and migrate. Each release of a genetically engineered organism is a round of ecological Russian roulette. Recently, Aventis' genetically engineered StarLink corn, a variety approved by the U.S. Department of Agriculture only for livestock consumption, entered the food supply by mixing in grain elevators and cross-pollination in the field.

- With the advent of genetic engineering, corporations are using new "intellectual property" rights to stake far-reaching claims of ownership over a vast array of biological resources. By controlling the ownership of seeds, the corporate giants force farmers to pay yearly for seeds they once saved from each harvest to the next planting. By making seed exchanges between farmers illegal, they also limit farmers' capacity to contribute to agricultural biodiversity.

The False Promise of "Golden Rice"

The biotech industry is taking great pains to advertise the humanitarian applications of genetic engineering. "[M]illions of people—many of them children—have lost their sight to vitamin A deficiency," says the Council for Biotechnology Information, an industry-funded public relations group. "But suppose rice consumers could obtain enough vitamin A and iron simply by eating dietary staples that are locally grown? … Biotechnology is already producing some of these innovations." More than $10 million was spent over ten years to engineer vitamin A rice—hailed as the "Golden Rice"—at the Institute of Plant Sciences of the Swiss Federal Institute of Technology in Zurich. It will take millions more and another decade of research and development to produce vitamin A rice varieties that can actually be grown in farmers' fields.

In reality, the selling of vitamin A rice as a miracle cure for blindness depends on blindness to lower-cost and safer alternatives. Meat, liver, chicken, eggs, milk, butter, carrots, pumpkins, mangoes, spinach and other leafy green vegetables, and many other foods contain vitamin A. Women farmers in Bengal, an eastern Indian state, plant more than 100 varieties of green leafy vegetables. The promotion of monoculture and rising herbicide use, however, are destroying such sources of vitamin A. For example, bathua, a very popular leafy vegetable in northern India, has been pushed to extinction in areas of intensive herbicide use.

The long-run solutions to vitamin A deficiency—and other nutritional problems—are increased biodiversity in agriculture and increased food security for poor people. In the meantime, there are better, safer, and more economical short-run measures than genetically engineered foods. UNICEF, for example, gives high-dose vitamin A capsules to poor children twice a year. The cost? Just two cents per pill.

Intellectual Property Rights and Genetic Engineering

In 1998, Monsanto surprised Saskatchewan farmer Percy Schmeiser by suing him for doing what he has always done and, indeed, what farmers have done for millennia—save seeds for the next planting. Schmeiser is one of hundreds of Canadian and U.S. farmers the company has sued for re-using genetically engineered seeds. Monsanto has patented those seeds, and forbids farmers from saving them.

In recent years, Monsanto has spent over $8.5 billion acquiring seed and biotech companies, and DuPont spent over $9.4 billion to acquire Pioneer Hi-Bred, the world's largest seed company. Seed is the most important link in the food chain. Over 1.4 billion people—primarily poor farmers—depend on farm-saved seed for their livelihoods. While the "gene police" have not yet gone after farmers in the Third World, it is probably only a matter of time.

If corporations like Monsanto have their way, genetic technology—like the so-called "terminator" seeds—will soon render the "gene police" redundant. Far from being designed to increase agricultural production, "terminator" technology is meant to prevent unauthorized production—and increase seed-industry profits. Fortunately, worldwide protests, like the "Monsanto Quit India" campaign, forced the company to put this technology on hold. Unfortunately, Monsanto did not pledge to abandon "terminator" seeds permanently, and other companies continue to develop similar systems.

Future Possible

From the United States to India, small-scale ecological agriculture is proving itself a viable alternative to chemical-intensive and bioengineered agriculture. In the United States, the National Research Council found that "alternative farmers often produce high per acre yields with significant reductions in costs per unit of crop harvested," despite the fact that "many federal policies discourage adoption of alternative practices." The Council concluded that "federal commodity programs must be restructured to help farmers realize the full benefits of the productivity gains possible through alternative practices."

Another study, published in the *American Journal of Alternative Agriculture,* found that ecological farms in India were just as productive and profitable as chemical ones. The author concluded that, if adopted on a national scale, ecological farming would have "no negative impact on food security," and would reduce soil erosion and the depletion of soil fertility while greatly lessening dependence on external inputs.

The country where alternative agriculture has been put to its greatest test, however, is Cuba. Before 1989, Cuba had a model Green Revolution-style agricultural economy (an approach the Soviet Union had promoted as much as the United States). Cuban agriculture featured enormous production units, using vast quantities of imported chemicals and machinery to produce export crops, while the country imported over half its food.

Although the Cuban government's commitment to equity and favorable terms of trade offered by Eastern Europe protected Cubans from undernourishment, the collapse of the East bloc in 1989 exposed the vulnerability of this approach. Cuba plunged into its worst food crisis since the revolution. Consumption of calories and protein dropped by perhaps as much as 30%. Nevertheless, today Cubans are eating almost as well as they did before 1989, with much lower imports of food and agrochemicals. What happened?

Cut off from imports of food and agrochemicals, Cuba turned inward to create a more self-reliant agriculture based on higher crop prices to farmers, smaller production units, urban agriculture, and ecological principles. As a result of the trade embargo, food shortages, and the opening of farmers' markets, farmers began to receive much better prices for their products. Given this incentive to produce, they did so, even without Green Revolution-style inputs. The farmers received a huge boost from the reorientation of government education, research, and assistance toward alternative methods, as well as the rediscovery of traditional farming techniques.

While small farmers and cooperatives increased production, large-scale state farms stagnated. In response, the Cuban government parceled out the state farms to their former employees as smaller-scale production units. Finally, the government mobilized support for a growing urban agriculture movement—small-scale organic farming on vacant lots—which, together with the other changes, transformed Cuban cities and urban diets in just a few years.

Will Biotechnology Feed the World?

The biotech industry pretends concern for hungry people in the Third World, holding up greater food production through genetic engineering as the solution to world hunger. If the Green Revolution has taught us one thing, however, it is that increased food production can—and often does—go hand in hand with more hunger, not less. Hunger in the modern world is not caused by a shortage of food, and cannot be eliminated by producing more. Enough food is already available to provide at least 4.3 pounds of food per person a day worldwide. The root of the hunger problem is not inadequate production but unequal access and distribution. This is why the second Green Revolution promised by the "life sciences" companies is no more likely to end hunger than the first.

The United States is the world's largest producer of surplus food. According to the U.S. Department of Agriculture, however, some 36 million of the country's people (including 14 million children) do not have adequate access to food. That's an increase of six million hungry people since the 1996 welfare reform, with its massive cuts in food stamp programs.

Even the world's "hungry countries" have enough food for all their people right now. In fact, about three quarters of the world's malnourished children live in countries with net food surpluses, much of which are being exported. India, for example, ranks among the top Third World agricultural exporters, and yet more than a third of the world's 830 million hungry people live there. Year after year, Indian governments have managed a sizeable food surplus by depriving the poor of their basic human right to food.

The poorest of the poor in the Third World are landless peasants, many of whom became landless because of policies that favor large, wealthy farmers. The high costs of genetically engineered seeds, "technology-use payments," and other inputs that small farmers will have to use under the new biotech agriculture will tighten the squeeze on already poor farmers, deepening rural poverty. If agriculture can play any role in alleviating hunger, it will only be to the extent that we reverse the existing bias toward wealthier and larger farmers, embrace land reform and sustainable agriculture, reduce inequality, and make small farmers the center of an economically vibrant rural economy. ❑

CONTRIBUTORS

Frank Ackerman an economist with the Stockholm Environment Institute, and a founder of *Dollars & Sense*. His latest book is *Can We Afford the Future? Economics for a Warming World* (Zed Books, 2009).

Jason Allen is a student at the University of Massachusetts-Amherst and a *Dollars & Sense* intern.

David Bacon is a writer and photojournalist based in California. He is an associate editor at Pacific News Service and writes for publications including *TruthOut, The Nation, The American Prospect, The Progressive*, and the *San Francisco Chronicle*.

Peter Barnes, co-founder of Working Assets, is a senior fellow at the Tomales Bay Institute.

Skip Barry, a member of the *Dollars & Sense* collective, worked at the Bristol Lodge homeless shelter in Waltham, Mass.

Marc Breslow is co-chair of the Massachusetts Climate Action Network and a former *Dollars & Sense* collective member.

Jan Clausen is a faculty member at Eugene Lang College.

Elissa Dennis is a consultant to nonprofit affordable housing developers with Community Economics, Inc. in Oakland, CA.

Laurie Dougherty is a *Dollars & Sense* Associate. She is the editor of *The Changing Nature of Work and The Political Economy of Inequality*.

Maurice Dufour teaches political science at Marianopolis College in Montreal, Quebec.

Alan Durning founded Sightline Institute (formerly Northwest Environment Watch) and is a former senior researcher at the Worldwatch Institute.

Bob Feldman is a former *Dollars & Sense* collective member.

Anne Fischel teaches media and community studies at Evergreen State College in Olympia, Wash.

Heidi Garrett-Peltier is a research fellow at the Political Economy Research Institute at the University of Massachusetts, Amherst.

Ross Gelbspan is a former reporter for the Boston Globe. He is the author of two books, *The Heat Is On* and *Boiling Point: How Politicians, Big Oil and Coal, Journalists, and Activsts are Fueling the Climate Crisis.*

Amy Gluckman is a former co-editor of *Dollars & Sense.*

Eugenio Gonzales is an independent consultant of the International Labor Organization, providing technical and financial assistance to small and medium community-based enterprises.

Monique Harden is the co-director of Advocates for Environmental Human Rights. She is an attorney and activist against environmental racism.

Lisa Heinzerling is a professor of law at Georgetown University Law School, specializing in environmental law.

David Holtzman is a former *Dollars & Sense* intern.

Mara Kardas-Nelson is a freelance writer currently based in Capetown, South Africa. She has written on health, the environment, and human rights for the *Globe & Mail* and the *Mail & Guardian.*

Sandra Korn is a student at Harvard College and a *Dollars & Sense* intern.

Jonathan Latham, PhD, is co-founder and executive director of the Bioscience Resource Project, which is the publisher of Independent Science News (independentsciencenews.org).

David Levy is a Professor of Management at the University of Massachusetts-Boston.

John Miller, a *Dollars & Sense* collective member, teaches economics at Wheaton College.

Anuradha Mittal is the founder and executive director of the Oakland Institute. She is an internationally renowned expert on trade, development, human rights and agriculture issues.

William Moseley teaches geography at Macalester College.

Kevin Murray is the Director of Advocacy and Communications for the Unitarian Universalist Service Committee.

Lin Nelson teaches environmental and community studies at the Evergreen State College in Olympia, Wash.

Laura Orlando is executive director of the ReSource Institute for Low Entropy Systems, a Boston-based nonprofit concerned with health and the environment and a former member of the *Dollars & Sense* collective.

William E. Rees is the Director for the School of Community and Regional Planning at the University of British Columbia in Vancouver.

Alejandro Reuss is an economist, historian, *Dollars & Sense* Associate, and a former co-editor of *Dollars & Sense*.

Peter Rosset is the former co-director of the Food First Institute.

Jonathan Rowe was a contributing editor at *Yes!* magazine and *The Washington Monthly* and staff writer for *The Christian Science Monitor*.

Abby Scher is a sociologist and journalist who was co-editor of *Dollars & Sense* in the 1990s. She is now a *Dollars & Sense* Associate and an Associate Fellow of the Institute for Policy Studies.

Samuel Scott is a maritime historian.

Jerome Segal is senior research scholar at the University of Maryland's Center for International and Security Studies and the author of *Graceful Simplicity: Toward a Philosophy & Politics of Simple Living*.

Michelle Sheehan is a Land Protection Specialist at The Nature Conservancy.

Liz Stanton is a senior economist with the Stockholm Environment Institute-U.S. and a research fellow at the Global Development and Environment Institute (GDAE) of Tufts University.

Bryan Snyder (editor of this volume) is a senior lecturer in economics at Bentley University.

Chris Sturr is co-editor of *Dollars & Sense*.

Jeannette Wicks-Lim is an economist and research fellow at the Political Economy Research Institute at the University of Massachusetts-Amherst.

Thad Williamson, a *Dollars & Sense* Associate, is assistant professor of leadership studies at the University of Richmond. He is the author of four books, including *Sprawl, Justice, and Citizenship: The Civic Costs of the American Way of Life* (Oxford, 2010).